HELL BEFORE THEIR VERY EYES

WITNESS TO HISTORY

Peter Charles Hoffer and Williamjames Hull Hoffer, *Series Editors*

ALSO IN THE SERIES:

HELL BEFORE THEIR VERY EYES

American Soldiers Liberate Concentration Camps in Germany, April 1945

JOHN C. McMANUS

Johns Hopkins University Press | *Baltimore*

© 2015 Johns Hopkins University Press
All rights reserved. Published 2015
Printed in the United States of America on acid-free paper

9 8 7 6 5 4 3 2 1

Johns Hopkins University Press
2715 North Charles Street
Baltimore, Maryland 21218-4363
www.press.jhu.edu

Library of Congress Cataloging-in-Publication Data

McManus, John C., 1965–
    Hell before their very eyes : American soldiers liberate concentration
camps in Germany, April 1945 / John C. McManus.
        pages   cm. — (Witness to history)
    Includes bibliographical references and index.
    ISBN 978-1-4214-1764-6 (hardcover : alk. paper) — ISBN 978-1-4214-1765-3
(pbk. : alk. paper) — ISBN 978-1-4214-1766-0 (electronic) —
ISBN 1-4214-1764-2 (hardcover : alk. paper) — ISBN 1-4214-1765-0 (pbk. :
alk. paper) — ISBN 1-4214-1766-9 (electronic) 1. World War, 1939–1945—
Concentration camps—Liberation—Germany. 2. World War, 1939–1945—
Personal narratives, American. 3. Ohrdruf (Concentration camp)
4. Buchenwald (Concentration camp) 5. Dachau (Concentration camp)
I. Title.
    D805.G3M4297 2015
    940.53'185—dc23
                            2014047681

A catalog record for this book is available from the British Library.

Special discounts are available for bulk purchases of this book.
For more information, please contact Special Sales at 410-516-6936 or
specialsales@press.jhu.edu.

Johns Hopkins University Press uses environmentally friendly book
materials, including recycled text paper that is composed of at least
30 percent post-consumer waste, whenever possible.

For the Victims and the Liberators

To Charles W. Johnson, Russell D. Buhite, and Larry D. Gragg, three great mentors

What you, my liberators, did in 1945 represented all that was good and kind in the world. Had it not been for your goodness, and kindness, and compassion, I would have died. A world would have died.

Andrew Rosner, Ohrdruf survivor

CONTENTS

I HAVE SPENT MOST of my career studying the experiences of American combat soldiers in the Second World War. As the years unfolded, and my work on a variety of books proceeded, I was struck by the frequency with which combat veterans ventured the opinion that the most unforgettable, and sometimes traumatic, aspect of their wartime service was the experience of liberating or witnessing a concentration camp. As a historian of combat, and one who appreciates what a visceral experience it is for the participants, I found these contentions startling. What could be more powerful than combat, I wondered? I had always been deeply moved by the Holocaust, though I had only studied it in passing, as a nonspecialist. I came to realize that seeing the concentration camps was a seminal moment, one that defined the entire war for many American soldiers. It brought them face to face with a dark and troubling world of human degradation, along with its sickening physical manifestations of terrible sights and smells. The act of liberating or witnessing a camp stood out from the workaday dangers of front-line action, when the objectives for a single day were generally the same as any other: stay alive, keep advancing, then repeat until the war finally ends. More than that, the camps represented for the soldiers an important moment of human trauma, human vulnerability, and redemption.

The liberation experience generated the full gamut of emotions and memories for them—similar to combat but, for many, even more affecting. As this sunk in for me, I realized that most Holocaust scholarship has focused on the victims, the perpetrators, or the larger mechanics of what happened, and comparatively little on the liberators. The relative paucity of work on American liberators is the main reason I decided to write this book—to fill that void and explore the combat soldiers in a new way.

There is another reason, though. I grew disturbed by the continuation of outright Holocaust denial and, more commonly, the tendency of some to see it as exaggerated. These views remain quite popular in some circles, and I regard them as troubling, ahistorical, and blatantly anti-Semitic. So I decided to focus on an aspect of the Holocaust that dovetails with my particular area of expertise and document the events beyond any possibility of denial or obfuscation. For the sake of brevity, I have opted to focus on the liberation of three camps—Ohrdruf, Buchenwald, and Dachau—as representatives of the larger whole and as emblems of the unfolding narrative of discovery as American soldiers experienced it in the spring of 1945. If I have made any errors or omissions in the process, I alone am responsible for them.

ACKNOWLEDGMENTS

I WOULD LIKE TO THANK my editor, Bob Brugger, at Johns Hopkins University Press, for originally approaching me about doing a book for the press's Witness to History series and for his steady, patient guidance throughout this long process. I also appreciate the useful input of the series editors, Peter Hoffer and Williamjames Hull Hoffer. Ted Chichak, formerly my literary agent and now retired, provided wise counsel and helped make this book a reality.

The book necessitated a tremendous amount of research and travel to multiple archives over the course of many years. Without the crucial assistance of a great many gifted professionals, I could not have written a word, so I have many people to thank. The military archivists at the National Archives in College Park, Maryland, and the U.S. Army Military History Institute in Carlisle, Pennsylvania, were as always extremely knowledgeable and helpful. The same is true for the dedicated folks at the National Personnel Records Center in St. Louis. While I visited the U.S. Holocaust Memorial Museum in Washington, D.C., Megan Lewis made a vast reservoir of material available to me, including letters and testimonies from the 1981 International Liberators Conference. Josh Caster from the University of Nebraska Archives and Special Collections is a great steward of the truly remarkable 42nd Infantry Rainbow Division Veterans Archive. Thanks to him, I was able to access hundreds of firsthand accounts from veterans who liberated or visited Dachau. Herb Pankratz and Kevin Bailey at the Dwight Eisenhower Library in Abilene, Kansas, helped me find a large amount of useful information, including Ike's personal correspondence about concentration camps, official documents, and other firsthand material from veterans. Carol Leadman and David Sun at the Hoover Institution went out of their way to make an important document about the Dachau death train available to me. The same goes for Claudia Rivers at the Special Collections Library, University of Texas El Paso, who dipped into the archives and personally forwarded me a copy of an obscure, but important, congressional report about Buchenwald and Dachau. Closer to home, the relentlessly knowledgeable Diane Everman at the St. Louis Holocaust Museum served as a singular font of information. Diane helped me access a treasure trove of firsthand material, photographs, and documents from the museum's underrated library.

My fellow Army historian and dear friend Kevin Hymel loaned me several relevant books from his personal collection. He also provided me with original copies of the diaries of General George Patton and his deputy chief of staff Colonel Paul Harkins. Flint Whitlock, author of multiple Holocaust-related books, was kind enough to share his well-informed perspective on the loathsome actions of Karl Koch, the one-time commandant of Buchenwald, and his infamous wife, Ilse. My colleague Theresa Ast, author of a truly first-rate dissertation about American liberators, unfailingly responded to my many questions with patience and wisdom. A special word of thanks goes to Beth and Miriam Feffer for their honesty and openness in sharing memories about their loved one, the sagacious Holocaust survivor Rabbi Abraham D. Feffer. My good friend Robert von Maier, editor of *Global War Studies*, spent many hours of his valuable time discussing this topic and putting me in touch with fellow scholars.

A grant from the University of Missouri Research Board helped defray many of the considerable travel costs during the preparation of this book. I would like to thank my colleagues in the History and Political Science Department at Missouri University of Science and Technology for their daily commitment to excellence: Diana Ahmad, Mike Bruening, Petra DeWitt, Patrick Huber, Tseggai Isaac, Michael Meagher, Jeff Schramm, and Kate Sheppard. The same goes to our distinguished emeriti: Lawrence Christensen, Harry Eisenman, Don Oster, Jack Ridley, and Lance Williams. I am especially grateful to my departmental friend and colleague Shannon Fogg, one of the world's leading experts on the Holocaust, for bringing me up to speed, over the course of many fascinating conversations, on topical historiography, background, and proper perspective. Robin Collier, the greatest secretary in recorded history, is a daily source of inspiration. I have dedicated this book, in part, to my three mentors: Charles Johnson, Russell Buhite, and Larry Gragg. Thanks in large measure to their wise tutelage, I am living my dream of being an author and a university professor.

I am blessed with many friends who, whether they know it or not, helped me through the many years it took to complete this work: Pat O'Donnell, Thad O'Donnell, Sean Roarty, Mike Chopp, Steve Loher, John Villier, Steve

Kutheis, Steve Vincent, James Gavin McManus, Tom Fleming, Dick Hyde, Stu Hartzell, Joe Carcagno, Ron Kurtz, Professor Dave Cohen, Professor Doug Kuberski, Norm Richards, John Brueck, Don Patton, Chris Ketcherside, Charlie Schneider, and many more than I have space to mention.

Family is my greatest source of support and inspiration. My in-laws, Ruth and Nelson Woody, are remarkable, giving people. The same goes for Aunt Nancy and Uncle Charlie. Doug, David, Tonya, and Angee are like brothers and sisters. My dear Aunt Helene has become remarkably educable now that she is retired and taking university courses. I would like to thank my older siblings, Nancy and Mike, and my brother-in-law John for a long litany of kindnesses, warmth, and friendship over the years. My nieces and nephews are a steady source of fascination, entertainment, and inspiration. I am beyond fortunate to enjoy the love and support of truly great parents, Michael and Mary Jane McManus. I have said on many occasions that nothing I do could ever really repay them, but I still like to try. Nancy, my wife and soul mate, endured long absences, both physical and mental, as I struggled to master this grimmest of all topics. She walked this journey alongside me. She too was deeply touched by such a tragic story of unimaginable human loss tinged with ultimate redemption. It is to her that I owe my greatest debt of gratitude.

HELL BEFORE THEIR VERY EYES

Prologue
Germany, April 1945

THE FAINTEST WHIFF OF SPRING tinged the cool morning air. On a quaint country road in Weimar, the heartland of Germany, a lone United States Army jeep rumbled steadily along, heedless of any danger in these waning days of war. One of the jeep's occupants, Corporal Charles Wilson, was lost in thought, studying the beautiful countryside. All around him were rolling, bouncy hills, green slopes, plateaus, sheep grazing in pastures, venerable stone bridges dating back to Roman times, charming little farmhouses standing like lone sentinels astride undulating plains that seemingly stretched to the horizon and beyond. Wilson, a pensive and deeply religious chaplain's assistant in the 46th Armored Medical Battalion, 4th Armored Division, was impressed with the scenic majesty of the German landscape. In his mind, he could hear the music of great German composers—Beethoven's *Pastoral Symphony*, the lilting melodies and hymns of Haydn and Mozart. As he imagined the music, he felt a kinship with nature, and he contemplated the richness of German culture. He thought of peaceful Bible passages. He watched as birds soared among the trees. After many months of war, Corporal Wilson felt a distinct sense of renewal. He was infused with hope for the future, one he imagined would be filled with Christian fellowship and brotherhood.

Then, all at once, the jeep arrived at its destination—Ohrdruf, a small concentration camp designed to house and exploit slave labor for the German war effort. Until this moment, Wilson had literally no concept, no understanding even in his wildest nightmares, of what the term "concentration camp" really meant. His ignorance was near total. Now, as he walked around and took in the terrible realities of Ohrdruf, engulfed in its powerful stench, his upbeat mood of hope and fellowship evaporated. "We see evidences of inconceivable human brutality, clumps of human debris, piled high and spread out in grotesque array," he wrote in his diary. "Men and women revealing evidences of long-lasting starvation in their emaciated bodies . . . systematically shot thru the head." In a long ditch were hundreds, possibly even thousands, of skeletal bodies, arms and legs poking out, heads too large for their skinny torsos, sightless eyes staring dully upward in supplication. Some of the bodies were partially burned. Others had been shot or clubbed. Some must have starved or died of disease.

Standing next to Wilson, another soldier—a tank crewman, according to his uniform—stared silently at the bodies. The tanker was so enraged at the incomprehensible sight of the corpses that he involuntarily dug his nails into his own palms, drawing blood. Wilson thought of this as "a stigmata in which bleeding anger fights with the knowledge of the awesome, unjust suffering of others." The foul odor of the place was overwhelming, so much so that Wilson felt dizzy and unbalanced, as if he would get sick. Only with a great effort could he fight off waves of nausea.

Hours earlier his eyes had taken in the beautiful splendor of nature. Now he had trouble focusing them well enough to see anything with clarity. Time lost its meaning. Minutes turned into hours. Finally he staggered away from Ohrdruf, back to the jeep with his comrades, to leave the place forever—physically but never truly mentally. In the space of those few hours, he and the others had seen "the unbearable evidence of human cruelty that would remain in our memories as long as we live." Wilson knew that the experience had changed him forever, leaving him with "provocative thoughts . . . [and] the effects of those thoughts . . . demand a moral response from me at every moment of my life."[1]

And thus, for Wilson and so many thousands of other American soldiers in the spring of 1945, that same struggle to discover, to bear witness, to strive for justice and meaning, began. . . .

The Setting

When American soldiers overran Germany in the spring of 1945, most had no idea what they were about to see. The average soldier disliked the Nazi regime and, in theory, understood the tyranny Hitler and his followers had imposed upon Europe. Very few, though, had any real notion of what that tyranny truly entailed.

The Nazi regime built and supervised thousands of concentration camps, all of which had distinct purposes. Some camps were for slave labor; others were incarceration centers for the regime's many enemies. These two types of camp tended to be located in Germany, close to the country's transportation networks and war production facilities. The worst camps, such as Auschwitz and Chelmno, were designed primarily as extermination centers—although they operated a good deal of slave labor, as well—and were located in occupied Poland. These camps and the other Eastern European killing centers accounted for the majority of Hitler's victims.

Although plenty of information had leaked to the Allied world about Nazi concentration camps—especially those in Poland which had been liberated months earlier by the Soviets—the ordinary American soldier knew little to nothing of them. Beginning in early April 1945, they began to see these hell-holes firsthand as United States Army units liberated camps like Ohrdruf. In the weeks that followed, thousands of U.S. soldiers came face to face with the horrors of Hitler's Germany. These men discovered, with their own troubled eyes, the very depths of human-imposed cruelty and depravity: railroad cars stacked with emaciated, lifeless bodies; ovens full of incinerated human remains; a gas chamber dedicated to the extermination of human beings; warehouses filled with stolen shoes, clothes, luggage, and even eyeglasses; prison yards littered with implements of torture as well as dead bodies; and, perhaps most disturbing of all, the half-dead survivors of the Nazi camps.

For the Americans who witnessed such powerful evidence of Nazi crimes (the totality of which are generally called the Holocaust), the experience was life altering. Most reacted with anger, revulsion, and abject disgust. They sympathized deeply with the victims even as they burned with hatred against those Germans whom they deemed responsible. Beyond these understandable emotions, almost all were haunted for the rest of their lives by what they had seen, for their experiences had taught them the troubling reality that human beings—even those considered "normal" by a supposedly civilized society—were capable of monstrous crimes. As a result, the American liberators were determined to bear witness, to testify to what they had seen, in hopes that it may never happen again.

At Ohrdruf, Buchenwald, and Dachau, a general pattern emerged. The first wave of soldiers discovered and liberated these horrible places. In the days that followed, as word of the camps spread among neighboring units, many other GIs (a World War II term for U.S. soldiers) converged on them to witness the atrocities for themselves. Others began the long, laborious cleanup. Doctors attempted to save patients wracked by disease and malnutrition. Engineers cleaned and sanitized the camp compounds as best they could and attempted to rebuild the infrastructure sufficiently to care for the considerable needs of so many thousands of half-dead survivors. Commanding officers served as reluctant commandants for the liberated prisoners. Somehow these officers had to make survivors understand that they must remain in place until they could be nursed back to some semblance of health and repatriated to their country of origin. (The latter was a serious difficulty for hard-pressed diplomats in the war's aftermath.) Often the commanders ordered local German civilians to tour the camps and witness the grisly handiwork of their countrymen; many military leaders also forced them to do the most unpleasant cleanup jobs, such as burying the dead, moving their skeletal remains, or cleaning latrines.

More than anything, the American liberators had to deal with the terrible memories of what they had seen, smelled, heard, and felt. Some lost their faith in humanity, others in God. Many experienced terrible feelings of guilt because of their inability to save more prisoners or to care for them properly; some felt self-loathing for their inward revulsion at the sight of them. For most, the shock and the trauma lasted a lifetime, even among the most battle-hardened combat soldiers. "The horror of that April day is still fresh in my memory," Clifford Barrett, an infantryman and Dachau liberator, wrote more than half a century later. He and his fellow soldiers emerged from the experience "totally different men. We just could not accept that human beings could do this to other human beings. We saw hell but those people had to live and die in it."[2]

For Barrett and many others, the liberations gave meaning and definition to the costly, bitter war they had fought to destroy Nazi Germany. Amid the nightmarish circumstances of the concentration camps, they found new purpose in the agony, sacrifice, and bloodshed of three terrible years of war.

Simply put, the soldiers now told themselves, "This is why we fought the war. This is why my buddies died. This is why I had to kill Germans." The discovery of the camps elevated the trauma of combat to a high moral plane, a source of lifetime pride for an entire generation of soldiers.

Allied Supreme Commander General Dwight D. Eisenhower visited Ohrdruf himself. "What I saw there beggars description," he later wrote to Army Chief of Staff General George Marshall. Eisenhower anticipated that the day would probably come when some would deny the existence of the concentration camps or at least their severity. He was determined to witness the horrors himself, and he encouraged every soldier under his command to do the same. He also arranged for representatives of the Allied governments and media members to visit the liberated camps and thoroughly document their terrible realities. History has proven Eisenhower correct. In the decades since World War II, denial—and its close cousin, ignorance—has ebbed and flowed, even among Americans, in spite of the fact that the Holocaust is perhaps the best documented event in human history.

Unlike the deniers, the GIs were actually there. They know what they saw and what they experienced. Following Eisenhower's lead, they have left us the rich treasure trove of evidence upon which this book is based—photographs, after-action reports, unit journals, official investigations, medical records, sworn testimony, letters, diaries, interviews, memoirs, books, and the like. Their story sheds light on just one aspect of this monumental and tragic event we refer to as the Holocaust. They were the ultimate witnesses to history.

Encountering Ohrdruf

IN EARLY APRIL 1945, Nazi Germany was on its deathbed, with only about a month left to live. Allied armies were in the process of overrunning and dismembering the country. In the east, Soviet troops had swept through Poland, Romania, Bulgaria, much of Hungary, and eastern Germany. The Soviets were now rapidly approaching the German capital of Berlin. In the west, the multinational western armies under the command of American General Dwight D. Eisenhower had breached the Rhine River and were knifing through northern, central, and southern Germany. Americans comprised about two-thirds of this force, and, by this time, the United States Army had become the most mobile military organization in the world. Even though plenty of hard fighting still raged, American units were advancing rapidly, often in combined arms convoys with infantrymen riding atop tanks or aboard halftracks (armored personnel carriers). Self-propelled artillery pieces and other mobile weapons rounded out these fast-moving columns. In general, the potent convoys rolled along at about 15 or 20 miles per hour and stopped only when they ran into roadblocks, mines, or armed resistance. Small reconnaissance forces, riding in jeeps, light tanks, or armored cars, often scouted ahead of the main force.

On April 4, after capturing the central German city of Gotha, heavily armed advance units from two U.S. divisions, the 4th Armored and the 89th Infantry, left Gotha and headed for the small town of Ohrdruf, some ten miles to the south, where composer Johann Sebastian Bach had once sung as an adolescent in the local church choir. Standing orders for the Americans were to take the town, capture an underground German army communications center, and establish a defensive perimeter in case of enemy counterattacks. Resistance in the area was minimal. When soldiers from Combat Command A, 4th Armored Division reached the communications center, they were dumbfounded at its immensity. "It turned out to be a complete underground building, nine stories high," Lieutenant Leavitt Anderson later wrote. "Every floor was jammed with the most sophisticated electronic switching equipment. There were thousands . . . of vacuum tubes, relays, generators, and miles and miles of wire."

Deep concrete tunnels, crisscrossed with strands of thick communication wire, led in every direction. There were enough telephone switchboards to serve an entire city. In fact, the complex had originally been built in 1938 as a headquarters for the German High Command, but the generals had never used it. In late 1944, Reichsführer Heinrich Himmler, head of the Schutzstaffel (the secret police and paramilitary arm of the Nazi Party, generally known as the SS) and, in effect, the man in charge of all Nazi concentration camps, had ordered the communications center expanded and refurbished as a possible redoubt for Adolf Hitler. Himmler's plan was to present the complex to the Führer on his birthday, April 20, but the arrival of the Americans had ended that hope.[1]

Nonetheless, from November 1944 onward, thousands of slave laborers had worked on the elaborate complex and a nearby railroad. They were housed in a crude labor camp located in a small valley just outside of Ohrdruf. This camp, usually called Ohrdruf (although some liberators originally referred to it as Stalag III or Ohrdruf Nord), was a satellite of Buchenwald, one of the original Nazi concentration camps. The practice of locating labor camps throughout the general area that surrounded the main camp (in this case Buchenwald) had become quite common within the vast Nazi slave-labor empire. It was not unusual for a main concentration camp to have dozens of satellites. Indeed, Buchenwald had 88 such subcamps.

Ohrdruf's prisoner population peaked at 11,700 people. As of March 25, 1945, there were 9,943 inmates remaining in the camp; 6,000 of them were

Jews; the rest were non-Jewish Russian, Polish, French, Belgian, Romanian, Hungarian, and German prisoners. They labored arduously on the communications center, digging tunnels and laying railcar tracks, from four in the morning until five-thirty in the evening. They were fed one loaf of unappetizing black bread per six men, some thin soup, and 25 grams of rancid margarine. Most had served time in other concentration camps before ending up at Ohrdruf. Beatings from the guards or kapos (prisoners empowered to supervise their fellow inmates) were routine. Clothing consisted of lightweight, crude, pajama-like, gray- and blue-striped, button-down tops and baggy trousers. Over the course of five months in the camp, prisoners only once had the opportunity to change clothes; nearly all of the garments were inundated with lice, dirt, and grime. "The Germans mocked them for their filth and pointed to their own cleanliness as proof of the master race theory," an American investigative officer later wrote in an official report on conditions in the camp.

On the morning of April 3, in response to the imminent arrival of the rapidly advancing United States Army, the SS rousted the emaciated survivors from their crude barracks and began forcibly marching them in the direction of Buchenwald, about 30 miles to the east. Anyone who could not, or would not, keep up was shot, beaten, or burned to death. Some survivors evaded the SS and melted into nearby forests, only to die near the road or among the trees. A comparative few managed to hide out among the shabby buildings of the Ohrdruf labor camp or its environs.[2]

A Terrible Discovery

Starting in the afternoon on April 4, combined arms advance units from the 4th Armored and 89th Infantry divisions arrived in the area. Their first inkling of Ohrdruf's horrors was the disquieting sight of inmates who had perished during the march to Buchenwald. "We encountered so many corpses they were beyond counting," Sergeant Ralph Craib, a 20-year-old squad leader in the 89th Division, later wrote. The bodies lay along the road, in nearby ditches, and among the trees. The Americans immediately noticed their wretched physical condition and the unique prisoner garb, though they had no idea what these sights truly meant. Next, the soldiers encountered haggard survivors who had managed to escape their German guards during the march. "They were like zombies," one of the Americans later said.

Most of the survivors were half dead and disoriented. Andrew Rosner, a 23-year-old survivor who had lain in a delirium along the side of the road for several days, wandered into Ohrdruf village and stumbled upon a group of American soldiers. "I was immediately surrounded by Americans, and, as their officers questioned where I had been and what had happened to me, GIs were showering me with food and chocolate and other treats that I had not known for almost five years," Rosner said. This sort of generosity was to become quite common, not just at Ohrdruf but in the many other liberation encounters in the weeks ahead. The Americans would soon learn that few of the former inmates were in any sort of condition to consume regular food. Indeed, candy and high-caloric, prepackaged C and K field rations were almost like poison to their malnourished bodies. In Rosner's case, the excitement of the moment and the rich food were collectively more than he could stand. He passed out on the spot only to awaken later in an American hospital.[3]

At the Ohrdruf labor camp on April 4, there was no definitive moment of liberation by one individual or group. Unlike other camps, Ohrdruf was largely empty of inmates and guards when the Americans arrived. Foot soldiers, tank (and tank destroyer) crewmen, and other vehicle-borne troops all converged on the area throughout the day. Such was the confusion of operations and events that both the 89th Infantry Division and the 4th Armored Division claimed to be the first to enter the labor camp. In that sense, Ohrdruf served as a forerunner for heated disputes that would erupt between units over liberation credit at several other camps (most notably Dachau, as described in chapter 4). Though these disputes can appear petty and irrelevant decades later, many veterans, and some historians, took them quite seriously as a matter of personal respect and proper documentation of the Holocaust. For these reasons, the United States Holocaust Memorial Museum and the U.S. Army Center of Military History eventually established clear parameters to officially recognize liberating units. Both organizations properly afford liberation credit for Ohrdruf to both the 89th Infantry and the 4th Armored.[4]

The labor camp was situated in a pine forest on a small hill just outside the town of Ohrdruf. As the Americans crested the hill, they first laid eyes on this little slice of hell. Enclosed by double-row fences of barbed wire, the camp occupied about 30 acres and consisted of little more than lines of ramshackle wooden barracks, painted a sickly dark green. Each barracks building was no more than 100 by 30 feet in size, yet most had somehow sheltered as many as 250 inmates. Just outside the wire, a rickety wooden guard tower stood about two stories high. Bathing facilities were nonexistent. A nauseating stench of death, sickly sweet and almost suffocating, permeated the area. In a square just inside the main gate, some 30 to 50 half-clothed bodies (estimates vary) lay haphazardly in clumps. These were men whom the Germans had executed, usually with a pistol shot to the head or throat, during the hasty evacuation of Ohrdruf.

Lieutenant Bob Cleary, commander of a reconnaissance platoon, could hardly believe his eyes. "There's nothing else that I can remember in my lifetime that remains as vivid and as horrible as that," he said. "You just can't believe how bad this place was. It was the worst day of my whole life, and the memories are imbedded [sic] in my brain." Private Bruce Nickols, another reconnaissance soldier, was nearly overcome by "the overpowering odor of quick-lime, dirty clothing, feces, and urine." In a vain effort to tamp down the smell, the Germans had sprinkled lime on some of the bodies. "Every time I smell lime since I get a 'flash back' of this horror," Herbert Lowe later wrote. Private Benjamin Fertig, a tank crewman, was so sickened by the stench of the place that he could not eat for several days. "I've gone by the places where they recycle sewage. That ain't half as bad [as Ohrdruf]." He felt a powerful urge to take a shower, but, under the circumstances, this was impossible. As Tech 4 (a rank equivalent to corporal) George Armstrong surveyed the awful scene, he felt a sense of guilt at being so free amid "so many dead people who must have suffered so much."[5]

Private Stanley Hodson intently studied the traumatized bodies at his feet. Their heads were shaved, and their upper legs were the size of his wrists. "They all lay in a pool of dried blood, right where they had been lined up . . . and shot," he wrote a few days later to his hometown newspaper in Maine. "They looked more like zombies than humans. Their skin was drawn taut around their heads, and their teeth were showing, like on a skull. Their mouths were open, as if cursing their murderers. They had no flesh on their bones, only skin. Their hip bones struck out tremendously and the skin hung loose. They reeked with disease."

Among the bodies was a corpse in significantly better condition than the others. The dead man wore a red plaid wool shirt, and he had a close-cropped, strawberry-blond beard. In red pencil, someone had written the words "American aviator" on a piece of paper and laid it on the body. "[He] had apparently been shot through the neck by a small caliber arm," Corporal Wencie Higuera said. "There were no dog tags or other identifying marks." Higuera estimated that the man had been in his early twenties. He had dark blond hair, a light complexion, and a medium build. The Americans later heard from German prisoners of war (POWs) that the aviator had been captured near Ohrdruf by the SS and subsequently executed because he had a broken ankle and could not make the march to Buchenwald. If this was true, it was unusual, as most downed American airmen ended up in prison camps supervised by the German air force.[6]

As the stunned liberators began to explore the camp, they soon encountered the few inmates who had managed to hide out and avoid the agonizing exodus from Ohrdruf to the mother camp at Buchenwald. "The thing I remember most is that the whitest part of their leg was the knee bone," Private William Charboneau, a 19-year-old GI in the 89th Infantry Division, remembered decades later in a voice choked with emotion. "I mean, their faces were so drawn out, and they tried to hold their hands up to us. It was horrible." Private William Coolman encountered one Russian survivor who "looked to be at least 60 yrs old [but] said that he was only 35. The living were terrible sights."

Inside one of the filthy, foul-smelling, claustrophobic barracks buildings, Tech 5 Dick Colosimo found a man who had evaded the marauding guards by hiding in his bunk. The building's only light came from one bulb near the door; there was no other electricity and no windows. "The bunks were stacked five high to the ceiling, so close to each other that one could not sit in an erect position in one bunk without bumping his head on the sideboard of the bed above," Colosimo wrote. The "mattresses" consisted of nothing more than crude, straw-filled gunnysacks. The skeletal, traumatized man told Colosimo that, when the guards began rounding up prisoners, he burrowed beneath his gunnysack, holding completely still while several of them searched the building. "Our sad-faced ex-prisoner indicated that he was trembling but he held his breath, not moving, just praying. He said that he didn't move an inch for a long, inestimable time, until he was sure it was all clear." To Colosimo, the man seemed to be in a daze, as if he could not quite comprehend that his terrible ordeal was finally over.[7]

In one small wooden building (the Americans thought of it as a shed or ice house), the soldiers found a room with a pile of about 30 gaunt, naked bodies stacked waist high. The bodies had been dusted with powdered lime, probably in an effort to curtail the stench and the rapidity of their decomposition. "Most of these corpses show the marks of brutality, bloody marks around the head, bruises on the back and kidneys, blackened testicles," one army officer wrote in a descriptive report from the site. Lieutenant Colonel Peter Majos, a physician, later wrote that several "showed evidence of traumatic injury such as broken ribs, contusions, and excoriations." In his professional opinion, most had died of malnutrition-related diseases.

For lack of any adequate language to convey the true horror of the scene before them, the soldiers tended to refer to the bodies as "stacked like cordwood." This banal phrase would become all too common among American liberators and witnesses at practically every camp. Michael Hirsh, author of a book on liberators, correctly pointed out that the use of such a phrase risked the danger of dehumanizing the victims or perhaps reducing such monstrous atrocities to the realm of the routine. The act of stacking cordwood, after all, is about as mundane and unremarkable a task as one can imagine. "It's very easy for the shock and horror of such a statement to evaporate into meaninglessness," Hirsh wrote cogently.

The lime emitted an acidic odor that could not even begin to diminish the powerful stench of decaying flesh. Most of the corpses were stacked on their stomachs; their sightless eyes appearing to stare at the dust and cinders of the ground below them. "It was really a gruesome scene," Tech 5 Abe Plotkin, a switchboard operator, later said. Lieutenant Colonel Albin Irzyk, the combat-hardened commander of the 8th Tank Battalion, was taken aback at the grisly sight. Over the course of many months in combat, he had seen a great deal of death and human suffering. None of it could compare. "I recoiled in absolute horror at the sight and smell," he later wrote. "This was such a shock that it was a moment before I could move." He almost passed out from the "telltale, stifling, indescribable stench of death. It was an awful sight combined with a horrible odor."[8]

Worse was to come. The troops soon realized that the shed was merely a storage place for bodies awaiting burial in the forest just outside the camp. According to survivor testimony, the storage shed had often been filled to the ceiling with the corpses during the winter. Army records estimated that between 2,000 and 3,000 such bodies had been hastily buried about a kilometer away. In reaction to the approach of American troops, the German guards had begun exhuming and quickly cremating the bodies, probably in an effort to conceal the evidence of their crimes. The guards had crisscrossed tree trunks, logs, and steel rails, liberally sprinkled with branches and brush, into a makeshift pyre on which to burn the bodies. "It appeared to be an extremely large hamburger grill fashioned from cross rails," Irzyk later wrote. This barbecue grill analogy was the only way the young colonel could begin to describe something that was for him so grotesque and unimaginable.

The Nazis had dug a pit between the rails and then ordered prisoners to stack as many bodies as they could into the hole. "A fire was still smoldering in the pit, and partially destroyed bodies remained on the rails and burnt parts were in the pit," Private Ralph Rush of the 355th Infantry Regiment recalled. In fact, the pit and the macabre pyre were littered with remains—"gray bone ash that was almost knee deep," in the recollection of another soldier. "It was still possible to distinguish a leg here, a head there," Sergeant Craib said. The flames had consumed many of the dead into blackened skeletons. Their shriveled extremities poked through the logs. Their scorched skulls hung downward into the ashy dirt. In some cases, the fire had not entirely consumed them; paper-white flesh could be seen in spots through the steaming rails. In small, quiet groups, soldiers stood gawking at the pyre, some with jaws dropped in shock or disgust. Among them, Private Hodson forced himself to look closely at the pit and saw "long poles with steel hooks on them used for turning the bodies over." The perpetrators had shifted the bodies around the fire like a cook moves meat around a grill. For the soldiers, this image was disturbing and life altering. They realized that only days earlier, other human beings—most of whom looked just like them and probably worshiped the same God—had stood over this bizarre grill, cremating these body parts with seeming detachment.

The smell of the dead was different here—and probably worse—than in the courtyard. It reeked of burnt wood and branches, scorched steel, gasoline fumes, and the acrid yet somehow sweet odor of burning flesh, bones, and hair. The awful odor made it difficult to breathe. Men dreaded the simple act of drawing their next breath of air. "The stench was overwhelming," Private Rush explained. Many years later, Private Charboneau soberly opined to an interviewer that "until you've smelled burnt flesh or decayed flesh, you have no idea what the odor is. I can still smell it today."

Rush was led away from the terrible scene by a young inmate, a Polish-Jewish man about his age, whom he had met a short time earlier. With tears in his eyes, the man handed him a silver watch and chain. "Here, this is all I have of value," the survivor said in broken English. "I can't take this from you," Rush replied. "The war will end soon, and you will need it." The man would not take no for an answer. Possessions apparently meant nothing to him anymore. The great gift of liberation and survival was all that mattered. Rush kept the watch though he never felt right about it. "I'm sorry I didn't get the young Pole's name," Rush said, "and I often wonder if he is alive."[9]

In addition to dragging bodies from the shed to the cremation pit, the guards and their prisoner labor force had exhumed remains of several thousand dead inmates from shallow mass graves and ditches in the forest, generally in the area adjacent to the pyre. At most, the Germans had cremated about one-third of them. The Americans now witnessed the grisly sight of half-clothed or naked remnants of the others, lying partially buried in pits and trenches. Here and there, the soldiers saw mounds of ash and dirt. Body parts protruded from some of the mounds. "The corpses were little more than skeletons," Captain Fred Diamond recorded in his diary. "Mere skin and bones, their arms and legs were not thicker than broomstick handles. Their ribs protruded greatly, and their abdomens were hollow pits. Their skin, now turned grey, was stretched like drums over their emaciated bodies." Many showed signs of extreme trauma. "Their bodies were covered with bruises," Diamond wrote, "and were enormously swollen, particularly in the region of the groin. The heads of many bore lacerations; others had had their eyes gouged out. Others had been stabbed in the chest approximately half a dozen times. Many had their misery ended with a bullet through their heads."

In another spot, Private Arthur Santa stared at a crude burial pit and noticed that "a leg was visible in a pool of bloody water." Lieutenant Colonel Morris Abrams, the 4th Armored Division's surgeon, was horrified. "It was so sad. You'd see young kids, older people, you'd see a skull half destroyed. You'd see bones scattered about . . . this God-awful stink. The smell . . . it was terrible." As the highest-ranking physician in the division, he was responsible for the health of every soldier. He worried about the spread of disease in such an unsanitary, pestilential environment. "If they expected us to billet right there, all I could think of was having an epidemic."

Elsewhere, Lieutenant Colonel Irzyk saw "an elliptical circle of bodies with the feet in and the heads out. I was absolutely stunned." Each corpse had a reddish colored bullet hole in the head or the throat. The surrounding ground was soaked with blood. Irzyk took a step back and gasped. Major John Scotti, a medical officer, angrily declared, "I tell you that German medical service is nil. This is how they have progressed in the last four years. They have now found a cure-all for typhus and malnutrition. It is a bullet through the head." As Lieutenant Thomas Curtin, a young liaison officer in the 4th Armored Division, stared in shocked silence at the awful sights before him, he thought of "the uncounted inmates as they heard the execution shots and then smelled the burning flesh of their comrades, and awaited their own similar fate."

Reacting to the Horror

In a way, the callous treatment of the victims' remains served as a final act of barbarism and dehumanization on the part of the guards. Thrown in such mass graves and disfigured so horribly, the dead lost their individuality, just as the Nazis intended when they robbed them of their names in favor of numbers tattooed onto their arms. The bodies resembled so much detritus, treated with the same disdain one might afford to last week's garbage. The very carelessness of the burial and cremation process practically screamed a message of hatred and contempt.

A brooding silence prevailed among the soldiers. They seemed reluctant, out of rage or respect for the victims, to say a word. "Some of the men were crying," Captain Jack Holmes of the 4th Armored Division recalled. "Others were wandering around like lost children." Holmes glanced at one of his friends and noticed his palms were bleeding because "he had shoved his fingernails in them so hard." In Private First Class Sol Brandell's platoon, a man who had a reputation as a devout Catholic stood at the edge of a pit loaded with corpses and "let out a loud wail, dropped to his knees, clasped his hands, and prayed to God amidst loud sobs, with tears running down his cheeks." Captain Ben Logan, a company commander in the 89th Infantry Division, was standing next to his first sergeant. The two men had become very close friends in the course of the war. The non-commissioned officer (NCO) looked at Logan and said, "I wish we could have gotten here earlier."[10]

Reaction to such horrible sights varied from individual to individual. The liberators felt a mixture of profound shock, distress, confusion, rage, and guilt at their own revulsion or powerlessness to help the survivors as much as circumstances warranted. One important point to bear in mind is that most of the men had arrived having no inkling of what Nazi concentration camps were really like. Unlike those who study the Holocaust from the distance of many decades, they had no historical base point against which to compare such horrid conditions and misdeeds. After all, for any latter-day investigator who is willing to confront the vast evidence of Nazi atrocities, the images and documented stories are plentiful. By contrast, the Americans at Ohrdruf (and soon many other camps) were the first witnesses to such a monstrous crime. Their brains found it difficult to process what was in front of their eyes. "There is no way I can fully describe the Ohrdruf camp except to say it was the most awful place I had ever seen, and I could not believe humans could be treated in such an inhumane manner," Corporal Ralph Dalton wrote. "I was shocked, and I will never forget it."

Lieutenant Colonel Irzyk was a consummate military professional who had seen a great deal of combat since the previous summer in Normandy. Like any commander, he was trained to maintain an even keel, but he knew that was an utter impossibility in Ohrdruf. "I had seen the most horrible of wounds, soldiers on both sides killed, dismembered. By this time, I believed I was somewhat hardened and understood deaths on the battlefield, but the examples of the deliberate and bestial suffering and death . . . was far beyond my comprehension." Numb and bewildered, he stood in silence, looking around in disbelief. "As I stared at the Nazi slaughterhouse, I just could not accept that human beings could have such utter and total disregard for other human beings and would callously, methodically, unemotionally *exterminate* them. What depravity!" Irzyk was emotionally overcome. He could not stand to see any more. "I had never before been in such an agitated state. I just had to get away."

William Charboneau, reflecting decades later on the terrible shock of discovery, said, "We thought we were hardened combat veterans. Some of us cried like babies. Some got sick. We couldn't believe what we were seeing. It was awful." One anti-tank gun crew took in the sights and hurried back to their truck. Once inside the truck, all of them simply sat in morose silence. "Each of us was lost in our own thoughts, each remembering what we had just witnessed," one of the crewmen later said. "The experience . . . was etched in every face. Over and over again the same cruel, brutal memories of carnage, torture, and disregard for life flashed through my brain." Private First Class Ladd Roberts, 19 years old, felt as if he passed from childhood to adulthood during the hours he spent at the camp. "As a teenager, viewing the Ohrdruf Holocaust aged me 10 years in one day," he wrote with piercing honesty. "I hope your teenager never has to see, smell, nor hear such a scene."[11]

Naturally, a wave of anger simmered among the soldiers toward the Germans, in or out of uniform, members of the Nazi party or not, whom they deemed collectively responsible for such madness and suffering. "This is eugenics as practiced by the Master Race," Captain Diamond wrote with condemnatory sarcasm at the end of a diary entry describing Ohrdruf. Private Santa was so upset by what he had witnessed that he warned his wife in a letter:

> This was all the result of a "cultured" and a "superman" race who have world rule ambitions. This all happened in OUR generation, and only a few days ago, at that. This was the result of a World [War] One Peace that didn't have permanency. This will be the result that will have to be fought by OUR little boy, IF the peacemakers don't smash Germany once and for all. I believe I would be very much tempted to assault anyone who professes sympathy for these bloodthirsty people. Any feeling I had for these people vanished when I viewed that horror camp. I didn't think I could hate anyone, but my feelings were severely jolted.

Lieutenant Curtin was so incensed that he summoned his driver, hopped in their jeep, drove to Gotha, and collared an arrogant German medical corps colonel whom they had briefly encountered the day before. "He was a man of slight stature but quite imperious. He spoke almost perfect English with a pronounced British accent." Curtin ordered the colonel onto the hood of his jeep and drove him to the concentration camp. The young lieutenant forced the enemy officer to "view all the horrors, but [I] was unable to get any reaction from him—except stony silence." The colonel later called Curtin "a cruel man" for making him ride on the hood of the jeep.[12]

Lieutenant Colonel James Van Wagenen, the military government and civil affairs officer of the 4th Armored Division, went into the town of Ohrdruf and found the mayor (or bürgermeister, as the Germans called him), a Nazi party member named Albert Schneider. Despite his status as a Nazi, Schneider had a good reputation among the residents of Ohrdruf as an honest and conscientious leader. He also had no direct ties to the SS. Van Wagenen personally led Schneider through the labor camp, making sure the mayor witnessed its many horrors. Schneider was shocked and visibly shaken by what he saw. "I did not believe that Germans were capable of atrocities like these," he told Van Wagenen. "We were told that the Russians were cruel and committed wholesale murder in a brutal way." In the next breath, though, he hinted that he did have some notion of what went on in the camp. "There were rumors in town, but we did not believe these."

Lieutenant Colonel Van Wagenen thought a visit to this grim place would be similarly illuminating for other citizens of Ohrdruf. He ordered Schneider to prepare a list of 25 men and women, representing a cross section of the town's population, to tour the camp the following day. The mayor agreed and departed. However, the next morning, he failed to show up at the appointed time. Van Wagenen sent a soldier to the home of Mr. and Mrs. Arthur Singer, where the mayor and his wife were staying because American troops were lodging in the Schneiders' house. On the back porch of the second floor, the soldier found the Schneiders lying dead, their wrists slashed. Alongside the corpses was a note, apparently meant for the Singers. "Forgive us for doing this in your house, but it cannot be helped." The Singers later told the Americans that the mayor had come home very depressed. He and his wife had eaten apathetically and then had retired upstairs to their room. Mrs. Schneider even told the hosts that, in the event of any nighttime shelling—the front lines were still only a few miles away—they would not take shelter in the basement. In retrospect, this was probably to make sure no one disrupted their plans to kill themselves.

News of the suicides spread rapidly through the ranks of the liberators. Interestingly, most of the soldiers mistakenly claimed that the mayor and his wife hanged themselves. In the World War II American military, death by hanging was considered highly dishonorable and distasteful, probably because it entailed more suffering than death by a firing squad. The latter was seen as more soldierly and certainly less painful. Hanging was meted out to spies, murderers, and war criminals. Perhaps the soldiers assumed the Schneiders had died by hanging because they thought of them, subconsciously or otherwise, as war criminals and felt they deserved that manner of death. Conversely, the people of Ohrdruf saw their mayor in a more honorable light, almost as a martyr. "[They] believe that the mayor felt responsible for the atrocities committed in the camp in his area," a United States Army intelligence officer who interviewed many of the residents later reported. "They assumed this to be the only reason for his suicide." But there might have been another factor. According to Staff Sergeant Andy Coffey, who was lodging in the Schneiders' home and got to know them a bit, the couple's two sons had been killed on the Eastern Front. "They cried a lot about [it]," Coffey later wrote. When he asked them about the labor camp right under their noses, "they claimed they had <u>no knowledge of the Ohrdruf Concentration Camp</u>."[13]

Forcing the Germans to Witness

With the mayor dead, Colonel Hayden Sears, commanding officer of Combat Command A, 4th Armored Division, renewed the order for Ohrdruf residents to view the camp. Under the supervision of the colonel and his soldiers, the civilians complied. Clad in long overcoats and wearing ties and hats, the stone-faced middle-aged and elderly civilians, all of whom were men, tromped among Ohrdruf's dreary buildings. A frightened-looking German army medical major accompanied them. Sears demanded that each of them individually enter the shed containing the bodies and take in the sight and smell of the place. Most had no reaction. One elderly man, though, did clap his hands once and shake his head in apparent consternation and disapproval. Sears looked at the medical major and said, "Doctor, you will observe that these men have either been bludgeoned to death or stabbed in the jugular vein. Does this meet with your conception of the German master race?"

"I cannot believe that Germans did this," the major replied.

"I presume your scientific mind still functions, Doctor," one of Sears's medical officers said. "You observe that these men have been dead at least a week—several days before American troops got here. Who do you think, then, committed these murders?"

"I would not have believed it if I had not seen it with my own eyes," the German doctor muttered.

Outside the camp, alongside the makeshift grill that had served as a crude crematory, the Germans were forced to stand grimly in place while the Americans read the list of atrocities committed in or near the camp. "Make them look at the hooked poles for turning the roasted bodies," Sears told an interpreter. "Make them stand closer and look!"

Everyone edged closer and stared somberly at the pyre. "The people of Ohrdruf were forbidden to come near this place," a paint merchant claimed. "They did not know about this. This is the work of only one percent of Germans, and you should not blame the rest."

"This is why Americans cannot be your friends," Sears replied. He turned to an interpreter and continued: "Tell them they have been brought here to see with their own eyes what is reprehensible by any human standard. Tell them we hold the whole German nation responsible because of its support and toleration of the Nazi government. Tell them so long as this kind of thing goes on, we must consider the German people our enemy."

One of the citizens, Karl Theuning, later told an army interrogator that the people of Ohrdruf had been angry with the SS for their behavior. "The population condemned the treatment of the prisoners," Theuning claimed. "Complaints were passed on by Bürgermeister Schneider through channels." Other citizens professed to be horrified but "helpless to do anything about it." But Gregory Kravchenko, one of the surviving inmates, claimed that "they did not have any human feelings toward us. At work, civilian Germans beat us to death." The full truth can never be known except by those who were there.

Most of the civilians simply professed ignorance. The Americans found these claims ridiculous and indefensible. When several Ohrdruf residents told Lieutenant Joe Friedman that they had no idea the camp existed, he responded, "How could you not know? Couldn't you smell it? What did you think they were doing, baking bread?" Still, the people claimed ignorance and powerlessness. "This Nazi ideology was inculcated into their minds so severely that it stayed with them for many, many years after the war," Friedman opined.

Like most of his comrades, Staff Sergeant Walter Seifert, a medic, had no sympathy for the local Germans. "The population of Ohrdruf knew very well what was going on," he wrote in his diary. "The slaves were working in the fields and factories and the people of Ohrdruf were rather well off because of their supply of cheap labor. Even now the people [have] no guilt whatsoever." When Seifert's unit, the Medical Detachment, 354th Infantry Regiment, occupied a house in Ohrdruf, the troops evicted the owners and would not allow them back inside, even to feed rabbits they were keeping in their backyard. The woman who had lived in the house told Seifert that he and the other Americans were cruel to allow the rabbits to starve to death. "When I told her she had the wrong conception of cruelty after having seen the things up on the Hill [a euphemism for the labor camp], she told me: 'That's different. They are only foreigners.'"[14]

The Brass Pays a Visit

The two generals with jurisdiction over the area, Major General Walton Walker, commander of the XX Corps, and Major General Troy Middleton, commander of the VIII Corps, ordered that the labor camp be left as the original liberators found it so that friend and foe alike could witness the stark truth of what had happened there. The generals also encouraged all soldiers who were not otherwise occupied to go to Ohrdruf. In the week that followed liberation, thousands of American soldiers visited the camp to see the appalling realities for themselves. "Of all the sights I have seen during this time, today I saw the most gruesome, a German concentration camp," Private Art Goldman wrote to his mother after paying a visit to Ohrdruf. "It is foolish for me to attempt to paint a word picture of what I saw . . . one must actually see such atrocities with his own eyes to believe them."[15]

The supreme commander, General Eisenhower, concurred with Goldman's sentiments. Eisenhower visited Ohrdruf on April 12 and was accompanied by two of his key commanders, General Omar Bradley and Lieutenant General George Patton. Dozens of soldiers, of all ranks, trailed along as the well-dressed and -groomed generals entered the compound. Eisenhower walked briskly with hands clasped firmly behind his back.

The three celebrity generals and their vast entourage were led around the camp by a squat, dark-haired, English-speaking man who said he had recently been an inmate. The man showed them the gallows where the Nazis had executed victims and a nearby whipping table where they had tortured prisoners. He himself had apparently once absorbed 25 lashes on this very table. Later, a story circulated—so widely that it could have been apocryphal—that the guide was actually a former camp guard who was subsequently recognized by former inmates and killed. In the meantime, though, the man led the somber group past the two dozen or so dead bodies still lying near the entry gate and to the shed where naked, emaciated, lime-dusted corpses lay piled in a mound.

By this time, Eisenhower, Bradley, and Patton collectively had seen much war, with all its inherent waste, destruction, death, and human tragedy. They were middle-aged military professionals at the peak of their proficiency. All three had previously known of the existence of Nazi concentration camps. And yet, like so many of their young soldiers, they were unprepared for, and quite taken aback by, seeing one firsthand. "All are men who have seen much of life in the raw, yet never on any human faces have I witnessed such horror and disgust," Lieutenant Colonel Charles Codman, one of Patton's aides, later wrote. For Bradley, the stench was almost too horrible to believe. "The smell of death overwhelmed us," Bradley wrote. "I was too revolted to speak. For here death had been so fouled by degradation that it both stunned and numbed us."

Bradley's revulsion was not unique. Eisenhower's complexion was chalky and his facial expression wan. "The visual evidence and the verbal testimony of starvation, cruelty and bestiality were so overpowering as to leave me a bit sick," Eisenhower wrote a few days later to General George Marshall, the United States Army's Chief of Staff. The stench emanating from the shed almost formed a physical barrier to entry. "As a reducer of smell, lime is a very inefficient medium," Patton later wrote in his diary. Near the door of the shed, he attempted unsuccessfully to fight off waves of nausea. He told Eisenhower he would get sick if he entered the shed so he refused to go inside. Eisenhower forced himself to go in. Patton—the iron-willed general whose men had nicknamed him "Old Blood and Guts"—quickly retreated around the corner and vomited. He and Eisenhower had been friends for more than two decades, and Eisenhower seemed to take a perverse pride in the fact that he entered the shed and Patton did not (possibly because the friendship had many ups and downs). He made a point of mentioning Patton's weak stomach in a letter to General Marshall shortly after the Ohrdruf visit and also in an interview with a journalist 20 years later, when he said that Patton had "heaved his lunch."[16]

Inside the shed, General Eisenhower grimly, and briefly, surveyed the bodies. At one point, he made eye contact with a soldier and said, "God, Sergeant, you have to have a strong stomach to take this."

The group moved on to the crude crematory and burial pits. Through an interpreter, Eisenhower listened to the testimony of survivors about the cruelty that had prevailed in this miserable place. One of the survivors remembered that the general "kept rubbing his hands together as we spoke of the horrors inflicted upon us and the piles of our dead comrades."

The supreme commander's expression was grim. Bradley, also gloomy-faced, peered closely at some of the human remains scattered about the area. "Lice crawled over the yellowed skin of their sharp, bony frames. A guard showed us how the blood had congealed in coarse black scabs where the starving prisoners had torn out the entrails of the dead for food." In the recollection of Major General Hobart Gay, Patton's chief of staff, Eisenhower commented that all of this was "beyond the American mind to comprehend." Indeed, it was so beyond comprehension and so repulsive that, after Patton returned to his headquarters, he immediately took a bath and scrubbed himself with lye soap. (His staff officers did the same.)

Eisenhower made sure to witness every last bit of Ohrdruf, barracks by barracks, burial pit by burial pit. Perhaps before anyone else, he understood that

Generals Dwight D. Eisenhower, Omar Bradley, and George Patton standing next to the make-shift crematorium just outside of Ohrdruf labor camp. Nazi guards incinerated innumerable bodies here. The area was littered with piles of ash and bone. (Dwight D. Eisenhower Library)

the day would come when some would attempt to deny the facts of what Nazi Germany had done—the killings, the gassings, the mutilations, the death marches, the starvation, the torture, the labor exploitation. The proliferation of cruelty was so staggering on such a titanic scale that no individual could ever truly grasp it all. Eisenhower was determined to see every part of it for himself. "I made the visit deliberately, in order to be in position to give first-hand evidence of those things if ever, in the future, there develops a tendency to charge these allegations to 'propaganda,'" he wrote to General Marshall on April 15. He reiterated the same message a few years later in a post-war memoir. "I felt it my duty to be in a position from then on to testify first hand," he wrote. In a 1965 interview, he said he toured Ohrdruf because "I'm not going to let anybody ever say again that all these stories are just made up."

Eisenhower came away from the experience very disturbed with the knowledge that "humans would get into this stage of degradation . . . physical degradation on the part of the inmates and spiritual degradation on the part of the people that inflicted it upon them." The barbarism and inhumanity generated a cold fury inside him. As a boy, he had often exhibited a volcanic temper; as an adult, he had learned to control it. This self-control was sorely tested at Ohrdruf. At one point, when he saw a GI bump into a German and, from sheer nerves, begin to giggle, he fixed the soldier with a cold stare and asked, "Still having trouble hating them?"

During a press conference a couple months later, he admitted, "I think I was never so angry in my life. It explains something of my attitude toward the German war criminal. I believe he must be punished and I will hold out for that forever." One of his aides described him at Ohrdruf as looking "very sick . . . and angry." During the tour, when someone told Eisenhower about the suicide of Mayor Schneider and his wife, he replied, "That is the most encouraging thing I've heard of. It may indicate that they still have some sensitivities."

Before Eisenhower left the camp, he gathered all of the GIs around him and spoke to them. "I want every American unit not actually in the front lines to see this place. We are told that the American soldier does not know what he is fighting for. Now, at least, he will know what he is fighting against." For soldiers like Tech 5 Richard Garrick, a radioman in the 355th Infantry Regiment, and the other men in his unit, the war had now taken on a new complexion. "The reality of this really struck home," he said. "It sobered them and they knew why they were doing what they were doing. It sort of stopped a lot of the bitching about why are we here."

Eisenhower spent that evening at Patton's headquarters in Hersfeld. The supreme commander made a point of sending messages to both the American and the British governments, urging them to send a random sample of newspaper editors and legislators to Germany to see the horrible facts for themselves. "I felt that the evidence should be immediately placed before the American and British publics in a fashion that would leave no room for cynical doubt," he later wrote.[17]

From Eisenhower on down, the precedent of documenting and witnessing the Holocaust was now set. As the general settled into a troubled sleep that early spring evening, he knew in his heart that Ohrdruf was only the beginning of the horrors his men would uncover as they overran Germany. Worse—much worse—was to come.

2 "The Smell of Death Was Thick in the Air"
Witnessing Buchenwald

ON APRIL 11, 1945, one week after the liberation of Ohrdruf, a combined task force from the 9th Armored Infantry Battalion, Combat Command A, 6th Armored Division captured a small town called Hottelstedt roughly 30 miles northeast of Ohrdruf. The task force was called Combat Team 9, and it consisted of two halftrack-mounted infantry companies, a tank company, and a mechanized headquarters company. Their job was to move fast, destroy or overtake any German defenders in their path, and to keep advancing as far as possible, bypassing any substantial centers of resistance. The 80th Infantry Division, advancing in the wake of the task force, was supposed to deal with any stubborn enemy holdouts. The commander of Combat Team 9 was Captain Robert Bennett. "Speed of advance was the essence of our attack to the East," he later wrote. Many such Allied armored forces were advancing through Germany in the same fashion. The complete collapse of the Third Reich was imminent even though plenty of fighting still raged.

On this day, Bennett's mission was to roll east to Ettersburg and seize a bridgehead over the Saale River. During the skirmish for Hottelstedt, his men had captured 15 SS troops. As the Americans lined their prisoners up to march to the rear, their attention was drawn to a nearby forest. Approximately 50 desperate-looking, bedraggled, armed men in shabby striped uniforms—Russians, apparently—emerged from the trees and attempted to attack the SS prisoners. "Of course we could not permit that although we . . . sympathized with the Russians," Bennett said. The Americans interceded and prevented the Russians from attacking the prisoners. Bennett's intelligence officer, Captain Frederic Keffer, spoke with the Russians and asked what was going on, where they had come from, and what they were doing. In disquieting and cryptic fashion, they pointed south and said they had escaped from a terrible place deep in the woods, not far away. The place was a concentration camp. It was called Buchenwald.[1]

The Origins of Buchenwald

By the time Keffer and the other members of Combat Team 9 encountered the escaped inmates, Buchenwald concentration camp was in its ninth year of existence. In July 1937, the SS had established the camp atop heavily wooded Ettersburg Mountain, some 1,600 feet in elevation. Throughout that summer, prisoners who were transferred from other concentration camps cleared trees, built barracks in rows of five, and enclosed the new prison with a ring of barbed wire. From these beginnings evolved one of Nazi Germany's most infamous labor and incarceration centers. Nazi leaders deliberately chose this Weimar locale because of its reputation as a place of German culture and political liberalism. Indeed, the camp was built on the exact forest retreat where eighteenth-century writer Johann Wolfgang von Goethe, one of Germany's most famous literary figures, had once spent many hours in contemplative solitude. The Nazis even preserved the celebrated oak tree where Goethe was said to have sought shade as he composed his works. The sturdy old tree remained standing alongside the camp's squat, dreary buildings—an odd juxtaposition of Germany old and new.

To the Nazis, the word "Weimar" carried more than just connotations of traditional German culture. It also brought to mind the shaky, fractious Weimar Republic the Nazi party had supplanted upon seizing power in 1933. For Nazis and German nationalists, the term "Weimar Republic" was disparaging. It was associated with a parliamentary style of government, societal permissiveness, and the hated Treaty of Versailles, the peace accord that ended World War I and imposed ruinous financial reparations on Germany, consigning it to the lowly status of a militarily weak third-rate power. The location of Buchenwald, therefore, conveyed a powerful symbolism for the Hitler regime: an image of a new, absolutist, rising, nationalist, politically intolerant Germany but one grounded in the greatness of traditional German culture.

Initially, the inmate population of Buchenwald consisted primarily of career criminals; they were soon joined by political opponents of the Nazi government. Over time, Buchenwald evolved into one of the most heavily politicized of all German concentration camps, not just because of the large number of political prisoners but also because of the competition for survival among differing political blocs. The dominant group was the Communists, many of whom had spent years fighting the Nazis and vying unsuccessfully for power in Germany. Following a nationwide Nazi-directed, anti-Semitic orgy of violence, property destruction, and roundups on November 11, 1938 (known as Kristallnacht), captured Jews were incarcerated in Buchenwald. The Jewish arrivals, along with political prisoners from newly annexed Austria, swelled the inmate population from about 3,000 to at least six times that many. Some of the Jews were later released. Some ended up in other concentration camps. Mortality rates spiked from about 2 percent in 1937 to nearly 13 percent in 1939. Prisoners worked long hours at backbreaking labor, constructing barracks, excavating earth to lay cables, digging and laying sewer mains, and clearing woods and building roads, all under poor conditions. Water was scarce, as was food. Latrine facilities were barely adequate. Tools were in short supply. Inhuman treatment by the sadistic SS guards only added to the nightmare. Beatings were routine, as was extreme verbal abuse. Prisoners were subjected to four separate roll calls each day; often that meant standing for hours in the heat or the cold.

The outbreak of war in 1939 brought an influx of foreigners into the camp. Initially, these foreigners came primarily from eastern Europe, but, as the war unfolded, they came from every German-controlled country on the continent. There were Soviet prisoners of war and forced laborers from Poland, Ukraine, Russia, Hungary, France, Italy, and Czechoslovakia, to name just some of the nationalities, in addition to many political prisoners from western Europe, including captured resistance fighters. Jews were always in the minority at Buchenwald; the Nazi policy of a "Jew-free" Germany meant that the majority of Jews were sent to ghettoes or death camps in Poland, at least until the last couple years of the war. Typically, though, they were treated the most harshly among the prisoners at Buchenwald. Conditions at the camp actually improved with the influx of prisoners. Atrocities declined for a year or two because wartime pressure and the larger collection of inmates served to distance the SS from their potential victims. Eventually, the growth of the prison population, the sheer desperation of total war, and the inherently brutal nature of Buchenwald led to a terrible climate of injustice, mistreatment, and horror.

The SS did not have the manpower to manage this many prisoners by themselves, so they implemented a system of self-administration within the camp. This led to the appointment of trustees among the inmates. The trustees and their allies wielded enormous power over their fellow prisoners. The trusteeships, and many other privileged positions, were dominated by German nationals. German criminals more or less controlled the trusteeships until 1942, when German Communists supplanted them in a savage power struggle. The Communists triumphed by establishing productive relationships with SS men, but, more than that, they prevailed because of their group discipline. The criminals tended to care only for themselves. "They grew fat on the rations of their fellows, clothed themselves with the garments of those they murdered," Captain Christopher Burney, a captured British special operative who ended up in Buchenwald, later wrote of the criminals, "and whiled away their long nights gambling and drinking, while their future victims lay on the straw and tried to recuperate enough strength and courage to carry them through the next day."

In addition to administrative competence, the Communists also tended to possess technical skills and mechanical know-how because many had once been industrial laborers. These skills made them indispensable in a camp focused on the exploitation of slave labor for the war effort. "Their advances were not made without resistance from the criminals, but gradually the criminals were eliminated from power, partly by intimidation, partly with the aid of the SS," said a United States Army report authored by Egon Fleck, a civilian analyst, and Lieutenant Edward Tenenbaum, an intelligence officer with the Publicity and Psychological Warfare section of Lieutenant General Omar Bradley's Twelfth Army Group. Based on immediate, on-site, post-liberation interviews and direct observations, their report chronicled the history, conditions, and liberation of Buchenwald in remarkable detail.[2]

An especially important ally of the Communists was Waldemar Hoven, a camp doctor, a relentless purveyor of opportunistic cruelty, and, in the estimation of Captain Burney, "a murderer of no ordinary talent." Hoven became such an advocate of the Communist prisoners that he willingly eliminated their criminal rivals by conducting medical experiments on them or simply killing them. "Numbers of the criminals were killed by beatings, hangings, or injections of phenol into the heart, or of air or milk into the veins," Fleck and Tenenbaum said. When these two analysts later had the opportunity to meet and interrogate Hoven, they formed the opinion that he was a psychopath. Hoven wept at the sight of several Jewish prisoners he claimed to have saved, yet he readily admitted his role in killing off the criminals and conducting grisly tests in the typhus laboratories, "where hundreds of healthy prisoners were burned with phosphorous for experimental reasons, dying in great pain."

For all their discipline and ostensible devotion to Marxist egalitarian ideology, the Communists relished their elite status and ruthlessly suppressed any challenge to their rule. In 1943, when thousands of Polish prisoners who had enjoyed a similarly privileged existence in Auschwitz arrived at Buchenwald and attempted to co-opt power, the Communists responded with a veritable reign of terror. According to Fleck and Tenenbaum, the Polish grab for power "was crushed by the killing of large numbers in the typhus experiment station," run by none other than Dr. Hoven.

The story was much the same for thousands of forced laborers, captured resistance fighters, and political prisoners from western Europe. Anyone who did not accede to the Communists' rule often suffered the camp's brutal justice, whether that meant becoming a guinea pig in the medical experiments, suddenly getting transferred to an even deadlier and more miserable camp, or, more commonly, not receiving as much food as the Communists and their allies. "The Germans had more to smoke and more to eat than any others, provided they belonged to the ruling party," Fleck and Tenenbaum wrote. They also had better medical care, clothing, and small articles of property such as watches and caps, much of which had been confiscated by the SS from other prisoners when they entered the camp. In the view of one analyst, the German Communists had the "power of life and death over all other inmates."

In this sense, the SS at Buchenwald had implemented a system in which they outsourced viciousness and ruthlessness, setting up a hierarchy among their victims which encouraged brutal behavior among prisoners rather than any sort of universal camaraderie. The block chiefs, or "kapos," who ranked just below the trustees and ran the lives of their fellow inmates much the way sergeants supervise soldiers in a military organization, could be especially harsh. Most of the chiefs were either Communists themselves or affiliated with them. They were under intense pressure from their Communist and SS overseers to keep their area of responsibility (mainly barracks) under control, free of rebellion, and productive.

Under these pressures, and with such power at their disposal, many trustees could not resist the temptation to terrorize and mistreat inmates. One leader was known for administering severe beatings and kicking prisoners in the testicles. Another assisted Dr. Hoven with executions. The majority personally beat their charges and even forced them to stand barefoot in snow for hours on end. "Remember first of all that they were fanatics," Captain Burney wrote. "Their minds had for many years been poisoned with the idea that they and they alone were the elite, that they and they alone had any right of authority over their fellows. Secondly, that idea had been instructed by the dogma of terror. Who is not with you is against you, and the simplest method of correcting him is to liquidate him." Their long-term goal was not just mere survival, but the realization of their dream of a Communist Germany. They were tantamount to a shadow government within the camp—highly organized politically, with a dizzying array of committees, divisions of responsibility, contacts on the outside, and even a militia of sorts, clandestinely armed with scavenged weapons.[3]

Of course, the depravity and relentless inhumanity of Buchenwald ultimately came from the Nazi regime and, more specifically, the SS. It was they who were responsible for creating such hell on earth and for finding seemingly endless ways to make that hell even worse for its victims. A terrible litany of atrocities and mistreatment took place during the camp's nine years of existence. Shootings, beatings, whippings (sometimes to the death), medical experiments, torture, overwork, overexposure to the elements, degradation, summary executions, and interrogations were all too common. One SS man liked to order prisoners to be buried alive. "Then he murdered them with blows from a shovel when they pushed their heads through the dirt," a surviving prisoner recalled. On occasion, this guard would stroll through the camp, select a prisoner at random, take him to the nearest washroom, and then hold his head under water until he drowned. Another sergeant would order a prisoner to bow in front of him. In the recollection of one witness, he would "then strike the prisoner on the base of the skull until his neck was broken."[4]

Colonel Karl Koch, the camp commandant from 1937 to 1941, had an especially notorious reputation, as did his wife Ilse. The two had met when Karl was commandant at another camp called Sachsenhausen and Ilse was one of his guards. She had joined the Nazi party in 1932 at the age of 26; he was a World War I veteran who had become a Nazi in 1930. Together they turned Buchenwald into their own exploitative playpen, robbing prisoners and fostering a climate of pitilessness and arbitrary punishment. Ilse was fond of riding her horse through camp and singling out prisoners for special whippings. Anyone who did not address her as "Gracious Lady" or some other respectful title was subject to brutal beatings. When one prisoner from the kitchen detail was found drunk from stolen liquor and, after a substantial beating, refused to identify who gave him the alcohol, Commandant Koch ordered every second prisoner in the detail to be whipped while everyone else stood at attention in the freezing cold. Still no one gave up the identity of the thief. Koch ordered the entire camp to go without rations the next day.

On another occasion, Kurt Dietz, a prisoner who served as the commandant's valet, stole two bottles of wine from the Kochs' personal stash. Ilse caught him and reported the infraction to her husband. The commandant's prescribed punishment was severe. Dietz was whipped in the face, forced to run and crawl over two high mounds of gravel, strapped to a block, gagged, beaten on the buttocks with 25 lashes, forced to do 100 deep-knee bends, and ordered to stand at attention on the gravel mound in the heat for several hours with no cap on his head. Finally, he was hung with arms tied behind his back on the door of his cell block for three straight hours. "The pain can scarcely be imagined," he later wrote. "For months afterward I could use my arms only with the greatest caution."

The Kochs were hardly a devoted, faithful couple. In 1940 the commandant traveled to Norway for a short trip and contracted syphilis. Ilse had affairs with several men, including the camp's deputy commander and Dr. Hoven. Karl, hoping to keep his case of syphilis confidential, sought treatment from Walter Kramer, a prisoner who served as a medical orderly. Kramer administered doses of the drug Salvarsan to Koch, and the treatment was successful. Thus cured and concerned that Kramer and another prisoner who knew of the treatments might disclose the news of his venereal disease, Koch ordered them both executed, supposedly for political crimes.

Koch also engaged in extensive embezzling, black marketeering, and outright thievery, usually at the expense of prisoners. His family lived in opulent splendor. For example, he ordered the prisoners to build a private horse riding hall (1,600 square meters in size) to be used exclusively by him and his wife. The cost was a quarter-million marks, paid for primarily with extorted or embezzled funds. Though such corruption was not unusual for SS concentration camp personnel, the Kochs took theirs to a particularly brazen level, creating many enemies within the Nazi bureaucracy and SS circles. In 1941 Karl was cited for tax evasion in Weimar and transferred to Majdanek concentration camp in Lublin, Poland. Later he was arrested, tried, and convicted in an SS court for corruption as well as for the unauthorized murder of Kramer and the other executed prisoner.

Like her husband, Ilse ran afoul of the authorities for her part in the rampant corruption and the routine mistreatment of prisoners. She was tried in an SS court but was acquitted. The most infamous crimes associated with her involve shrunken human heads, preserved organs, and lampshades made out of human skin, the evidence of which was found by Buchenwald's liberators. According to prisoner testimony, Ilse collected the macabre lampshades, handbags, and even gloves made from the skin of dead inmates, many of whom she had personally ordered to be killed for this very purpose. Some of the shades featured elaborate tattoo patterns. The accusers claimed that, on morning rides, Ilse often inspected inmates for interesting tattoos and then ordered them killed and skinned for her grisly keepsakes. Although posterity has generally taken these gruesome stories as factual, giving Ilse the somewhat sexist nickname "the Bitch of Buchenwald," no other hard evidence of her guilt has ever come to light. Nonetheless, the witness testimony was damning enough to leave little doubt that she was involved with these bizarre crimes in some fashion. Though acquitted by the SS court, Ilse was tried and convicted of lesser war crimes by the Americans after the war and then released in 1947. At that point, the German government convicted her of crimes against German citizens. She spent the rest of her life in prison, committing suicide in 1967. Karl was executed by the SS in 1945.[5]

The demise of the Kochs slightly improved conditions in Buchenwald under the stable and more honest command of SS Colonel Hermann Pister. Even so, the place was still ruled by terror, injustice, mistreatment, and brutality. (Pister was later convicted and executed by the Americans as a war criminal.) As the war unfolded, Buchenwald's importance grew as a source of slave labor for the German war effort, spawning some 88 subcamps, one of which was Ohrdruf. In hopes of creating a way station and, thus, streamlining transit from Buchenwald to these subcamps, the SS built a new enclosure within Buchenwald which came to be known simply as "the Little Camp." Ringed by barbed wire, this enclosure comprised some crude tents as well as windowless horse stables improvised into barracks. The tents were drafty and extremely muddy with their dirt floors. The stables were designed to house 50 horses; many contained nearly 2,000 human beings. There was only one latrine for the entire compound. There was no running water, no heat, and little food. Each prisoner ate about 500 calories per day. Many people simply lay down and died, their corpses sprawled unattended for days or even weeks.

The Little Camp was originally populated by Polish, Russian, French, and Dutch prisoners. Eventually, it also became a dumping ground for children, Gypsies, and Jews. The Little Camp reflected not only the casual savagery of the Nazis' slave labor system but also the pronounced hierarchical stratification among Buchenwald's prisoners. Physically separated from the main camp by barbed wire and guards, the Little Camp and its degraded residents were seen as a veritable leper colony by the other prisoners, especially the ruling Communists. "All were reduced to an unbelievably low common denominator by the torture and starvation," Fleck and Tenenbaum wrote. Another commentator described it as "a place of deepest despair for those left to be forgotten and to die from cold, starvation, dehydration, debilitating labor, torture and rampant epidemics of diseases that went untreated."[6]

By February 1945, Buchenwald's population had swollen to 112,000 prisoners, with sharp separations among the different classes of prisoners. Conditions in the Little Camp were deteriorating while the Communists, their allies, ethnic Germans, some western Europeans, and prisoners who had logged the most time in Buchenwald still lived in relatively stable barracks, with some semblance of an adequate food supply. The disintegration of Nazi Germany and the imminent approach of the United States Army threatened to destabilize the entire power structure of the camp. Heinrich Himmler, Reichsführer of the SS, ordered his concentration camp commandants to kill or evacuate their prisoners. Evacuation was almost equivalent to a death sentence because it often meant that hordes of diseased, malnourished, disoriented prisoners would be driven on "death marches" by sadistic, desperate guards for long distances, all the while exposed to the elements with little shelter, little food, and no medical care. Alternatively, evacuation could mean that prisoners would be packed onto trains bound for other spots in the crumbling Nazi empire, again with no basic care of any kind. Survival under such conditions was at best problematic, at worst unlikely. Horrible though Buchenwald was, prisoners were still better off staying because at least the camp provided crude shelter, a tiny food supply, and some level of stability.

In early April, with the Americans only miles away, Colonel Pister, who was ordinarily a disciplined man inclined to follow orders to the letter, instead temporized. In effect, he was caught between two power centers: his superiors in Berlin, whose power was diminishing by the day, and the menacing specter of the United States Army, whose proximity and prodigious strength empowered the Communist hierarchy and resistance-minded prisoners within Buchenwald. If Pister executed all of the prisoners, the Americans would see him as a cold-blooded murderer and punish him accordingly. Plus, he would face the real possibility of a prisoner uprising. (In fact, the Communists and former resistance fighters had hidden caches of stolen weapons and were already planning a mutiny.) If he openly disobeyed Himmler's orders, he risked arrest and execution at the hands of the SS security police. Instead he tried to pursue a middle course and play one side against the other. On April 2, he met with the trustees and announced his intention to stay at the camp and hand it over, along with the whole inmate population, to the Americans. The following day, though, he issued an order for Jews to be separated and prepared for evacuation.

For the next week, tense, extraordinarily stressful events ensued, with Pister issuing multiple evacuation orders and the prisoners doing their best to delay or defy the orders, all against a backdrop of rumors about the impending arrival of the Americans. According to Fleck and Tenenbaum, the trustees "spread the word that all inmates were to continue to resist evacuation, and that they were to be assisted by the trustee organization. Since much of the internal police of the camp was in the hands of the Communist trustees, this order made it almost impossible for the SS to find specific individuals." Even so, the SS could and did round up masses of people, particularly those who were new to the camp, had no connections, or were too weak to resist. Over the course of that week, some 20,000 prisoners, half of them Jews, were herded out of Buchenwald and sent away, mainly on overloaded trains. One scholar estimated that most of these unfortunate people died on the way to the Flossenbürg, Theresienstadt, and Dachau concentration camps.

At last, on the morning of April 11, with the sounds of small arms fire echoing in the distance and the arrival of the Americans a matter of mere hours, Pister summoned the ranking inmates and told them, "I am leaving now. I hereby turn the camp over to you." He urged them to say nothing of this to anyone lest it incite anarchy and chaos. Pister promptly fled, along with most of the other SS troops, though a skeleton force of guards, who either did not receive the withdrawal order or were deemed expendable, did remain at various posts around the camp for a few hours. At 12:10, the roll call officer announced on Buchenwald's public address system, "All SS men leave the camp immediately!" The prisoners were concerned that this was a ruse and that the hated guards would soon attempt to kill everyone. Instead, quiet prevailed. Some of the prisoners were already armed, waiting to be attacked or to take over the camp. Nothing happened. By mid-afternoon, American tanks could be seen and heard rolling by on the roads outside of camp.

Post-war Communist propaganda, particularly in what became East Germany, asserted that the Communists rose up at this point, fought the remaining SS troops, and took control of the camp, in essence liberating themselves. In fact, there was little if any real fighting. The sentries who remained after the withdrawal order began to abandon their posts around 3:00 p.m. and head for the woods. The "uprising" took place only after most of the Nazis had fled, though the armed prisoners did chase down 76 SS men, mainly in the surrounding woods, and take them into custody. The main Communist motive was probably to take control of Buchenwald before the Americans arrived, not to engage in a real battle with the SS. By 3:15 p.m. (a time still frozen on the camp's clocks to commemorate the moment of liberation), they were in nominal control of Buchenwald. Prisoners seized control of the SS barracks and armory. Armed patrols roamed the camp and nearby villages. "They were very childish, forming bands of different nationalities and marching about looking as if they had defeated the entire Wehrmacht," Captain Burney, the British special operations prisoner, later wrote with ill-disguised contempt.[7]

The First Americans Enter Buchenwald

It was some of these newly armed former inmates, clad in either their striped uniforms or scrounged clothing, who made contact with Captain Robert Bennett's Combat Team 9. The puzzled Americans did not know what to make of these disheveled, bony, desperate-looking men. The two groups communicated through a mixture of Russian, English, and German. Bennett absorbed their main message: 21,000 surviving prisoners were nearby at Buchenwald. "He was also told that most of the SS troops who administered the camp had fled, but that some had been held in an uprising of the prisoners," Lieutenant Hollis Alpert, an army historian, wrote ten days later after interviewing Bennett. Otherwise, the captain had little idea of what any of this really meant. "I could not spare many troops to investigate this report," he wrote. He detached Captain Frederic Keffer, his intelligence officer, to check out the camp while the rest of Combat Team 9 resumed the advance. For the expedition, Captain Keffer chose Tech Sergeant Herbert Gottschalk, a German-speaking soldier from his intelligence section, as well as Sergeant Harry Ward and Private First Class James Hoyt, plus two prisoners to function as guides.

With Hoyt driving, the group piled into an M8 armored car and set off. "We had been told by our intelligence that we might overrun a large prison camp," Keffer later wrote, "but we—or at least I—had no idea of either the gigantic size of the camp or the full extent of the incredible brutality." They arrived just outside Buchenwald. Hoyt carefully maneuvered the vehicle through a hole in the camp's fence and through a double-barbed, electrified wire fence that stretched some 12 feet high. The vehicle rolled to a stop in the main compound. Keffer and Gottschalk dismounted, and, before they could even take in their surroundings, they were excitedly greeted by—and found themselves enmeshed among—thousands of jubilant prisoners. "What an incredible greeting that was," Keffer said. "I was picked up by arms and legs, thrown into the air, caught, thrown . . . until I had to stop it. I was getting dizzy. How the men found such a surge of strength in their emaciated condition was one of those bodily wonders in which the spirit overcomes all weaknesses of the flesh."

Once Keffer calmed the inmates down, he and Gottschalk gave them all the C rations in their possession and promised that other Americans would soon arrive with more food and medical aid. The prisoners gave the Americans a brief tour, including a look at several captured SS guards who, in Keffer's recollection, "were securely staked down alive to the ground." They did not get to see the inside of the prisoner barracks or the Little Camp, where conditions were the worst. The four Americans were under orders not to linger. Their job was reconnaissance, not occupation, although it is fair to say they were the first liberators to arrive at Buchenwald.

They spent less than an hour at the camp before heading back to the group and reporting what they had seen to Captain Bennett. For his part, Bennett had only glimpsed the camp when his vehicle passed it during the combat team's advance that day to Ettersburg. "Our mission required that we do nothing more than report the facts that we had ascertained." He dutifully

The main entrance gate at Buchenwald, shortly after liberation. Today the clock remains permanently set at 3:15, the moment of liberation. (National Archives)

informed his superior, Colonel Albert Harris, commander of Combat Command A, and Harris informed Major General Robert Grow, the division commander. Grow made sure that his superiors at the corps and army level also were informed. This set the wheels in motion for infantrymen, medics, and military government troops to head for Buchenwald, though many would not arrive for several more days.[8]

In the meantime, two other Americans, Mr. Egon Fleck and Lieutenant Edward Tenenbaum, the analysts from Twelfth Army Group, encountered escaped prisoners, realized that Buchenwald was no longer under SS control, and decided to head for the camp. As their jeep rolled through the gates at about 5:00 p.m., they were greeted by prisoner sentries and then large numbers of excited prisoners who "cheered at the sight of an American uniform, rushed out to shake hands, and threw valuable binoculars from their slave workshops." While armed inmates kept order, the Communist leaders greeted the two Americans. After a brief orientation and tour, the Americans attended a meeting of the camp council, an authoritative body of about 50 former prisoners which now purported to govern Buchenwald. Each member of the council represented between 500 and 1,000 inmates from one section of the camp or a certain nationality. They met in a long room that had once been an SS mess hall. "German was the predominant language, but each group had its own interpreter who translated as the meeting progressed," the Americans wrote. "When a speaker finished a sentence, a low murmur of French, Russian and Czech could be heard from the interpreters." The main topic was how best to organize the newly liberated camp. Commissions were appointed to take care of sanitation, food, clothing, administration, security, and information.

An incident at this meeting revealed the continued stratification within the ranks of the now-liberated inmates. When the floor was thrown open for discussion and questions, one of the council members contended that "bandits" were breaking out of the Little Camp and asked what the leadership was going to do to control them. The new leaders had already posted guards around the barbed-wire perimeter of the Little Camp, and they promised to increase their number. Thus, instead of assisting their less fortunate brethren in the Little Camp, they continued to oppress them.

Fleck and Tenenbaum were the first Americans to visit this horrible place. "A trip through the Little Camp is like a nightmare," they wrote. In a matter of seconds, scores of skeletal, lice-ridden, diseased inmates converged on the two men "like magic, pouring out of doorways as if shot from a cannon. Almost all wear striped convict suits, covered with patches or grey-black remnants of Eastern clothing. The universal covering is a little black skull cap. They doff these ceremoniously to the visitors. Some are crying, others shouting with joy." With bony hands they touched and hugged the Americans. In this crowd of degraded humanity, Fleck and Tenenbaum were especially saddened to see children, most of whom were probably between the ages of six and fourteen.[9]

The stench of the place was overpowering, as Fleck and Tenenbaum described:

> The smell of death is thick in the air. In the main camp there are solid barracks, clean and well made. In the small camp there are twenty-seven low wooden barns. In these are three to five tiers of wide shelves running the length of the building. On them are sacks of rotten straw, covered with

vermin. In the center of the camp are open sheds, covering deep concrete-lined pits. These are the latrines, from which pour an indescribable stench.

Beyond the tidal wave of starving survivors of the Little Camp, just outside the barbed wire that surrounded the compound, Fleck and Tenenbaum could see armed inmates from the rest of the camp patrolling menacingly, keeping the residents of the Little Camp imprisoned in their terrible place. They wrote:

> To many of the self-styled aristocrats of the big camp these are all "bandits." The "bandits" carry lice and disease to a greater extent than other inmates. They seek to break out of the terribly crowded corner of the camp in which they are, into the more comfortable clean blocks of the main part. They are brutalized, unpleasant to look on. It is easy to adopt the Nazi theory that they are subhuman, for many have in fact been deprived of their humanity.

In their report, Tenenbaum and Fleck cautioned their Twelfth Army Group superiors not to fall into the trap of continuing this Nazi-inspired but prisoner-supervised practice of veritable apartheid. "It would be easy to continue favoring the big camp in the distribution of food, as has been done in the past, and, more important for the wretches of the small camp, in the distribution of medicine."

Decades later, one senses that even such sympathetic observers as these two men could not bring themselves to stay in the Little Camp for long. The terrible condition of the Little Camp inmates created a disturbing tendency to dehumanize them, even in the minds of these caring visitors. Many other American soldiers would experience the same difficulty envisioning these survivors as full-fledged human beings similar to themselves. Perhaps this lends some insight as to how ideology-tainted guards could so regularly mistreat and brutalize their prisoners.

Buchenwald council members provided Fleck and Tenenbaum with clean beds in Block 50, where Dr. Hoven had once conducted his medical experiments. Fleck and Tenenbaum spent a quiet night there. In the morning, they were awakened by the incongruous, melodious sounds of a brass band, which played for them until they got up and "appeared at the windows to be cheered by several thousand inmates." Later that morning, the Americans observed a liberation parade—the celebration did not include people from the Little Camp—and Lieutenant Tenenbaum even addressed the former prisoners over the camp's loudspeaker system in what one of them termed "American

German." Tenenbaum and Fleck then left Buchenwald and returned to their unit, where they prepared an 18-page report that still stands as the finest original source on the camp's inner workings and the conditions when Americans arrived. "It was an incredible experience," they wrote. "The rebirth of humanity in a bestial surrounding."[10]

Liberators and Witnesses at Buchenwald

In the hours and days that followed these first instances of contact, more Americans arrived at the camp as liberators, caregivers, and, most commonly, observers. Staff Sergeant Martin "Dick" Renie was a squad leader in A Company, 317th Infantry Regiment, 80th Infantry Division, the unit that was trailing the 6th Armored Division's task force. When he and his soldiers got to Buchenwald (probably around midday on April 12), they were engulfed by the stench of rotting flesh and sewage that permeated the camp. As Renie and his men laid eyes on the former inmates, they were stunned into a puzzled silence. "As ragged a group of men as I've ever seen," Renie later wrote. He conversed with one of them in a rough mixture of French and English. He was able to glean enough to understand the basics about Buchenwald and the sheer number of liberated inmates, many of whom were of course armed. Renie's squad gently disarmed as many as they could and then set about distributing food. This was a common American tendency—the generous but misguided impulse to give food, alcohol, tobacco, and other goodies to such stricken people. "The men were in very poor shape," Renie wrote. "One man showed me his hip bone actually exposed through the skin which had worn off by the weight of his belt. They were unbelievably thin with hollowed eyes and sunken cheeks."

People in this kind of condition were in no shape to digest the calorie-rich American C and K rations that Renie and his squad passed into so many bony hands, and most of the food was vomited right back up. Renie saw some survivors—undoubtedly alumni of the Little Camp, now released—shuffling aimlessly with a half-dead gait, "most of them completely devoid of energy and motion. They really hadn't the will to do anything. These people were horrifyingly thin, emaciated skeletons covered with skin."

Some prisoners took Renie and the other soldiers on an impromptu tour, a common occurrence as former prisoners began to interact with Americans following the camp's liberation. It was as if the survivors knew how unbelievable their surroundings would seem to those who had not experienced such hell. Or perhaps they were already compelled to bear witness, in no uncertain terms, even to such compassionate liberators. Renie's group toured the barracks, and they got a firsthand look at Buchenwald's infamous body disposal plant, or crematorium, which consisted of six sturdy, fire-brick ovens. "Troughs leading to the furnace doors allowed for sliding the bodies into the brick furnaces," Renie said. "It was all so fantastically unbelievable that we were in complete shock." With the shock came emotion. In Renie's case, he struggled to keep from breaking down and sobbing. The horror he felt was indescribable and unforgettable. "I was ashamed of the whole human race," he later said. Although this was not necessarily a universal sentiment among the liberators, many of the young soldiers were shocked to realize that human beings were capable of such calculated savagery.[11]

According to one United States Army report, Buchenwald's ovens could incinerate up to 400 bodies in a ten-hour period. The SS had actually devised a clear-cut method to dispose of the bodies of their victims. After roll call each evening, prisoners were ordered to collect and strip the bodies of anyone who had died in the previous 24-hour period. A truck or wagon then circled the camp to pick up the bodies and haul them to the front yard of the incinerator plant. Prisoners hauled the bodies into the building, extracted any remaining valuables such as gold teeth, and then shoved the remains into the ovens. "The floor of each incinerator consisted of a coarse grate through which the boneash fell into an ashpit about 16" deep," the report stipulated. Directly below the ovens was a torture chamber, the floor and walls of which consisted of cool cement. The walls were equipped with sturdy rows of meat hooks on which the SS hung and beat rebellious prisoners. As Victor Geller, a philosophical soldier and a Jew, studied the impersonal concrete wall, he mentally engaged it in an imaginary conversation.

"How could you be a party to this?" Geller asked.

In Geller's mind, the wall answered, "Like everything else here, like everyone else here, I was made part of the system. Like the gallows and the whipping posts, like the ovens upstairs, I was used. I was just one of the tools of a bureaucracy that devised a scheme which forced the victims to carry out their own destruction."

Geller thought to himself, "This place . . . is the ultimate point of transition, an assembly line that moved people until they became things, from subject to object. This machinery converted the human being into visible puffs of smoke, from fullness to void. Here, evil was not even deserving of emotion, just sound procedure."

One survivor told Herman Cole, a medic from the 6th Armored Division, that "some were . . . hung on the . . . meat hooks to die while . . . others were being cremated." On these frequent occasions when the Nazis strangled, tortured, or beat their victims to death, the bodies were immediately and easily disposed. "An electric elevator, with an estimated capacity of 18 bodies, ran up to the incinerator room, which was directly above The Strangling Room."

From the testimony of liberated prisoners, the soldiers learned that in March a coal shortage had forced the guards to shut down the ovens for ten days. In the interval some 1,800 bodies accumulated in the yard outside the incinerator. At the same time, the weather warmed. The rising number of dead bodies combined with the warmth exacerbated the already insufferable stench permeating the area. Instead of waiting to cremate the bodies, SS guards organized a work party of prisoners to gather the corpses and bury them in a huge communal pit in the forest outside the camp. When the job was finished, the SS simply shot the members of the work party, threw them in the pit, and hastily covered their remains with dirt. Even though a new coal supply allowed for the resumption of cremations, so many prisoners were dying that, by the time the Americans arrived at Buchenwald, corpses were still stacked up, awaiting incineration. The Americans estimated that about 120 bodies were still "parked in a truck in the front yard." The terrible sight of these bodies, so unceremoniously and anonymously packed together on this truck—or wagon, really—was heavily photographed by many soldiers and remains one of the most infamous images associated with Buchenwald. The ovens themselves still contained some remnants of the people they had devoured. "The incinerator grates had not yet been cleared of un-consumed hip-bone joints and parts of skulls," an American observer later wrote.[12]

Lieutenant Colonel Jim Moncrief, the 6th Armored Division's personnel officer, visited Buchenwald because of the cryptic reports Major General Robert Grow and division headquarters had received from Captain Bennett. "I had staff responsibility to represent the General in matters dealing with people—including prisoners." With absolutely no notion of the horrors ahead, Moncrief took several moments to process what he saw as he entered the compound. There were several inert bodies at his feet. "I remember thinking, at first, that these men were taking a nap. But I soon discovered that they were dead." Even more troubling for Moncrief was the sight of those who

Starved corpses lying in a pile at Buchenwald, where prisoners and guards had stacked them for cremation in the camp's infamous ovens. In general, the practice was to shove the bodies through the windows on the left and then haul them into the ovens. (Lester Figus Collection, St. Louis Holocaust Memorial Museum)

were near death, emaciated to the point where they lacked the energy required to raise their heads or smile. Their eyes seemed to stare right through him . . . or perhaps past him. "By this time in the war I had been quite accustomed to seeing death. But I had never seen walking death. I will never forget the expressionless stare in their eyes."

News of the camp's liberation and the humanitarian crisis it presented traveled up the chain of command to General George S. Patton. As at Ohrdruf, the general was determined to witness the terrible reality with his own eyes. Alongside his subordinate, Major General Walton Walker, commander of XX Corps, Patton arrived at Buchenwald. The two generals inspected the camp, taking in the various sites including the crematorium and the barracks. Patton also came face to face with survivors of the Little Camp, some of whom tried to cheer him but were too weak to emit more than a few stilted cries. Though Patton did not become sick as he had at Ohrdruf, he was revolted by their degraded physical condition. "The inmates looked like feebly animated mummies and seemed to be of the same level of intelligence," he wrote, with characteristic insensitivity, in his diary.

The awful panorama of tragedy moved Major General Hobart "Hap" Gay,

Patton's chief of staff, to opine bitterly, "The sight and stench of these living dead . . . was entirely too much. No race and no people other than those which are strictly sadists could commit crimes like these." Another Patton aide, Lieutenant Colonel Charles Codman, felt more sadness and disgust than anger. "I have taken a bath, changed my clothes, smoked two packs of cigarettes, but the overpowering moral and physical stench . . . remains in my nostrils—the sour-sweet stench of death, dysentery and despair," he wrote in his diary later that evening.[13]

When Sergeant Howard Cwick, a Jewish GI, got to Buchenwald, he stood gaping at the horrors of the Little Camp. Tears streamed down his cheeks. He encountered a skeletal man who reached out and wiped the tears away. In German he told the man, "I am a Jew!" The man's expression turned to wonderment. "A Jew? You are a Jew?" They clung to each other, sobbing and shaking. Other inmates converged on them as the word spread that Cwick was Jewish. "They closed in around me," Cwick wrote. "Arms came out from everywhere—to touch my uniform, my face. Several grabbed my hands—and began kissing them." Another man clung desperately to Cwick's leg, as if he feared that letting go might mean he was only hallucinating about the arrival of liberators. Cwick felt "overwhelmed by the enormity of the horror that I was witnessing."

The man who had wiped Cwick's tears turned and nudged a friend who was in such poor shape that he only had the strength to lie on the ground. "Nachum, we are free," the man exclaimed in German. Nachum did not respond. The bony man squatted down and cradled Nachum's head in his arms. "It's over; we are free," he murmured. But his friend did not smile or move a muscle—he was dead. He had expired at the very moment of liberation. The survivor gently laid the body aside, rose to his feet, looked at Cwick, and cried out, this time in English, "You are too late! This is my friend! He couldn't wait for you anymore! Why couldn't you have come sooner?"

Sergeant Cwick was at a loss for words. He felt only guilt and sadness. As if to compensate, he approached a pair of wary-looking inmates who backed away as he neared them. One of them pointed at his canteen and asked for water. (Dehydration was as life-threatening for the survivors as malnutrition.) Cwick handed him the canteen and said in Yiddish, "I am an American soldier. I am a Jew." The inmate gulped eagerly, nearly draining the canteen, and handed it back. Moments later, he gripped his stomach and, in Cwick's recollection, "heaved convulsively. He had drunk too much and too fast. His vacant body just wasn't up to it."

What happened next was revealing. Alarmed cries spread among the inmates that Cwick had poisoned the man. These survivors had been brutalized and traumatized for so long, and with such craven callousness, that even now they had difficulty trusting a U.S. soldier. Many other Americans would encounter the same dysfunctional legacy of the camps as they met the survivors. The only way Cwick could counter their doubts was to drink from the canteen himself while declaring, between sips, that he was a Jew and an American soldier.

Upset by this sequence of events, Sergeant Cwick left that group of inmates and began exploring the rest of the Little Camp. He smelled the enclosure's one latrine before he saw it. Nearly overcome, he buried his nose in the crook of his arm. A stooped-over shell of a man came up to him, tugged at his sleeve, and began excitedly yelling in Polish or Russian. He motioned for Cwick to take a look inside the latrine, which he did. "The filth . . . was indescribable," he recalled. Still the man kept gesturing and pointing downward. Cwick glanced down and nearly recoiled in abject horror. "At the top of that nearly filled pit of human waste lay an almost submerged rotting body of a man. That poor soul must have lost his balance and fallen off the two encrusted boards that served as the seat. Being far too weak, he must have been unable to claw his way back up, and so, down there, in that cesspool of human filth, he lost his fight for breath, and either suffocated or drowned." In far too many instances, prisoners had been unable to even make it to the latrine. With their stomachs in severe turmoil, wracked by diarrhea and dysentery, many had no control over their bowels. "So, wherever we went," Cwick said, "there was feces, feces, feces, the major cause of even more serious illnesses."

When he could no longer stand the terrible odor, Sergeant Cwick left the Little Camp and took in the equally awful sight of the crematorium and its surrounding area. Outside the building, Cwick noticed another soldier kneeling in front of some sort of pile, about four feet high, poking at it with his bayonet. "Is that what I think it is?" Cwick asked with a sense of dread.

The other GI nodded. "Yeah. It's ashes from the ovens inside."

He took what looked like a chicken bone from the pile and handed it to Cwick. The terrible realization that this little bone came from an anonymous human being unleashed a fresh stream of tears from his eyes. Clutching the bone in his hand, he sank to his knees and cried out, "Why, God, why?!" There was no answer, only the cold, eerie silence of Buchenwald and a pile of incinerated human remains. He stared at the mound in front of him. "I found myself wondering, how many fathers, how many brothers, how many sons are in that pile?"[14]

Nearly every American who witnessed the aftermath of Buchenwald's liberation felt some mixture of shock, dismay, and horror. "Even after combat and its conditions, no word can describe it rightfully," wrote Sergeant Alex Kormas, an artilleryman. "The smell, stink, depression, remain with me and others to this day." Some men were also quite angry, certainly with the Nazis but, in a larger sense, with all Germans. "The true nature of fascism was too incredibly vicious for acceptance by decent people," one civil affairs officer wrote. In his view, it brought into focus "the degeneracy of the German people under Nazism." When Warrant Officer John Glustrom, a member of an engineer battalion, stared in shock at the remnants of the Little Camp, he felt little besides hatred and contempt for the Germans—to the point of dehumanizing them (a common tendency). "I felt the captors were less than human beings. The system was so clever, and I felt the country was run by a madman, who had a lot of willing accomplices. We all felt deep hostility toward the Germans before we saw this concentration camp . . . and this just added fuel to our flames." Warrant Officer Dwight Pearce, a reconnaissance soldier from the 6th Armored Division, summed up the sentiments of many: "I had a feeling of revenge." However, there is no record of any American reprisals at Buchenwald against the captured guards or other Germans.

The same could not be said for the liberated inmates, whose hatred was of course much more personal and more intense than anything the Americans could imagine. Thus, at times, liberators witnessed the survivors carrying out reprisals against their former tormentors. Warrant Officer Pearce was stunned to encounter a battered wreck of a man, whom he assumed had been an SS guard. "Why he wasn't killed I don't know, but I've never seen a person so beat up in my life. He didn't look like a human being. He couldn't see, his nose was broken and so was his jaw, he was just a bloody mess." Pearce and several other soldiers took him into protective custody. Far more commonly, though, the Americans did not interfere with the vengeance of the former prisoners.

In many cases, the victims of reprisals were not just SS men but also fellow prisoners who had functioned as cruel supervisors (or kapos) over their peers.

Jewish kapos, almost all of whom were in the Little Camp, were especially vulnerable because they were not part of the Communist organizational system of mutual protection and highly disciplined unity. Moreover, the kapos were far more likely to mistreat prisoners on a daily basis than the SS, who at times were remote, almost Olympian figures to the average prisoner. Kenneth Gerber saw a group of liberated, armed Jewish prisoners execute several kapos. "These were wild men bent on revenge," he said of the vigilantes. Their hatred for the kapos was visceral, of the kind reserved for traitors.[15]

One group of prisoners hunted down a hated kapo and presented him to a group of American soldiers that included Sergeant Cwick. "If I ever saw pure animal terror, I saw it written all over his contorted face," Cwick said. "He knew his end was near. His eyes pleaded for help." A crowd gathered around and screamed for the man's blood. "Give him to us!" they roared. Here was a serious moral dilemma for the Americans. They were inclined to treat all liberated prisoners with compassion and humanity, as they knew nothing of the inner workings of the camp and the horrible atrocities this man might have committed. Even if he was a criminal and scoundrel—judging by the mood of the survivors, he must have been—they were still bound to protect him from reprisals. However, they were attempting to establish trust and rapport with the survivors. If they protected the kapo, the crowd might well turn on the Americans or at least feel alienated from them. After all, what right did they have to deny these long-suffering victims their greatly anticipated moment of retribution? Of course, if they gave in to the crowd's blood lust and delivered the kapo to their clutches, the man would undoubtedly be tortured and killed, thus making the Americans party to an atrocity, no matter how justified it might have been in their minds. Also, the prisoners probably could have killed the kapo on their own, but they brought him to the Americans, almost as if they were seeking validation for revenge.

Instead of taking a stand and making a decision, the Americans turned away to discuss the matter. In so doing they failed to protect the kapo. The inmates apparently interpreted their indecision as de facto permission to do what they wished with the man, and they set upon him. "They punched, they kicked, they pummeled, and stomped that man to death," Cwick remembered. They tore his clothing off and smashed his head with rocks, boots, and fists until the grotesque, misshapen carcass lay inert at their feet. Cwick felt an almost strange sympathy for the dead man. "I would like to say I would never have worked for the Germans," he later reflected, "but no one knows his own 'breaking point.' No one knows how much pain or horror he could suffer or witness before he would 'change.' The need for survival is powerful! Until we walk in someone else's shoes . . . we aren't qualified to judge him!" In Cwick's opinion, the moment he and the other soldiers turned away from the crowd, they all knew what would happen; in that sense, they chose to indulge the blood lust of the vigilantes. Cwick carried the guilt of the kapo's death with him for the rest of his life. "I was as responsible for his death as I would have been had I put my pistol to his head and fired. To my dying day, I will see his terror-filled eyes pleading for our help." Even the knowledge that the kapo had turned against his fellow Jews was never enough to abate Cwick's terrible sense of guilt.[16]

In one of Buchenwald's administration buildings, Victor Geller struck up a conversation with a hardened survivor—a fellow Jew—who excused himself every 15 minutes, picked up a wooden club, and left the room. After several such instances, Geller finally asked the man where he was going. The man gazed at Geller and explained that the club had once belonged to Nazi guards. He, himself, had once been beaten with it. Now one of the guards was in custody elsewhere in the building, under the control of his former victims. The man told Geller:

> During my turn on duty here, I used this club to beat the Nazi several times an hour. You want to know why I beat him? Maybe you want to know why I don't kill him? Let me tell you because you should understand. As an American, as a soldier and especially as a Jew. A human being, no matter who he is, deserves dignity and justice. He very rarely gets his fair share, but he can hope and struggle. The man in the cell should be brought to justice, but not yet. Justice would mean putting him to death. That is too nice, too orderly. Before he shares death with his victims, he must first share their loss of dignity and a little of their pain. So I beat him, but I do not talk to him. I don't care what he feels as long as he also feels pain.

Geller passed no judgment on the man and his actions. Nor did he intervene to put a stop to the beatings. He hadn't suffered what the survivor had suffered, which probably made him reluctant to interfere in any way; or maybe he agreed that the Nazi deserved to be tortured in such fashion. Reflecting later on the man's words and actions, Geller felt a powerful kinship with him, one that even transcended the strong bond he shared with his fellow soldiers. "Maybe the Jews of Buchenwald were brothers that I had never met, to whom I was linked by blood, shared and shed," Geller opined. Even though he spent only a few hours at the liberated camp, he felt as if a part of him would always remain there.

The same was true for Captain Herschel Schacter, a rabbi and chaplain with VIII Corps headquarters. As the son of a Jewish immigrant, he was drawn to the Little Camp to comfort and care for the battered survivors with whom he felt a deep sympathy and kinship. Filled with anger and revulsion, he rushed around the compound, yelling in Yiddish that they were now free. "I remember their eyes, looking down, looking out of big, big eyes . . . haunted, crippled, paralyzed with fear. They were emaciated skin and bones, half-crazed, more dead than alive." Some approached Schacter and touched him, as if to convince themselves that he was real. "Is it true?" they asked. "Is it over? Does the world know what happened to us?" Rabbi Schacter confirmed that they were indeed free. As he spoke, he could not help thinking to himself, "If my own father had not caught the boat on time, I would have been there."[17]

3 Treating Buchenwald
Medicine and Murrow

As word spread around Twelfth Army Group of the awful conditions prevalent in Buchenwald, medical units began to converge on the camp. Soldiers from the 120th Evacuation Hospital arrived on April 15, 1945. Their outfit's mission was to care for wounded soldiers on the battlefield. Instead, they now found themselves caring for people whose physical condition was arguably unprecedented in human history. Needless to say, the medics were shocked at what they saw. "The greatest problem facing the unit was one of sanitation," the 120th's history recorded. "The water supply had been cut off due to the destruction of one of the mains by explosives." The dearth of water presented a dire threat to the lives of the prisoners, and the retreating SS had cut off the water supply for this very reason. "The devilish cruelty of this action can be more readily understood when one realizes that a large number of the inmates were seriously sick, many at the point of death, and the lack of water if only for sanitary facilities was equivalent to a death sentence," Major Ralph Wolpaw, a physician in the 120th, later wrote. The filth resulting from such a lack of water for 21,000 people only added to their misery. "Latrine facilities in the camp were virtually nonexistent," states the unit's history, "and hygiene of any kind was apparently unknown. Prisoners' barracks were in the worst possible condition. Lighting was inadequate, barracks were filthy . . . overcrowded, inmates underfed and underclothed."

Lieutenant May Horton, a nurse, was greeted by grateful survivors who seemed so deteriorated that she wondered how they could still be alive. They were "thin, bony, and terribly undernourished, a gaunt look. One man knelt down and kissed my combat boots. I can never think of this without tears." The commander of the 120th, Colonel William E. Williams, took one look at the awful conditions and decided Buchenwald was no place for Horton and his 40 other female nurses. (Perhaps this is more of a commentary on gender attitudes in 1945 than on the conditions in the concentration camp.) He ordered them transferred elsewhere while the other troops remained at Buchenwald.

Remarkably, some of the medics either were ignorant about the dangers of giving rich food to the starving inmates or simply gave in to their generous impulses. One truck driver, nicknamed Tex, handed out C rations to the desperately hungry prisoners. "He was just a good, decent person," said one of his friends, Tech 5 Warren Priest. "He was this good-natured kid from Texas, friendly to everybody." Unfortunately, the food was like poison to the fragile systems of the prisoners. Several devoured the contents, passed out, and apparently died. Tex was devastated by this terrible turn of events and never fully recovered emotionally. "It has haunted him all his life," his wife later told an interviewer. "The idea that they survived the horrors of the camp only to die there . . . because of what should have been an act of kindness." Another soldier, Jerry Hontas, claimed that his superior officers initially set up a buffet-style food line for the prisoners in one of the former SS barracks. The menu apparently included "hot meat and vegetable soup, potatoes, bread and the like. The food was simple in itself, but too rich for the shrunken stomachs and digestive organs of the starved men. Several spontaneous deaths occurred. The lesson was quickly learned; feeding starving people in a spirit of compassion is a task that requires patience." According to unit records, the menu soon changed to a "soft and liquid diet . . . soup, milk, oatmeal, and meat stew." The American food was augmented with German fare appropriated by GI search parties in nearby towns.[1]

The medics set up a hospital in the former SS barracks buildings. Although they were quite used to this job, they had seldom encountered such unsanitary, wretched conditions. "Displaced personnel [former inmates] had been sleeping in these barracks and the furniture, rugs, and bedding were undoubtedly infested" with vermin and disease, the 120th's history explained. "All furnishings were immediately discarded and drapes removed. The walls and floors which were of tile construction were thoroughly scrubbed with soap and water. New Army canvas cots were installed with new German Army Store blankets where possible and of United States issue when necessary." The Americans were also assisted by those liberated inmates who were in good enough physical condition to work.

With the barracks converted into makeshift hospital wards, the soldiers of the 120th now surveyed the camp to begin the arduous job of gathering and moving those who needed medical attention away from their squalid circumstances and into the clean hospital. "This was accomplished by separating the men by nationality and putting a doctor of that nationality in charge," Lieutenant John Lafferty, one of the American doctors, recalled. Thus categorized, and organized by the level of need and urgency for care, the patients were moved by truck, hauled by stretcher teams, or, for those who could walk, simply escorted to the SS barracks. "I was hauling desperately sick and dying prisoners, or what remained of once strong and healthy men, to the hospital," Private Hence Hill wrote in a letter to his wife. "The sight of those near death was almost beyond belief—thighs the size of my arm, buttocks no longer visible, pelvic bones seen at any angle, as were other human bones. You can imagine the odor." In one instance, Hill started to pick up a seriously ill young man who could barely move. "Leave him; he will die in an hour or so; let's take only the ones we can help," said a doctor who had been a prisoner for many years. Hill turned away, leaving the sick man to be hauled away with the piles of dead bodies slated for burial in a mass grave outside the camp, when one of the American officers stepped in and overruled the prisoner-doctor. "He goes and will be treated as long as there is life in him."[2]

Some of the surviving prisoners were children. Approximately 900 inmates were below the age of 18, and they were generally housed in one overcrowded barracks building in deplorable conditions. Most were cared for after the fall of the camp by their fellow prisoners and then evacuated by the Americans. Tech 5 Priest received orders to check their building and make sure no one was left. He ducked inside and was nearly overcome by the powerful stench of decay and rot. "I remember the litter everywhere, piled one or two feet high in places, making access to several parts of the barracks impossible," he said. "Everything was covered with excrement, urine, vomit—blankets, clothing, shoes, jackets, underclothes—to call the scene indescribable is inadequate." All of these terrible odors, mixed with the residue of burned flesh still wafting from the crematorium, were, in his estimation, "beyond the human capacity to forget."

Priest held his breath and briskly walked along the rows of rickety beds, past piles of debris, hoping to sweep through the vile building as quickly as possible. He reached the end, saw nothing, and turned to go back to the entrance. Just then, he noticed a slight movement amid a pile of clothing in one of the beds. His first thought was that a rat had found an appropriate home in the filth. No sooner had this thought flashed through his mind when he heard a whimper. He picked up a stick and poked the pile to investigate. "A small child, a girl, perhaps five or six, [was] huddled in a fetal position . . . barely conscious." Astounded, he gently pulled her from the bed, wrapped her in his field jacket, took her in his arms and rushed from the barracks. "I have to get her to the aid station as soon as I can!" he thought desperately. She was unbelievably light; so much so that he kept glancing down to make sure she was still in his arms. She whimpered again and then he heard nothing. "The little girl died in my arms on the way to the aid station." Deeply moved, saddened beyond description, defeated, and discouraged, he laid her little body down. She made such an impression on him that he gave her the name Angela to indicate that she was an angel in the middle of hell. "She lives still in my memory, that little human form . . . and since then she has become a constant companion of mine. Angela lives on my shoulder and close to my heart."

Before patients were allowed to enter the new wards, they were deloused and disinfected with DDT powder (a pesticide) that was sprayed by soldiers from hand and vehicle tanks. According to the 120th's history, "selected German personnel, if available, were instructed as to the use of the spray on incoming patients. The infested patients were brought to the door of the building and unloaded on the litter [stretcher] from the ambulance. They were thoroughly sprayed . . . over the body, the axilla and pubic area, being given special attention." Medics gently removed the inmates' tattered, filthy clothing. In a few instances, they steam-deloused the clothes and returned them. More often, they simply burned the filthy rags and scoured the surrounding areas and nearby army supply depots for pajamas and other appropriate clothing. "The patients were then carried to one of the new cots with fresh blankets," the 120th's history said. The blankets were largely scrounged from U.S. and German army stocks.

The troops administered more DDT dustings for the next couple of days.

Ideally, these delousing efforts should have been accompanied by soap and water baths, but running water was not available. In the meantime, the DDT alone proved quite effective in containing vermin. Once the water was running again, some three days after the relocation, orderlies began administering daily soap and water baths to the patients. In addition, the soldiers took steps to make sure they themselves did not get infected. According to original hospital records, "insecticide powder for Body Crawling insects, in two ounce cans, were amply supplied; this was sprinkled in the axilla, over the chest, abdomen, pubic region and thoroughly rubbed into the hair of the exposed personnel." In all, the troops deloused at least seven buildings. Anyone who was exposed to the patients took a thorough hot water and soap bath at the end of his shift. The 120th experienced no recorded infestations.[3]

Practicing a Different Kind of Medicine

The doctors, technicians, and orderlies were trained for combat trauma; they knew how to treat healthy young men with combat wounds. Surgeons who were used to operating on soldiers instead found themselves functioning as caregivers to people on the verge of death from dehydration, disease, and malnutrition. No one was prepared to salvage human beings who had been mistreated and degraded in such a sinister, ruthless manner. Few members of the unit had ever even seen a malnutrition case, save for some of the doctors who had witnessed alcoholism-induced muscle degeneration during their stateside residencies.

The condition of these living skeletons was beyond what the young soldiers could comprehend. Private Bill Whipple was so appalled at the appearance of the inmates that he reported to his family in a letter, "There isn't enough flesh left to even look human." One doctor shared this sense of stunned revulsion: "At first I couldn't believe what I saw. We were sort of horrified." Walter Mason, a soldier in the pharmacy section, was so staggered by the terrible state of the patients that he wondered how they could possibly have lived for even a few days like this, much less months or maybe even years. "One wonders how they had survived to this point in time," he later commented. "Many of these patients had open sores which were covered with what appeared to me to be toilet tissue, but actually it was a type of bandage in common use there. I am sure most patients were not fully aware of what was going on as each patient seemed to have that vacant stare in their eyes which made it impossible to read in their eyes any emotional reaction." Deeply moved by the plight of so many people near death, Dr. Lafferty wrote to his family that "malnutrition was severe . . . pneumonia, scarlet fever, and every disease imaginable. There were leg ulcers, bed sores, and wounds that were not healing. Probably the average weight was not over 80 pounds."

As Dr. Lafferty indicated, diseases such as typhus, dysentery, scurvy, and even tuberculosis were a real problem. Most of the victims were badly dehydrated; their chronic diarrhea magnified the suffocating odor of feces, rot, and disease that engulfed them like some sort of toxic cloud. According to the 120th's records, the unit hospitalized and treated some 5,490 patients, with only 445 surgical cases. The rest were treated for their deteriorated physical condition and associated maladies, including 330 tuberculosis cases, 208 dysentery cases, 62 typhus cases, 49 pneumonia cases, and 98 patients with "contagion." In a few instances, the doctors administered scarce reserves of penicillin to carefully selected patients in an attempt to control infections. Seventy soldiers donated blood for transfusions. The 120th's journal recorded 51 deaths among the hospitalized patients in a six-day period, with dozens, or possibly even hundreds, more dying in the compound, either before they could be admitted or because they had never accessed treatment.[4]

If there was one thing the doctors and other medics did know from their combat experience, it was how to prioritize the treatment of patients according to their condition, a practice generally known as "triage." Their policy was to afford top priority to those who were in the worst condition. "The first thing we had to do was pick out the most severely ill patients," explained Captain Philip Lief, whose 3rd Auxiliary Surgical Group had joined forces with the 120th, "and to try heroic measures such as transfusions, intravenous feeding and therapy . . . and supportive therapy in order to try to help these people to survive." In addition to feeding the survivors a diet of liquid or soft, mild foods, they administered blood transfusions, though it was often difficult to find usable veins in the arms of such malnourished individuals. "Most of the inmates had signs of malnutrition that meant very little skin on the face, sunken bones . . . eyeballs sunken in the eye sockets, very little muscle tissue on the legs or arms," Dr. Lief recalled. "One could see all the thoracic cage, the ribs very prominent. If the inmate took off his shirt, you could see the spinal column very, very prominently."

The Americans made extensive use of any physicians they could find among the liberated inmates. Some of these doctors had been incarcerated at

Buchenwald for years; although they were hardly in great shape themselves, they nonetheless were in an ideal position to provide the Americans with vital information about the medical history of patients and, in general, assist them in any way they could. They also were instrumental in the task of organizing the patients by nationality and performing triage. Dr. James Mahoney worked with a former prisoner who had once been a preeminent surgeon in Austria. According to some of the patients, this man was such a skilled and valuable doctor that he had at times persuaded the camp authorities to afford sick inmates with food, medicine, and hospital treatment similar to what the SS men received. "This surgeon's moral and professional courage, in the face of death . . . , remains an inspiration to me to this day," Mahoney later commented. "He was most curious about what was going on in the field of medicine in the outside world since he had been out of touch for five years."[5]

Nursing the victims back to physical stability was one thing; healing their devastated mental and emotional state was quite another. Bodies could be replenished over time—especially young ones—with good food and decent medical care. The same might not be true for their minds. Some were suffering from acute neurological and psychological problems. Some were so traumatized and so dazed from dehydration and hunger that they hardly knew what was happening around them. Some were in such a fog and so crazed with thirst that, in the recollection of one doctor, "they opened bottles of plasma and started to drink the plasma, although we told them this had to be given intravenously." At times, language barriers inhibited meaningful conversation; ironically, German tended to be the unifying language for the various nationalities. For the GIs who did not speak German and the patients who did not speak English—the majority in both cases—the next resort was usually a pidgin-type of speech or simple sign language.

Many of the patients had experienced so many months and years of dehumanizing and horrible treatment from practically everyone around them that they found it difficult to trust the American medics. "The mental disturbance of the inmates was very, very apparent," Captain Lief said. "It took anywhere from a week to three weeks for most of the inmates to realize the significance of the fact that they were now among friends and Americans who had liberated the camp. They were happy to see us but at first they distrusted everyone." When he and his colleagues tried to ask them about what they had gone through, they found that, psychologically at least, a part of nearly every survivor was still stuck in the horror of captivity. They were "living like in a nightmare. A lot of them wanted to repress what they had seen." Lief noticed their aimlessness and helplessness, as if they had been robbed not only of their individuality but of their ability to make any decisions for themselves. "They reminded me of children, of people who wanted to be cared for, of people who did not want to assume responsibility, people who had been or- dered about and had become conditioned to be ordered to do certain things rather than to think for themselves."

Many patients had been separated from their families and loved ones. They wanted to know what had happened to them, but the Americans could pro- vide no information. This only deepened the sense of depression and help- lessness for those patients. "They were afraid of anything and everything," Captain Samuel Riezman later said. As a Jewish-American physician, Riez- man felt a special sympathy for the survivors whom he met and treated. "I don't think they were able to think. I felt that all of their humanity, all of their spirit, was gone. A lot of people in that condition did recuperate but, at the time, I did not see how it was possible."[6]

Gradually, as their physical condition improved and they saw how hard the Americans were working to care for them, the distrust diminished and was replaced by strong bonds of gratitude and friendship. As author and professor Elie Wiesel, recipient of the Nobel Peace Prize and one of the teenage survi- vors of the Little Camp, once wrote:

> They gave us back our lives. And what I felt for them then nourishes me to the end of my days, and will do so. When we first met at the threshold of a universe struck by malediction, we spoke different languages. We were strangers to one another. We might as well have descended from different planets, and yet a link was created between us. A bond was established. We became not only comrades, not only brothers. We became each other's witnesses.

Wiesel eventually made a practice of attending 120th Evacuation Hospital reunions. Pierre Verheye, a former Belgian resistance fighter who spent more than three years in concentration camps, including four months at Buchen- wald, later wrote to Sergeant Dick Renie of the 80th Infantry Division: "I will be eternally grateful to you and the members of your unit." Captain Christo- pher Burney, a British survivor of Buchenwald who was in much better shape than most of the other former inmates, opined that "the Americans were beyond common praise" because of the dignified respect with which they treated people who had literally forgotten the nature of such basic human decency. "This was just the natural gift of the kindest people in the world treating others friendly [sic], as if they were kind too. This was something I had not really seen for years."

The medics were deeply committed to the rehabilitation and recovery of their charges, not just because of common professionalism but also from a sense of altruism. "Our unit worked hard on this special assignment to save as many victims as possible, and we are very, very proud of the care they received," Hence Hill wrote his wife. Some, like Dr. Wolpaw, were amazed to see tangible results in the face of such seemingly hopeless circumstances. "The degeneration of years could not be undone in a few days, but an effort was made and the improvement in the short time we were there was very gratifying to all of us." There is, of course, no way to quantify how many lives the medical units saved in the aftermath of the camp's liberation, but the number was certainly substantial. It is fair to say that without their efforts, the human catastrophe of this infamous camp would have been significantly worse.[7]

Telling the World about Buchenwald

As the medics worked to save lives and nurse the survivors back to health, word of the terrible conditions at Buchenwald began to circulate throughout the Allied world. The Allied governments were reasonably well versed on Germany's genocidal efforts and the extreme brutality of the concentration camps. There had been some reportage of these crimes in the media. Even so, the average American—soldier or citizen—either knew little about the topic or viewed such stories with great skepticism and as little more than wartime propaganda. The truth of Buchenwald's unimaginable depravity thus spread quickly in Britain and the United States, prompting visits from a wave of media and dignitaries. General Dwight D. Eisenhower, true to his post-Ohrdruf commitment to document the realities of the camps, arranged for such visits and encouraged the high-profile witnesses—media, government, or otherwise—to tell the world what they saw.

One of the first reporters to arrive was Marguerite Higgins, a correspondent for the *New York Tribune*. She had already heard many stories of gruesome Nazi crimes and she doubted their veracity. Raised on spurious World War I tales in which Allied propaganda claimed that German soldiers had carried out mass executions of civilians including priests and nuns, she was determined not to be taken in. Also, like any good journalist, she was deeply skeptical of unsourced rumors; she trusted only what she could see and corroborate herself. So, initially, when she questioned camp survivors whose physical condition seemed okay, her tone was distrustful and brusque, almost to the point of rudeness. However, when they showed her around the camp and she witnessed the ovens and the stacks of bodies, she softened considerably. (Later in life she would feel great shame at her initial insensitivity.)

Higgins was especially struck by the indignity of the emaciated corpses and the mercilessness of their continued exposure to the elements. "As if to emphasize the horror, the frosty spring nights had frozen into ghastly stalactites the trickles of blood and yellow bubbles of mucus that oozed from the eyes and noses." Though she was disgusted by such a macabre sight, and the camp as a whole, she did not allow herself to dwell on such emotions. As a reporter, she had to maintain some distance from the natural emotions elicited by such horrors. She compared her mindset to that of a surgeon operating on a patient or a military commander who must order comrades into danger. "At Buchenwald all my energies were concentrated on obtaining the pertinent facts of the case against the Nazis in the shortest possible time."

Corporal Howard Katzander, a correspondent for *Yank*, the U.S. soldiers' weekly magazine, also struggled with the surreal nature of reporting the unthinkable. "This camp is a thing that has to be seen to be believed, and even then the charred skulls and pelvic bones in the furnaces seem too enormous a crime to be accepted fully," he wrote. "It can't mean that they actually put human beings—some of them alive—into these furnaces and destroyed them like this. But it means just that."[8]

Undoubtedly the most famous and influential reporting from Buchenwald was done by Edward R. Murrow, the revered CBS broadcast journalist. Four years earlier, he had earned the trust and esteem of the American public for his reporting during the German bombing of London. (The broadcasts had also engendered tremendous sympathy among the American people for Britain.) Murrow possessed a deep, resonant, steady voice that was ideal for radio. Although he was anything but a sensationalist, he understood the power of descriptive words, cadence, and tone of voice. On-site reporting through electronic media was in its relative infancy during World War II; radio conveyed a certain immediacy that was lacking in even the best print sources.

Murrow was one of the first true masters of this newer mode of wartime communication in what was still largely a pre-television age. Shocked beyond measure by what he saw and smelled at Buchenwald, Murrow sat down with a microphone and, in effect, functioned as a set of eyes and ears for millions of Americans. "Permit me to tell you what you would have seen, and heard, had you been with me," he intoned. "It will not be pleasant listening. If you are at lunch, or if you have no appetite to hear what Germans have done, now is a good time to switch off the radio." He discussed the camp's location and described his interactions with liberated inmates, along with a tour of the barracks buildings. "The stink was beyond all description," he said of one building. He described his visit to the body disposal plant and the adjacent courtyard:

> As we walked out into the courtyard, a man fell dead. Two others—they must have been over sixty—were crawling toward the latrine. I saw it but will not describe it. There were two rows of bodies stacked up like cordwood. They were thin and very white. Some of the bodies were terribly bruised, though there seemed to be little flesh to bruise. Some had been shot through the head, but they bled but little. All except two were naked. I tried to count them as best I could and arrived at the conclusion that all that was mortal of more than five hundred men and boys lay there in two neat piles.

His concluding statements were especially powerful: "I pray you to believe what I have said about Buchenwald. I have reported what I saw and heard, but only part of it. For most of it I have no words. If I've offended you by this rather mild account . . . I'm not in the least sorry."

Murrow's moving broadcast dramatically increased international awareness of Buchenwald's realities. At the same time, Eisenhower was cabling his military superiors and the Allied governments, urging more visits from prominent members of the media and government officials for the purpose of documenting Nazi crimes and bearing witness for posterity. He arranged for a distinguished group of 18 journalists, led by Joseph Pulitzer, publisher of the *St. Louis Post-Dispatch*, to fly to Germany for a firsthand look at Buchenwald and other liberated camps. The group included Julius Ochs Adler of *The New York Times*, Stanley High from *Reader's Digest*, John Randolph Hearst from Hearst Publications, Ben Hibbs from *The Saturday Evening Post*, and William Chenery from *Collier's Magazine*. "They landed in Paris—a rather cocky lot," said Boyd Lewis, a correspondent with United Press who greeted them at the Scribe Hotel, the headquarters for war correspondents in the European theater. "They were a little patronizing."

Like so many other Americans, the reporters wondered if the ghastly reports about Buchenwald might be distorted by exaggeration or the emotion of liberation. "I came here in a suspicious frame of mind," Pulitzer later wrote. "It is my grim duty to report that the description of the horrors of this camp . . . have given less than the whole truth. They have been understatements. The brutal fiendishness of these operations defies description." Pulitzer and the others were just as stunned and repulsed as Higgins, Katzander, and Murrow had been. The headline of Adler's story claimed, "Buchenwald Worse Than Battlefield." Hibbs wrote in *The Saturday Evening Post*, "It isn't a pretty picture. But it was seen and is recorded here by one who believes this nation must know all the truth." The piles of dead bodies made the deepest impression of all on Pulitzer. "My impression was that I was looking at caricatures of human bodies." By the time he and his colleagues returned to Paris, they were considerably chastened; all of them wrote descriptive personal stories for their respective publications about what they had witnessed. "We looked upon men who had gazed into the jaws of hell," Lewis wrote, "and they believed. Believe you me, they believed."[9]

Seeing was also believing for government officials. On April 24, 1945, separate delegations from the British Parliament and the U.S. Congress toured the camp. "Although the work of cleaning the camp had gone on busily for over a week before our visit and conditions must therefore have improved considerably," the parliamentary report declared, "our immediate and continuing impression was of intense general squalor; the odour of dissolution and disease still pervaded the entire place." They were appalled by the sight of the preserved human organs in what had been a laboratory for the Nazi doctors (and possibly a collection for Ilse Koch). Two of the ten British legislators were themselves physicians; the group spent a considerable amount of time inspecting the makeshift hospital barracks buildings. They reported that, when they entered a building,

one half-naked skeleton, tottering painfully along the passage as though on stilts, drew himself up when he saw our party, smiled and saluted. The medical members of our Delegation expressed the opinion that a percentage of them could not be expected to survive, even with the treatment they were

Bodies stacked on top of one another at Buchenwald, probably in the Little Camp. (Harry L. Smith Collection, United States Holocaust Memorial Museum)

now receiving, and that a larger percentage, though they might survive, would probably suffer sickness and disablement for the rest of their lives.

The Britons made a special point of commending the American medics. "It would be impossible to praise too highly the selfless exertions of the 120th Evacuation Hospital."[10]

The congressional delegation arrived on the same day, though the Americans do not seem to have crossed paths with their British counterparts. The delegation was composed of 12 members, half from the Senate and half from the House of Representatives. There was an even distribution of Democrats and Republicans, all of whom were chosen by the leaders of their respective parties. The delegation's de facto leader was Kentucky Senator Alben Barkley, a ranking Democrat and future vice president during the presidency of Harry Truman.

After receiving a preliminary dusting of DDT, the group slowly made the rounds of the camp. They took in the terrible sights of the crematorium, the hospital buildings, the prisoner quarters, the Little Camp, the laboratory where medical experiments had taken place, and the piles of skeletal bodies. Though such sights were becoming depressingly routine for the soldiers who had spent any amount of time in Buchenwald, they were shocking in the extreme for the politicians. "We saw the barracks, the work places, the physical facilities for torture, degradation, and execution," they wrote in a joint report prepared primarily by Barkley, Representative R. E. Thomason, and Representative Edouard Izac, a California Republican and Naval Academy graduate who had received the Medal of Honor for his valor during World War I.

> We saw the victims, both dead and alive, of the atrocities practiced at these camps. We saw the process of liquidation by starvation while it was still going on. We saw the indescribable filth and smelled the nauseating stench before it was cleaned up, and we saw a number of victims of this liquidation process actually die. Pictures and descriptions of the conditions at this camp cannot adequately portray what we saw there, and it is only when the stench of the camp is smelled that anyone can have complete appreciation of the depths of degradation to which the German Nazi Government and those responsible for its agencies, organizations and practice had dropped in their treatment of those who had failed to embrace the doctrines of the "master race."

The congressmen felt that these were crimes against humanity and that "those who were responsible for them should have meted out to them swift, certain, and adequate punishment." All of the congressmen were, of course, deeply troubled by what they saw. Izac later told an interviewer, "The truth is that we can never describe sufficiently the degradation that people were subjected to by the Nazis." The members of the British Parliament also struggled to convey the revulsion and disgust they felt. Similar to the liberating soldiers, they had no reference point to begin processing such calculated, extreme mistreatment of one group of human beings by another. Even for politicians whose tradecraft was the effective use of words, there were scarcely any to properly describe a place of such unimaginable degeneracy. "In preparing this report, we have endeavoured to write with restraint and objectivity, and to avoid any personal reactions or emotional comments. We would conclude, however, . . . that such camps as this mark the lowest point of degradation to which humanity has yet descended. The memory of what we saw and heard at Buchenwald will haunt us ineffaceably for many years." A United Nations War Crimes Commission, visiting a couple days later, reported that "the whole impression created by the inspection of the camp was one of cold-blooded, scientific and premeditated savagery calculated to degrade, dehumanize and exterminate the inmates."

By the end of April, Buchenwald had become a kind of macabre museum. Allied authorities forced 1,200 Germans from nearby Weimar to view the terrible handiwork of their countrymen. Their reaction was not much different than that of their countrymen who had seen Ohrdruf—a mixture of chagrin and supposed ignorance. Other outsiders—military or otherwise—were curious to get a firsthand look at this place that had become infamous. So many of these observers descended on Buchenwald that medics and other soldiers with a job to do in the camp began to resent their presence as ghoulish and voyeuristic. (In fairness to these visitors, many were following the recommendations of their senior leaders and their own compulsion to bear witness.)

By and large, the camp had been cleaned up, primarily by Army engineers. The bodies had been buried. Those patients who were still in the hospital were probably going to survive. Clergymen and relief agencies were hard at work trying to relocate survivors back to their homes and reunite them with their families; many, however, had no homes to return to and no surviving family members. The healthier survivors were only too happy to guide the gawking visitors on tours of the camp and to relate horrifying tales of their experiences. To be sure, Buchenwald's air remained malodorous, and the sights of the camp and its survivors were still troubling and unforgettable for any visitor. But there was already a distancing from the worst of what had gone on in the camp and from the terrible aftermath witnessed by the initial liberators and the first witnesses. The later witnesses tended to relate atrocities they had heard about from survivors or descriptions of Buchenwald's infrastructure because they had not personally seen these horrors. Yet, like so many others, they had difficulty finding the right words to bear effective witness to what they *had* seen. Percy Knauth, a correspondent for *Time* magazine, summed up the feelings of these men and so many others who came into contact with Buchenwald: "I saw death reduced to such a state of ordinariness that it just left me numb and feeling nothing. You just can't understand it, even when you've seen it."[11]

4 Dachau
The Approach

THE LITTLE MARKET TOWN on the Amper River has existed for nearly 1,200 years, dating back to the time of Emperor Charlemagne in the ninth century. The town's name, Dachau, refers to the union of rich clay soil with the pure glacial waters of the Amper. In the late nineteenth century, Dachau was home to a burgeoning colony of writers and artists who took to the surrounding countryside and painted well-regarded landscapes. By 1900, artists had proliferated in Dachau to the point where a common yarn claimed that at least one of ten people on the quaint streets was a painter.

Two factors combined to change forever the nature of the small town. First, the rise of neighboring Munich, some ten miles to the southeast, as a metropolitan and industrial center turned Dachau into a suburb of the bigger city. Second, and more importantly, World War I created a great demand for industrial munitions production. In 1915, Dachau became home to the Royal Gunpowder and Munitions Factory, a seminal event in the history of not just the town but, as things turned out, Germany itself. Such was the voracious wartime demand for ordnance that the factory eventually employed 8,000 workers, most of whom came from elsewhere in Germany. The growth of the plant led to the expansion of Dachau's railroad line and changed the composition of the population. Dachau was now heavily tied into the larger German economy. Thus, when Germany lost the war and its economy collapsed, Dachau plunged into depression and social upheaval, much like the rest of the country. The Royal Gunpowder and Munitions Factory abruptly closed, consigning thousands to the unemployment line and leading to a restive mood of anxiety and near desperation.

This turmoil throughout Germany was a significant factor in the rise of Nazism. Munich, in particular, became a Nazi stronghold and a major administrative site for the party. In March 1933, shortly after Hitler and the Nazis came to power, they began to round up and imprison Communists and Socialists who comprised their most committed, implacable political opponents. With grotesque irony, the Nazis referred to this incarceration as "protective custody." Nazi leaders settled on the abandoned munitions factory in Dachau as an ideal place to jail their new prisoners. However, contrary to popular belief, Dachau was not the first Nazi concentration camp. That dubious distinction belongs to Nohra in Thuringia, established some two weeks before Dachau. Oranienburg, near Berlin, was also older, if only by a day or two.

The Establishment of Dachau Concentration Camp

The first detainees were brought to the industrial complex at Dachau on March 22, 1933; two days earlier, Heinrich Himmler, the Reichsführer of the SS, had announced the establishment of the prison. The local authorities in Dachau and the residents had no say in Himmler's decision to confine prisoners in their locale. Initially the inmates were guarded by officers from the Bavarian State Police, who treated them well. On April 11, the police officers were supplanted by SS troopers, who had rather different ideas about how to treat their prisoners. Forty-year-old SS Oberführer (Colonel) Theodor Eicke, whom Himmler appointed as commandant in June, took the lead in formalizing methods of terror, exploitation, and degradation. "Tolerance is weakness," Eicke once wrote. "Knowing this, we will act ruthlessly wherever we must to defend the Fatherland." Rudolf Höss, a colleague of Eicke's who spent four years with the Dachau SS garrison and later became infamous as the commandant of Auschwitz, wrote of Eicke's methods: "[His] intention was to lay a foundation of hostility in his SS men toward the prisoners, to stir them up against them, to repress any flicker of sympathy."

Eicke's proscriptions only served to harden the attitudes of men who were already prone to fear and dislike anyone who disagreed with the Nazi vision of a hyper-nationalist and racially pure Germany. In addition, Eicke was an effective organizer; he was the architect of the doctrine of dehumanization around which a vast network of concentration camps would gradually develop. At Dachau, corporal punishment, including flogging, now became standard, as did supervised torture and the withholding of food and mail for recalcitrant inmates. Eicke cut rations, implemented hard labor, and authorized his men to use deadly force on anyone who attempted to escape. He created a mature administrative structure, assigning his subordinate commanders responsibility for distinct departments. For example, one dealt with the admission, interrogation, and release of prisoners; another handled the discipline and supervision of the inmates. Himmler was impressed enough with Eicke's work that he appointed him inspector general for all concentration camps. This promotion afforded Eicke the opportunity to disseminate his structure and ideas. Thanks to his influence, Dachau served as the model camp that other SS men emulated before the war and later as the Nazi empire expanded during the war years.[1]

Originally, the Dachau detainees were housed in the old munitions factory and then in the crude concrete barracks. As at Buchenwald, they were put to work razing old buildings, expanding the camp, and constructing their own housing, all under miserable conditions of hard labor and privation. "Chunks of cement from a demolished building were broken up with pneumatic drills and the men had to carry the pieces on their bare shoulders under the hot sun," recalled one political prisoner. By 1938, Dachau had grown into much more than a concentration camp. It was now a sprawling complex, occupying several square miles, with dozens of factory and workshop buildings. Dachau had also evolved into the main training ground for the SS and the organization's key administrative nerve center, with barracks buildings, a parade ground, office buildings, and clean, modern quarters for officers and their families. Here SS men of all ranks—from guards to clerks to executioners to the planners and the commanders—learned their grisly trade and exported their knowledge to other miserable places in Hitler's empire. The military arm of the organization, commonly known as the Waffen-SS, also trained at Dachau.

The concentration camp itself, called the "protective custody compound," occupied just one segregated and walled-off section of the complex. In addition to the solid concrete walls, the area was ringed with guard towers, electrified barbed-wire fencing, and, on its western side, a canal with water from the Wurm River that essentially functioned as a moat. Within the compound, there were 34 rectangular wooden barracks buildings, each designed to house about 200 prisoners. Each building contained toilets and washing facilities. Prisoners slept on open-sided wooden beds that were stacked three tiers high. The compound contained a library, a canteen, a quarantine block for new arrivals, a crude infirmary, and a special block that would eventually be used for gruesome medical experiments. Just across the canal from the compound stood a squat brick crematorium with a gas chamber, though the latter was probably never used for executions.

The Expansion of Dachau

Other targeted groups soon joined the original complement of Communist and Socialist political prisoners in the compound. The Nazis rounded up and imprisoned men they thought of as lazy: vagrants, beggars, people with mental illnesses, alcoholics, prostitutes, and homeless people. Added to these were Gypsies, Jehovah's Witnesses, homosexuals, and inveterate common criminals. Although there were some Jews among the first group of prisoners, the real influx came after Kristallnacht in 1938 and later, when the German government began apprehending as many Jews as possible. Even so, Jews were never the majority in Dachau. The different categories of prisoners were forced to wear identifying emblems: a red triangle for politicals, yellow for Jews, black for social outcasts, green for criminals, purple for religious, and pink for homosexuals. With the outbreak of war and a dramatic rise in the number of foreign prisoners, they were sometimes forced to wear special delineations such as a "P" for Polish and "F" for French.

Predictably, the treatment of prisoners throughout Dachau's terrible life span under the guidance of multiple commandants was generally harsh. Life was grim and regimented. Days began at sunrise with reveille (a military bugle or trumpet call). They did not end until 9:00 p.m. Prisoners endured long roll calls at least twice a day. Most commonly, they were used as slave laborers, working long days (12 hours or more) at hard physical work. The Nazis coined the phrase "arbeit macht frei," or "work makes (you) free." The iron entry gates to the Dachau compound bore those words. (Rudolf Höss also emblazoned them at Auschwitz, and the phrase is most famously associated with that camp.) Höss and other Nazis later claimed that the saying was

An aerial view of Dachau in May 1945. The Protective Custody Compound is on the right. It was only one part of the larger administrative, training, and factory complex that comprised the Dachau concentration camp area. (National Archives)

designed to afford concentration camp inmates a sense of dignity and hope by occupying their minds and bodies with productive toil. In reality, though, the words conveyed little more than mockery, as only a small minority of prisoners ever earned their freedom. Those who were "rehabilitated" and released were threatened with dire consequences if they were too talkative about the realities of their prison experiences. Furthermore, Eicke and his colleagues wanted the name "Dachau" to have a sinister and foreboding connotation for ordinary Germans, lest they be tempted to oppose the regime.

Dachau: The Camp Versus the Town

Among the German people, the residents of Dachau were the most deeply affected by the growth of the camp. In only a few decades, they had seen their village transition from a quaint market town and artist colony to an economically flourishing industrial incarceration center. This transition created a tragic paradox within the town of Dachau: in the space of a mile, charming old homes gave way to the grim walls of the concentration camp. In this and other ways, Dachau had two faces. Undoubtedly many of the civilians profited directly from slave labor, the growing economy, or, most commonly, from the presence of the SS whose members patronized local bars, hotels, restaurants, tailors, tradesmen, and the like. Few civilians had access to the protective custody compound, but, as time went on, they had many opportunities to see or smell something of the camp's realities. Trainloads of starving prisoners ran straight through town, right past many private houses; "they ate grass and drank from puddles," a horrified resident later told an American interrogator about one such train of captives. In many instances, the new prisoners were offloaded at the town's train station and walked two miles through Dachau to the camp. Work details of inmates were a common sight in town, especially during the war. As conditions in the camp worsened, the stench of death could be smelled for many miles.

Many of the civilians, out of either fear or indifference, simply turned a blind eye to these horrors. Josef Engelhard, a local Socialist who openly protested the government and somehow managed to maintain his freedom, claimed that, among his fellow Dachau residents, "ninety percent are dirty and have daubed themselves with the blood of innocent human beings." Another man, who publicly refused an SS recruiting call, said of his neighbors, "They were all too cowardly; they really didn't want to risk anything." Certainly, that was true of many people who professed ignorance or simply did not want to get involved. "What could we have done?" they often asked rhetorically.

However, there was substantial tension between the locals and the SS men, quite a few of whom behaved with arrogance, brutality, and boorishness in town during their off-duty hours. Part of the conflict was religious. Most of Dachau's residents were Catholic, so they deeply resented the hostility of SS troopers toward Christianity. At times the tension boiled over into violence, such as during the early morning hours of New Year's Day, 1941, when SS men brawled with locals in three separate drinking establishments. "The SS really beat up the civilians," one Dachau mother wrote to her son who was serving in the German army. "They punched one man's eye out and tore out a piece of flesh from the back of his neck. The pubs were all full of glass. The windows were also broken." Freida Keller, the wife of an SS officer, said that the two groups avoided each other whenever possible. She and her family spent most of their time within the complex, away from the town and its residents. "The people of Dachau were really sick of the SS," she claimed. "They didn't want them there."

At times, residents risked severe reprisals—and perhaps even imprisonment—to slip food, drinks, or cigarettes to prisoners who were part of work details. One group of women was so appalled at the condition of prisoners who were working near their street that they used their own ration cards to acquire bread for them. The women retrieved apples from their own cellars, spread jam on the bread, and attempted to give the food to the prisoners. But the guards pushed the women away, cursed them, and angrily confiscated the food. One former prisoner said of Dachau's citizens, "They were always good to us, secretly gave us what they could and most of them hated the SS." Maybe so, but their efforts to help were either too little or too ineffective to make much of a difference in the life of the average prisoner.[2]

Before the war, food in the camp was unappetizing but sufficient to sustain life; after the war began, rations diminished as the cruelty of Nazi camps increased under the pressures of wartime. When prisoners entered the camp, the SS confiscated their clothing and property, often stealing it outright and selling it for their own profit. Beatings and whippings were fairly common. Torture consisted of forcing prisoners to stand at attention or squat for hours, hanging them on meat hooks, or chaining them in solitary confinement with no food or water. Contact with the outside world was limited. No visitors were allowed. Letters were restricted and heavily censored. In spite of the tough regimen, deaths averaged just two per year in the 1930s, although not all were documented. Similar to Buchenwald, the SS delegated much of the day-to-day discipline and brutality to kapos, many of whom were common criminals. At higher levels of the inmate population, German political prisoners tended to occupy positions of the greatest power and influence, though they did not necessarily rule the camp with the same sort of rigidly organized hierarchy that had made their counterparts inmate masters of Buchenwald.

Within the concentration camp system, Dachau had a reputation as a relatively mild camp. That would soon change. As the war unfolded and Dachau grew, conditions worsened for its prisoners. Medical care was next to nonexistent. Only prisoners with temperatures above 104°F were excused from work and sent to the infirmary. Even there, there was little medicine or professional treatment. Hygienic standards declined. Disease rates soared. At various times, typhus and dysentery swept through the compound. The worst afflicted were often left to die in filthy quarantine blocks. The annual death rate climbed to 2,100 in 1941 and then more than twice that the next year. Four thousand Soviet prisoners of war were brought to the SS shooting range and executed. As this incident indicates, brutality and inhumanity steadily rose. Prisoners starved to death, were severely beaten, and were subject to arbitrary executions or torture.

Life and Death in Dachau

Some of the most unfortunate inmates were used in medical experiments. Fortified by orders from Himmler, 70-year-old Dr. Klaus Schilling, a leading expert in tropical medicine, subjected more than 1,000 criminals, Russians, Italians, and Polish clergymen to experiments designed to find an antidote for malaria, which was claiming the lives of German soldiers in the North Africa campaign. By means of injections and insect bites, Schilling and his charges infected their subjects with the disease. As patients inevitably became feverish and ill, the doctors studied the effects of the disease on their bodies and tested drugs on them to see which might be used to combat malaria. Hundreds of prisoners either died from fever or dehydration or were weakened to the extent that they succumbed to other diseases.

In 1942, Dr. Sigmund Rascher, a Luftwaffe (German air force) physician and SS lieutenant, became interested in high altitude and pressure experiments. In hopes of learning how best to save downed German pilots who parachuted from heights of 10,000 feet or more, he secured Himmler's permission to conduct research on about 200 prisoners. Rascher put the prisoners into a decompression chamber under extreme pressure and oxygen-deprived conditions. Some 70 to 80 of them did not survive. When the Luftwaffe became interested in how to save pilots who landed in cold water, Rascher expanded his operations to conduct hypothermia tests on prisoners by dressing them in flight clothing and immersing them in ice cold water. Once their body temperatures plunged to dangerously low levels—a process that usually took well over an hour and involved great agony—Rascher and his cohorts attempted to warm them with blankets, physical contact with animals or women, or a hot water bath (the most effective method).

Eventually Rascher eschewed water and simply exposed the prisoners to dry cold by stripping them and leaving them outside in sub-freezing weather.

"I have carried out intense chilling experiments on thirty human beings by leaving them naked from nine to fourteen hours, thereby reducing their body temperature to 27–29 degrees [Centigrade]," he wrote. He claimed that hot baths rapidly warmed the subjects enough to save them, even those with limbs so frozen they had turned white. He passed along a steady series of reports on his work to Himmler, including one chilling missive in which he urged relocation of his experimental group to Auschwitz. "It is colder there and because of the very size of the grounds, less attention will be attracted . . . the subjects cry out when they are freezing." According to the post-war testimony of eye-witnesses, about 400 prisoners were used in these experiments, of whom between 80 and 90 died.

But this was not the extent of the medical barbarism. Other Nazi doctors at Dachau conducted human subject research on tuberculosis, sepsis, and phlegmon. The common method was to artificially induce these maladies in their subjects. The consequences were devastating. Even those who survived were often permanently disabled or their health forever ruined. One such patient, Father Stanislaw Wolak, a Polish priest, was injected in the leg with a range of substances, including three cubic centimeters of phlegmon pus. He immediately sickened to the point where he was near death, in a state of abject misery. "I begged them to amputate my leg, not to save my life, but to lessen the pain, which I really cannot describe," he later wrote. The experimenters refused. He managed to survive but he was never the same again. "My health is ruined. My leg will never return to its normal state. I feel great pain especially during changes in the weather." Nineteen other priests were part of these experiments. Wolak claimed that seven of them died horrible, painful deaths.[3]

Dachau's Final Days

As the ruthless calculus of Germany's war created an ever-rising, voracious demand for labor, Dachau spawned more than 100 satellite slave labor camps or detached work parties of prisoners at such places as Allach and Kaufering, where prisoners were often worked to death to produce weapons and materiel for the German war effort. The proliferation of such places would one day lead to great confusion among a bevy of U.S. military units who claimed to liberate Dachau when in fact they had liberated satellite camps. The main Dachau protective custody compound became not just a place of incarceration, but an overcrowded holding area from which thousands of people, including many Jews, were parceled out to the various slave labor enterprises.

The prison barracks grew quite overcrowded, especially in the camp's final months as the compound turned into a veritable dumping ground for prisoners whom the SS were evacuating, often by rail, away from the approaching Allied armies. Most of these newcomers were filthy, verging on starvation, and near the end of their physical limits; many had endured indescribable conditions aboard crowded trains or on death marches under the prodding of heartless guards. Their arrival led to even more miserable conditions at Dachau. Barracks buildings designed to house 200 people now contained as many as 1,600. Disease rates spiked. A typhus epidemic claimed hundreds of victims. Malnutrition grew significantly worse, making the prisoners that much more vulnerable to disease. Four thousand prisoners died in March 1945. By April, as many as 200 per day were dying. "Every morning at dawn we carried out the dead," Stephan Ross, a 14-year-old inmate later recalled. "We placed the bodies by the electrified fence. Then they were piled on flat carts and taken to the Crematory." Food grew increasingly sparse, especially among the newcomers who were in significantly worse physical condition than the longtime inmates (particularly ethnic Germans who now comprised something of an elite group among the prisoners). Many of these transients were subsisting on 600 to 800 calories per day. Ross even claimed that many of the inmates eventually resorted to cannibalism.

By the last week of April, with the Third Reich almost finished and Hitler's empire now plunged into near total chaos, the compound contained more than 40,000 inmates and about 30 different nationalities. Tension was high. Many prisoners were worried that the Nazis would simply kill them all rather than allow them to be freed by the Allies. This was no idle fear because, according to Rudolf Höss, Hitler had issued Himmler strict orders that no prisoners were to be left alive. Apocalyptic rumors swept through the compound. "The whole camp was to be blown up!" Sidney Glucksman, a survivor, said of one rumor. "It was said that the explosives were all in place." This hearsay was not true. What was accurate, though, was the SS intention to forcibly evacuate prisoners, just as they had attempted a couple weeks before at Buchenwald. And evacuation often meant death because it entailed either hellish train rides or long marches while exposed to the elements, with little food, water, and shelter. Bad as Dachau was, it was preferable to an itinerant life of privation and ill treatment.

On April 26, the guards attempted to evacuate the camp. The inmates had previously formed an International Prisoners Committee (IPC) as a clandestine resistance organization and shadow government of sorts. Now they were mainly concerned with maintaining discipline, health, welfare, and services during this dangerous transition period. The IPC did everything it could to impede and thwart the prisoner roundups, and it was largely successful. Such was the confusion and chaos in Dachau that most of the prisoners defied the SS. The guards did succeed in rounding up about 7,000 Jews, Gypsies, Russians, Italians, and Austrians. They passed out rudimentary blankets and provisions and then marched them out of Dachau, to the south, bound for Tegernsee. One source, based on the testimony of a survivor, claims that in a forest about 15 miles outside of Munich, the SS men turned their guns on the prisoners and massacred all but 60 of them. According to another source, the SS killed anyone who could not keep up, which amounted to several hundred people, but eventually American military columns overtook and liberated the surviving majority of exhausted prisoners.[4]

Back at Dachau, the regular SS garrison was preparing to flee the camp. Their leadership was in flux. The United States Army was only a few miles away. The sound of artillery and even small arms fire could be heard in the distance. The guards knew exactly what this meant. They did not intend to stick around and face the consequences of their actions in the concentration camp. Most of the guards left, as did Wilhelm Weiter and Martin Weiss, two men who had alternately handled commandant duties during the final days.

At the same time, SS Untersturmführer (Second Lieutenant) Heinrich Wicker and about 200 SS troopers arrived and assumed responsibility for guarding the compound. Wicker was a 23-year-old concentration camp guard and veteran of the invasions of France and the Soviet Union. Tall and lean, with a chiseled jawline and a prominent nose, he personified the popular image of an SS officer. He had once been part of the guard contingent at Natzweiler-Struthof, a labor camp in France that the United States Army had liberated in the fall of 1944. More recently, he and his men had spent much of April evacuating labor camps and supervising death marches in southern Germany. Another SS force of similar size was now guarding the rest of the Dachau complex. Amid the leadership void, young Wicker became the de facto commandant. In assessing the disorderly situation, he decided to wait for the right moment and then simply abandon the camp and its prisoners to whatever diseases, hunger, and anarchy might consume them.[5]

The actions of Dr. Victor Maurer from the International Red Cross prevented this human catastrophe. In March, the Red Cross had finally received consent from Ernst Kaltenbrunner of the powerful Reich Main Security Office to enter concentration camps. In late April, Maurer traveled to Dachau with a convoy of trucks containing food parcels and other relief supplies for the inmates. The guards would not allow him to inspect the compound, but they did give him permission to hand out the parcels. Maurer spent the evening of April 28–29 in quarters located just outside the compound. In his recollection, it was "a restless night." All night long, he heard the sounds of combat in the distance and the comings and goings of guards in nearby buildings.

On Sunday morning, April 29, he explored his surroundings. A white flag fluttered from one of the main towers. Maurer soon realized that only Wicker and his men were still keeping watch over the protective custody compound. (Maurer was unaware of the presence of more guards in the administrative complex.) "He had intended," Maurer said of Lieutenant Wicker, "along with his troops, to abandon the camp . . . and it was only after much discussion that I prevailed on him to change his mind. It would have been disastrous had thousands of deportees, lusting for revenge, managed to get out. The population for miles around would have suffered, and no one could tell what damage would have been caused by the spread of epidemics."

Much to Maurer's relief, Wicker agreed to turn the camp over to the Americans, but only under three conditions: guards would remain posted in the towers to keep the inmates under control until the Americans arrived; all the other SS men would lay their arms aside and wait to surrender; Wicker and his men would then receive safe passage back to their lines. In reality, there were hardly any German lines to speak of in the vicinity of Dachau at this stage, and the guarantee of safe passage was not Maurer's to make. Only the Americans could decide such a thing. Nonetheless, Wicker and Maurer agreed to the conditions, and, as that crisp spring Sunday morning unfolded, they settled in to wait.

Inside the compound, the prisoners were practically mad with anticipation. The IPC knew the Americans could arrive at any moment. (Several sources claim that the committee had already sent several members on clandestine missions to make contact with the army.) The inmates stayed in their barracks but kept a close watch on the guard towers. "Ten times a day, we thought we saw the Americans coming," wrote Nerin Gun, a Turkish journalist whom the Germans had imprisoned for publishing anti-Nazi stories. "The least sign was interpreted as the harbinger of imminent liberation." Other prisoners, like Gleb Rahr, were in such bad shape that they were barely aware of the imminent liberation: "I was in a state of semi-consciousness, lying on my wooden bed, without any mattress or coushon [sic]." Even so, he could hear shells exploding in the distance.[6]

Within two miles of Dachau's walls, the Americans were on the move. Major General Wade Haislip's XV Corps was advancing south against sporadic resistance with the mission of taking Munich. Haislip had lined up three infantry divisions for this task: the 3rd, the 45th, and the 42nd. Two combat commands from the 20th Armored Division also spearheaded the advance. The Germans were in headlong retreat. The situation was fluid and confusing. Units were moving so quickly that commanders found it difficult to keep track of who was where. In the course of these rapid military operations, the 45th and the 42nd converged on the town of Dachau at more or less the same time on April 29. Haislip and his staff knew of the existence of the concentration camp, but they were not certain of its exact location. Haislip notified both division commanders, Major General Robert Frederick of the 45th and Major General Harry Collins of the 42nd, that they should be prepared to secure the camp. The inmates were to remain in place. "It was known that disease was rampant in the camp, and a certain number of murderers, rapists, and other undesirables were in the place," said Captain William McCahey, General Collins's aide de camp, of the briefing he and his boss received from Haislip's headquarters group.

Thus, the same orders flowed confusedly downward in two separate divisions, neither of which was coordinating closely with the other. The overwhelming majority of the combat soldiers had never heard of Dachau. Among the few who had, most thought of it as similar to a POW camp. They were highly suspicious of atrocity stories because they tended to associate them with wartime propaganda. In spite of the fact that Ohrdruf, Buchenwald, and several other camps had been liberated weeks or days earlier, amid great media fanfare, none of the 42nd and 45th soldiers had any true notion of the terrible realities of German concentration camps. They had little access to newspapers and no access to civilian radio sets. They saw, heard, smelled, and knew what was in front of them and little else. Such was the myopia of the combat soldier's world.[7]

The town of Dachau, with its orderly cobblestone streets, wood-framed, gingerbread-like homes, and colorful flower beds was, for the soldiers, just one more place they had to conquer on the way to final victory. So April 29 began for them as just another day in action, carrying out a mission, hoping to survive to see another sunrise. Private First Class Sid Shafner and the seven jeeps of the Intelligence and Reconnaissance Platoon, 222nd Infantry Regiment, 42nd Infantry Division, were patrolling one street when two odd-looking figures flagged them down. "These young boys wore black and white striped clothes and quite frankly, we were startled and surprised at first glance." Both boys were teenagers. They were gaunt and dirty. Shafner and the other soldiers did not know what to make of their shabby clothing and poor appearance. The two boys attempted to converse with Shafner in Greek, German, and Spanish, but he knew none of these languages. Finally they settled on Yiddish. They made him understand that nearby was a concentration camp where thousands of prisoners were hungry, sick, and desperate, just struggling to survive. They contended that many of these unfortunate people were being killed in cold blood. Shafner was skeptical. He sternly told the boys not to play games with him. "I explained we were American soldiers and if they were with a circus or a carnival, we had no time for pranks. They insisted that they were serious and were telling the truth."[8]

It is interesting that Shafner formed the impression that they were part of a circus group. In his mind, and to many other soldiers from that generation, circus kids were runaways who spun tall tales to drum up interest in the oddities of the trade. At least initially, Shafner believed that only this could account for their shockingly poor appearance. When he realized the two boys were serious and that they were anything but circus performers, he grabbed his handheld radio and reported their claims to his boss, Lieutenant Irving Short, who dutifully passed the information up the chain of command.

Similar reports were filtering in to other leading units, thus affecting the direction of the advance. At the vanguard of the 45th Division was Lieutenant Colonel Felix Sparks's 3rd Battalion of the 157th Infantry Regiment. His battalion was supported by a combined arms task force of tanks from the 191st Tank Battalion and a battery of artillery pieces from the 158th Field Artillery Battalion, plus some engineers. He began the day under the impression that he was supposed to push for Munich. Then he unexpectedly received a coded radio message from his regimental commander, Colonel Walter O'Brien, ordering him to proceed directly to the Dachau concentration camp. O'Brien's message concluded with the XV Corps order to seal off the place. "Upon capture, post an airtight guard and allow no one to enter or leave."

Sparks was perturbed at the change of plan. He had seen a lot of combat since he participated in the invasion of Sicily almost two years earlier. He was a 27-year-old survivor, a hardened fighter who cared deeply for his soldiers and who had little patience for anything he perceived as extraneous, unnecessary, or injurious to their welfare. Because of his personal courage and his aura of competence, men tended to follow him closely in combat. He checked his map and saw that the camp was about a mile to his left. With his lead companies already committed to the push for Munich, he knew he could not hope to extract his entire task force and head for the camp. This could mean only one thing: he would have to split his unit up. Naturally, he did not like this one bit. He detached I Company, his reserve outfit, plus a machine gun section from M Company, an artillery forward observation team, and some reconnaissance soldiers for this new mission. Sparks decided to lead this ad hoc force himself, a fateful choice that would significantly affect the rest of his life. "At that time I knew virtually nothing about Dachau," he later commented, "except that it was a concentration camp near the city of Dachau."[9]

Discovering the Death Train

As Sparks made his arrangements, Lieutenant Colonel Don Downard, commander of the nearby 2nd Battalion, 222nd Infantry Regiment, 42nd Infantry Division, received a report from a civilian about the concentration camp and where to find it. The 31-year-old colonel had never heard of the Dachau camp, but he immediately understood that it was an important objective. With great alacrity, he took elements of his F Company, a platoon of tank destroyers from the 692nd Tank Destroyer Battalion, and set off for Dachau. (He also informed his other companies about the report and warned them to be wary of a potential trap.) Many of the infantrymen rode on the tank destroyers. Downard rode in his jeep. According to Downard and several other men from this force, they soon came under fire from a platoon-sized German unit of about 40 men who were dug into a small hill overlooking the road. "We halted, dispersed and dispatched the offending Krauts," Downard wrote cryptically. As the tank destroyers and mortar men laid down fire support, riflemen overran the hill and subdued the enemy resistance. In all likelihood, this small unit action took place near Webling, a tiny farm village about a mile west of Dachau. The enemy troops were apparently Waffen-SS men whom someone at the concentration camp had recently dispatched to Webling to delay the Americans as long as they could. After capturing the enemy position, the victorious riflemen may have summarily executed the surviving SS men and a local farmer, though this has never been conclusively proven.

Downard's force resumed the advance through the town of Dachau. At one point, one of the tank destroyers engaged in a gun duel with what the crew thought was a German tank on their left flank. In reality, it was an American Sherman tank attached to the 45th Infantry Division; the tank blew up but fortunately the crew escaped unharmed. The incident illustrates just how much confusion existed within the two divisions about their respective locations and the line of demarcation. Sometime in the early to mid-afternoon, Downard's group arrived at the rail line that led into the camp. They noticed a long, stationary train of some 39 cars spread out along the track. Some were boxcars; others were open gondolas. The Americans could see that something was heaped inside the cars, but they did not know what. They stopped and dismounted.

Sergeant Olin Hawkins was primarily concerned not with the train but with perimeter security. He felt like a sitting duck in the open alongside the railroad tracks. As he peered anxiously around for places that might conceal enemy soldiers, one of his men called out to him, "Jesus Christ, Sarge! Look at this!" Hawkins turned and, for the first time, saw the contents of the train cars. Emaciated, traumatized, grotesque dead bodies were heaped in every conceivable position. "Their cadaverous arms and legs seem disproportionately long compared to their sunken abdomens, narrowed bony chests, visible ribs, protruding shoulder blades, and withered necks—all signs of starvation," wrote one soldier. Some were clothed in blue-and-white-striped prison uniforms. Others wore shabby coats. Still others, in the recollection of one lieutenant, "were naked and all of them skin and bones. Their legs and arms were only a couple inches around and they had no buttocks at all. Many of the bodies had bullet holes in the back of the neck." Trash, excrement, and abandoned clothes littered the cars and the surrounding area. Shriveled raw potatoes were tucked pitifully under and alongside some of the bodies. The corpses seemed to stare through half-closed eyes at the stunned Americans, most of whom were speechless. There were hundreds, perhaps even thousands, of bodies. (Estimates vary from 500 to 2,300.) There were men and women, children too.[10]

None of the soldiers had any idea who they were, where they came from, what had happened to them, and what they were doing there. But the troops did clearly understand that these were victims of Nazi savagery. A few of the soldiers later found out the full story of their horrible odyssey. This particular train, now known to history as the "death train," originated at Weimar, near Buchenwald, on April 7. With American forces nearing that camp, the SS had rounded up 4,500 French, Italian, Russian, Polish, and Austrian prisoners and loaded them aboard 59 train cars for evacuation to Flossenbürg. Some of these prisoners might have come from the group that had been force-marched a few days earlier from Ohrdruf to Buchenwald. They received only a small amount of food—15 small boiled potatoes, a few ounces of bread, and a bit of sausage—for what their captors expected would be only a short journey. People were packed tightly together, with each person having no more than a few feet of space. The prisoners were guarded by 130 SS NCOs and enlisted men under the command of Obersturmführer (First Lieutenant) Hans Erich Mehrbach.

Instead of a quick transfer to a new camp, the journey degenerated into a haphazard trek across Germany because of damaged rail lines, attacks by Allied fighter planes, and the chaos resulting from the inexorable advance of Allied armies. Believing that Flossenbürg had already been taken by the Americans, Mehrbach decided to reroute to Dachau. At various times, the train went to Leipzig, Dresden, and even Pilsen in Czechoslovakia. The only resupply of provisions came during a stop at Nammering, when a Catholic priest collected food from his parishioners and distributed it to the prisoners as best he could. By then, hundreds had already died from starvation, exposure, and disease. Moreover, at Nammering, the SS troopers removed at least 800 inmates and executed them. As with those who had already died, their bodies were abandoned or burned in a nearby stone quarry. Trees were cut down by the prisoners to feed the cremation fires. Some tried to escape, but the SS shot them down. Those who could not work quickly enough were also shot. Some 524 bodies were buried locally. Another 270 were burned in the quarry.[11]

For the living, the terrible journey resumed. "How to describe the life—and death—on those trains!" wrote Gleb Rahr, a survivor. "The constant, unrelenting hunger. The pain of the cramped position—being unable to move. The stench of too many unwashed bodies lying in their own waste. Unceasing, almost casual, brutalities of the SS. This became the whole world." Pierre Verheye, a Buchenwald survivor who spent decades researching the story of the death train, wrote:

Some inmates [were] drinking their own urine, others lapping water from rain puddles on the floor of railroad cars—floors which were the resting place of dead bodies, bodily wastes, and dirty clothes crawling with lice. Crowded conditions did of course change these railroad cars into human zones where the law of the jungle reigned at all times and most particularly during the night at which time fights to the death took place . . . not only over space but also over such personal belongings as blankets and shoes.

By the time they reached Dachau on April 27, the majority had died. At most, only about 800 were still alive. The train was down to 39 cars. "I had become a skeleton," recalled Joseph Knoll, a 20-year-old Hungarian Jew who somehow managed to survive. "I weighed 70 pounds. My mind was clear, but there was scarcely a glimmer of life within me. My hands and feet were frostbitten." With their last reserves of strength, he and the others tramped from the railroad into the compound, where they were herded into the quarantine barracks.[12]

Two days later, incredulous at the terrible sight of the train and muttering in low voices to one another, the American soldiers patrolled along the cars, studying with morose introspection the mounds of corpses. As if in a daze, Lieutenant Colonel Downard began to walk the length of the train. "It was all I could do to believe it," he said. About 15 yards behind Downard, Tech 4 Anthony Cardinale, a radioman with regimental headquarters, was just as stunned as everyone else. He and Staff Sergeant Joe Balaban, the regiment's radio chief, walked the length of the train, shaking their heads at the surreal scene. In Cardinale's recollection, both men felt "deep disgust and horror at what we saw." For Cardinale, the sight provoked something of an awakening about the purpose of the war. He kept thinking to himself, "We had to get in here and stop the wholesale slaughter of human beings. We have to be here."

Car by car, Cardinale stopped and peered inside to inspect the gruesome contents. As he gazed at one pile of bodies, his eyes detected movement. "I saw this hand weakly waving back and forth. It was poked up between some of the bodies on top of it. It was quite evident that its owner was alive, and had heard our voices, and was desperately trying to attract our attention." Cardinale stopped short. For some reason, whether out of revulsion or fear, he could not bring himself to climb into the rail car. He called out to Downard, "Hey Colonel, here's a live one!" Lieutenant Colonel Downard turned around and ran over to see for himself. "There, almost buried under a mass of dead bodies, was a hand that was waving so feebly you could hardly notice it. But it was moving!"

Downard and the tank destroyer commander, Captain Roy Welbourn, strode toward the car. Before they could climb inside, Sergeant William "Hap" Hazard, a photographer from the division newspaper, asked Downard if he could wait a moment while he readied his camera to capture the moment. "It took me less than fifteen seconds to get focused and insert the flash bulb in my 4 X 5 Speed Graphic [camera]," Hazard wrote. The idea of delaying the rescue for the sake of a photograph seems rather insensitive and self-centered. However, in retrospect, it is fortunate that Downard assented because it allowed Hazard to document the important moment for history.

Downard and Welbourn clambered into the car and rummaged through the bodies until they found the survivor. He was young, probably a teenager, though it was difficult to tell for certain because he was so severely underweight. As gently as they could, the two officers took hold of him, with Downard on his left and Welbourn on his right. Welbourn shook his right hand, patted him on the shoulder, and assured him he would be okay. The inmate stared upward at the two men. Private First Class Cliff Lohs vividly recalled "the worshipful look in that prisoner's eyes." Carefully, Welbourn and Downard handed him down to Cardinale and Balaban. "He was just skin and bones," Cardinale said. Dazed and bewildered, but also hopeful, the man looked at Cardinale and asked in German, "Frei? Frei?"

Cardinale nodded vigorously. "Du ist frei," he said several times, assuring the man that he was now free. Balaban tried to explain in pidgin German that they were American soldiers and they had freed him. "Frei, frei . . ." the young man kept repeating, as if trying to make himself understand that it was true. He was so skinny that his pants slid off. His legs were mere sticks. His hip bones were visible. Cardinale clutched him awkwardly and carried him along for several paces. The survivor's hands grasped the radioman's shoulders. His bony bare feet hovered inches off the ground. At some point, another soldier wrapped him in a GI blanket and took him from Cardinale. Sergeant Joe Hazel, with a cigarette poking from his mouth, picked the survivor up, cradled him in his arms, and placed him in Lieutenant Colonel Downard's jeep.

Although no one knew whether the man was actually near death, they all understood that he needed immediate medical attention. "To make sure he got to the Aid Station, I decided to take him there, myself," Downard wrote. With the stricken man in the passenger seat, Downard hopped in the back and ordered his driver to head for the aid station. On the way there, they took some sniper fire. The driver swerved and collided with an army ambulance. Downard was thrown unconscious from the jeep. The young man bashed his head on the windshield, opening up a nasty gash. "When I regained consciousness, I was lying on a litter [stretcher] in the Aid Station," Downing said. "On another litter, on my left, was the survivor." Medics treated Lieutenant Colonel Downard for concussion and the former prisoner for the bloody cut. "I didn't think he had that much blood left in him," said Cardinale, who drove past the scene. "Poor guy was totally shocked and bewildered."[13]

In the confusion of the moment, none of the soldiers thought to get the name of the young man they had saved. Nor did any of them have the opportunity to find out if he lived or died, and they spent the subsequent decades after the war wondering what happened to him. Downard and a few others tried but failed to locate him. "I pray that the man we saved is still living and well," Balaban wrote in 1995. "It would be a most happy and emotional scene to re-unite with him." The incident and the young man's fate were never far from Cardinale's mind. "Since that day the Sun has not set on any day that I have not thought of him and said a prayer."

Fortunately, enough information has now come to light to surmise, with some degree of probability, the identity of the death train survivor. Born in 1928, Abraham D. Feffer grew up in a Jewish family in the shtetl (a small Jewish town) of Drobin, Poland. When the Germans took over the country, they eventually rounded up the Feffers and put them in various work farms and ghettoes. In 1942, the family ended up in Auschwitz, where Abraham's mother and sister were immediately gassed and his father soon worked to death. Through sheer resolve, excellent people skills, and an inherent facility with languages, young Abraham managed to weather more than two years in the camp. In January 1945, he was evacuated, like so many other prisoners in eastern European camps, to Germany. Somehow, he survived those perilous months and the odyssey of the death train. After his liberation, American medics nursed him back to health. (One soldier estimated that he weighed only 78 pounds when he was found on the train.)

Fifty members of his family had been killed in the Holocaust. He was destitute and alone in the world. In his distant memory, he recalled having an uncle in New York. A soldier helped him place an ad in the Yiddish press. The uncle saw the ad and arranged for Abraham to immigrate to America as a displaced person. For a time he worked as a bus boy at a resort. Feffer's family had nurtured the hope of him becoming a rabbi, and this was now his dream. Because he had witnessed the near destruction of Judaism, he now wished to spearhead its rebirth. But the long years of Nazi incarceration had interrupted his education. He did not even have a high school diploma. Through persistence, hard work, dedication, and the help of many kind individuals, he managed to fulfill his dream. He finished high school in two years, college in three, and seminary in four. In 1956, he was ordained a rabbi and joined the United States Army as a chaplain. "What a great day of justified pride this was for me," he later wrote. "Finally, my wish to 'pay back' the United States Army of 1956 for having liberated me from a pile of corpses on a train destined for death near Dachau in 1945 was recognized. What a feeling of fulfillment it was! I remember how good it felt whenever I wore my uniform." He went on to a long, productive career as a prominent rabbi who enriched the lives of thousands, not just at his own synagogues in Toronto and Akron, Ohio, but in many other places during his extensive international travels and interfaith outreach. Having never reunited with the men who saved him from the death train, Feffer died of cancer in 2005.[14]

Coping with the Sight of the Death Train

The 45th Infantry Division soldiers were also shocked and sickened when they came upon the death train. They probably reached it sometime shortly after Downard's group, though they believed they were first on the scene, before the 42nd Division men. For many years, veterans from the two divisions engaged in something of a feud over which unit reached Dachau first as the supposed true liberators. "Let me be frank, we consider this dispute as childish and ridiculous," Arthur Haulot, a Dachau survivor, once wrote, expressing a nearly universal opinion among the former inmates. In fact, the 42nd and 45th converged on the Dachau complex at nearly the same time, albeit in different locations. (Elements of the 20th Armored Division were also involved in the operation.)[15]

When Lieutenant Colonel Sparks and his soldiers arrived at the site of the train, they found it difficult to comprehend the terrible sights that greeted them. "The bodies were lying . . . hanging out the open doors," said Staff Sergeant Jack Hallowell. "Some people had been able to get out and then had fallen in the field and died. They were just little skeletons within their prison clothing." Among the bodies, there were even indications of cannibalism. One of the soldiers peered into a boxcar and "actually saw one person's teeth . . . embedded into another person's flesh." There were bullet holes in some of the boxcars, indicating that the guards had turned their machine guns on them. Sparks could not help but stare sadly at several bodies lying alongside the tracks. These victims had either gotten out of the cars themselves or been dragged out by their tormentors. "Their heads had been crushed in, apparently with a rifle butt and their brains were scattered around on the pavement." A few other bodies had bullet holes in their heads.

With wide, dazed eyes, the men circulated along the tracks, still wary of any danger they might face but largely transfixed by the horror of their surroundings. As First Lieutenant William Walsh, the commander of I Company, stared at the bodies, he could not help but wonder about their personal stories and the monumental individual tragedy that each body represented. "Their families don't know this," he thought. "Their fathers, their mothers, their sisters, their brothers, their children don't know they're here. Nobody will ever know what happened to them."

Walsh and many of the other men were experienced combat soldiers. Many had been fighting since Sicily, Salerno, or Anzio. Even the relative newcomers had logged several months in combat. As a group, they had fought in many battles and seen a great deal of death and destruction. They had seen their buddies torn apart by machine gun fire and shell fragments. They had seen entire towns leveled into little more than choking rubble. They had seen civilians killed and maimed in the crossfire of combat, their blood and gristle spattered onto venerable European streets. They had become calloused to violent death. But they had never witnessed anything that compared with the sight of so many horribly mistreated human beings. Nor, in their ignorance, did they have any conception that something of this nature could even be possible. "This was the culmination of something that I had never been trained for," Walsh commented. "Nobody had ever said this goes on."[16]

No one was more hardened than Sparks, a man who had endured about 500 days of front-line action. Even he was stunned into silence. He recalled, "I couldn't think of a thing to say and I'm not one who lacks for words. The scene there robbed the human mind of reason. It was such a horrible, terrible, unbelievable scene, that it was even difficult for me to think rationally. I was not prepared for what I saw in Dachau. Nothing could prepare you for that." Almost like an electric current, a mood of revulsion and anger surged through the men. "Some turned their heads, white-faced and sick," the 157th's after

A group of American soldiers force their Hitler Youth captives to view the Dachau death train. (National Archives)

action report stated. "Others with horrible fascination looked at the piles of dead." One of the longest serving of these veteran infantrymen turned to a buddy and said, "I've been in the Army for thirty-nine months. I've been overseas in combat for twenty-three. I'd gladly go through it all again if I knew that things like this would be stopped." Many felt a palpable sense of guilt that they had not gotten there sooner.

The infantrymen did not linger at the rail site for long. Sparks gave the order to keep going into the camp. His line of advance was straight ahead, toward the administrative and training complex, not the protective custody compound. This complex was vast and multifaceted, with dozens of buildings including barracks, offices, laboratories, clothing factories, assembly shops, a porcelain factory, machine shops, ordnance plants, garages, warehouses, and a hospital. For the sake of security, each building had to be cleared. Inside the warehouses and some of the other structures, there were huge quantities of looted items and goods that had been produced in the complex. There was perfume, silk, lace, linen, alcohol, chinaware, silverware, uniforms, robes, porcelain figures, weapons of nearly every type and description, coats, suits, shoes, watches, and food.

Most of Sparks's soldiers assumed that the atrocities against the death train victims had been perpetrated by whoever was in charge of guarding the camp. The troops were emotional now, their anger and sorrow boiling over into a rage. "You try to hold yourself together," said Private First Class John Lee. "You try to tell yourself that you can control yourself. Well, I looked at my buddy [Private] Bobby McDonnell and he was just in complete tears so then I busted out. And looking around, I think most of the guys were all . . . teary eyed. You almost start getting a savage feeling out of it yourself . . . wondering if there's some sort of way of getting revenge." Even as many sobbed, others raged or sputtered with indignation. "The effect of it just opened up a flood of raw emotions," Sparks recalled. "Some men were screaming. Some were cursing. Some were silent." Some bellowed darkly, "Don't take any SS alive!" or "Let's kill every one of these bastards!"[17]

No one was more upset than Lieutenant Walsh, a 24-year-old Newton, Massachusetts, native who spoke with a thick New England accent. He was absolutely dumbfounded by what he had seen. He could not begin to comprehend how such cruelty and destruction of human life could even be possible. Thoughtful, glib, but often inarticulate and overly opinionated, Walsh struggled in vain to control his emotions. "I'll be honest with you, I broke down," he told an interviewer 45 years later. "I started crying. The whole thing was getting to me. You get pretty shaken. I'm shaking right this minute just talking about it and I didn't know if I could talk about it. I tried to forget about it for years." Cursing the Germans and raging in front of his soldiers, he lost control of himself, sobbing and shouting.[18]

By now, Sparks had come to realize that the Dachau camp was a much larger place than he had envisioned. He decided to spread out his men to cover the area with sufficient attacking force. He ordered Walsh to take two platoons from I Company and follow the train tracks while he dismounted from his jeep and proceeded a few hundred yards to the east with another platoon. No one was to go straight through Dachau's railroad gate because Sparks figured it must be covered by machine guns. He also cautioned his soldiers to watch out for booby traps. Nonetheless, the men of both groups moved with almost reckless abandon. "I never saw anything like it," said Lieutenant Harold Moyer, one of the platoon leaders. "The men were plain fighting mad.

They went down that road without any regard for cover or concealment." In no time, they scaled the masonry wall that ringed much of the complex.

Soon after surmounting the wall, Walsh and his men encountered a German who was carrying a flag adorned with a red cross. Walsh described him as "an SS trooper," about six-foot-four with Red Cross armbands. "He had beautiful blond hair. He was a handsome looking bastard." In the context of what Walsh and the soldiers had just seen at the railroad tracks, the appearance of this strapping young medic only served to make them even more upset. Walsh thought, "You sonofabitch, where the hell were you five minutes ago, before we got here, taking care of these people, with your red cross armbands and all that shit?"

The mood was dark and menacing. Walsh's soldiers were angry and in no mood to afford decent treatment to the man. He attempted to explain something in German, but no one understood, and they were hardly of a disposition to listen anyway. For a time, they herded him along, all the while murmuring threats and imprecations. According to Walsh, "he made a break . . . and one of our men shot him." If this is true, then the German must have picked up on the malevolent mood of his captors and decided that escape was his best chance of survival. After all, only a few minutes earlier, he had surrendered of his own volition, with the apparent intention of placing himself in the care of the Americans. (He might even have been hoping to arrange surrender of the entire garrison in that part of the Dachau camp complex.) Or perhaps he did not actually try to escape; perhaps the men of I Company simply executed him on the spot. The whole truth of the incident will probably never be known.

As Walsh's group pressed on, four more SS troopers emerged from a hiding place and, with hands folded on their heads, surrendered. If anything, Lieutenant Walsh's state of mind was even worse now after seeing the man with the Red Cross armbands. The atrocities Walsh had witnessed were beyond inexplicable. He could not understand how human beings could treat others of their own species with such ruthlessness. In his mind, the perpetrators deserved no quarter. "I had strong feelings against the Germans after that camp," he later said. The sight of the four new prisoners apparently sent him into a fury. By now, he had lost complete control of himself. He personally took charge of the prisoners, herded them back to the site of the train, and vigorously motioned them into a gondola car. "[He] was quite angry and upset . . . and called for a machine gun," recalled Private Fred Randolph. Walsh also called for a Browning Automatic Rifle (BAR). The BAR could fire 20-round clips of 30.06-caliber bullets at a full automatic rate, as fast as the rifleman could pull the trigger. Private First Class Harry Crouse, a nearby BAR man, started for the boxcar.

Within a few seconds, though, the lieutenant apparently changed his mind about what weapon he wanted. According to Randolph, the young company commander herded the prisoners into a neighboring boxcar that happened to be empty. Then he shot each of them with his .45-caliber pistol, but he failed to kill all of them. Some were wounded and howling in pain. "I figured there was no use letting them suffer so I finished them off," Private Albert Pruitt later told Lieutenant Colonel Joseph Whitaker, the Seventh Army assistant inspector general who conducted an investigation into the mistreatment of captured guards at Dachau.

Pruitt climbed into the boxcar and saw that one German was lying near the door. The other three were inside, lying face down. He leveled his rifle at the wounded men and pulled the trigger several times. In an apparent attempt to make himself look humane, while inadvertently revealing something of his innate anger at the Germans, Pruitt explained to Whitaker, "They were all hollering and taking on and I never like to see anybody suffer, and I had one brother killed by them [the German army] and one lost his leg, so I didn't like to see them suffer. I don't know whether any were dead or not, but they were taking on." Regardless, when Walsh and Pruitt were finished with their brand of vigilante justice, the four prisoners were dead.

The company resumed its advance deeper into the complex, entering and clearing the factory workshops, warehouses, barracks, and administrative buildings, where they engaged in a series of sporadic firefights against small groups of SS guards and military personnel. They had already been through a lot, yet they still had not seen the worst of Dachau.[19]

"My Heart Was Going a Mile a Minute"
Liberating Dachau

To THIS POINT, the Americans had discovered only the outlying portions of the Dachau concentration camp complex. Before them still lay the
heart of this malevolent place. At nearly the same time that Lieutenant Colonel Felix Sparks's unit cleared out the administrative areas, yet another group
of Americans reached Dachau (the town and soon the camp). Earlier that
morning, Major General Harry Collins, commander of the 42nd Division,
had ordered Brigadier General Henning Linden, his assistant division commander, to take a small reconnaissance group and secure the concentration
camp until medical help and relief supplies could be brought in by support
columns. Born in Mound, Minnesota, the stocky 53-year-old Linden was the
son of Swedish immigrants and a graduate of the University of Minnesota. As
a child, Linden had spoken Swedish as his first language. He had spent the
majority of his adult life in the army, earning a reputation as a reliable and
courageous leader. Tech 5 Guido Oddi, one of his bodyguards, thought of him
as a "caring man who was very interested in the people who were associated
with him." Tech 5 William "Pat" Donahue, another one of his bodyguards,
thought he was strict but caring. "He was made to command. He scared the
daylights out of an eighteen-year-old kid like me. But as we got to know and

understand him, he became a father image to us. He has been a great influence on my life." Tech 4 Harry Shaffer, his driver, "felt secure every minute I was with Gen. Linden due to his strong leadership and commitment. He was a General who took charge of the troops under him and looked after them." Each morning, the men would ask him, "How are you, sir?" He would reply, "One step ahead of a cold." This idle exchange became part of their daily routine.[1]

In hopes of finding out the location of the camp and the disposition of front-line units, Linden and his small command group climbed into three jeeps and drove to the command post of the 222nd Infantry Regiment. The regimental commander, Lieutenant Colonel Lucien Bolduc, had little to offer. The situation was fluid and confusing. Most of Bolduc's companies were out of touch or had passed along only sketchy reports. Liaison with neighboring units, such as the 45th Division, was practically nonexistent. Nor did Bolduc even know the concentration camp's exact location. About all he could tell Linden was that Lieutenant Colonel Downard's group had already advanced to the town of Dachau and perhaps beyond. Linden decided to resume his quest. To facilitate coordination with whatever 222nd Infantry units the general might encounter—Linden especially hoped to find Downard—Bolduc gave the general two of his staff officers, four enlisted men, and two more jeeps.

As Linden emerged from the command post, he met Paul Levy, a Belgian war correspondent for Agence Belga and the British Broadcasting Corporation (BBC), and Raphael Algoet, a photographer for the Belgian government. After the German conquest of Belgium, Levy had been arrested by the Nazis and incarcerated for a year. During his imprisonment, he had vowed to tell the world how people were treated in Nazi camps and to be among the first to enter a liberated camp. Moreover, he was determined to find his dear friend Arthur Haulot, whom he knew was incarcerated at Dachau. While Linden was in the command post, Levy had struck up a conversation with two French prisoners of war who claimed to know the way to Dachau. "According to them, the camp had been destroyed, the SS guards had killed everyone and had set the place on fire before leaving," Levy wrote. The correspondent approached the general, reported what he had just heard, and suggested they use the two Frenchmen as guides.

They set off immediately—five U.S. Army jeeps, plus Levy and Algoet's jeep with the two former prisoners aboard. Along the way, another jeep carrying

Marguerite Higgins and Sergeant Peter Furst, a *Stars and Stripes* correspondent, joined the group. Higgins had reported extensively on Buchenwald only a couple weeks earlier, and she was determined to witness Dachau as well. Thanks to the guidance of the Frenchmen, the group had no trouble finding its way. They arrived at the death train, slowed their jeeps, and were just as sickened and shocked at the sights as the previous groups of American soldiers had been. Tech 5 Donahue was sitting in the passenger seat of the lead jeep. Horrified, the 19-year-old Wisconsin native stared at the dead bodies. He never forgot the terrible sight of "emaciated arms, legs the size of a curtain rod, gaunt faces, sallow skin stretched across the bones." The jeeps lingered for only a few brief moments at the death train. "Long enough to lose about ten pounds and a gallon of tears," Donahue later quipped.[2]

Linden gave the order to press on. Though there was no sign of Lieutenant Colonel Downard, the general still expected to encounter him at any moment. Just past the train, the group turned right onto Avenue of the SS and rolled past the Eicke Platz to within sight of Dachau's main entrance. (By contrast, Sparks's unit had kept going straight and thus ended up in the administrative and training section of the camp.) "Three people approached down the road under a flag of truce," General Linden later wrote in an official report. The three individuals were Victor Maurer, the Red Cross representative, Lieutenant Heinrich Wicker, the acting commandant, and one of his SS aides. Maurer was carrying the flag, which amounted to little more than a broomstick with a white sheet or towel affixed. He also wore a Red Cross band on his left arm.

Lieutenant William Cowling, Linden's aide de camp, was in the lead jeep, a couple hundred yards ahead of the others, acting as a scout. He ordered the driver, Tech 5 John Bauerlein, to stop. They dismounted and approached the three men. Behind them, the other American soldiers and the media people were doing the same. Cowling unslung his Thompson submachine gun and tensely aimed it at Wicker. After what the young lieutenant from Leavenworth, Kansas, had just seen at the train site, he was in anything but a generous mood. "I was just hoping he would make a funny move so I could hit the trigger of my tommy gun," he later wrote in a letter to his family.

No such "funny move" was forthcoming. Wicker had only surrender on his mind. He asked to speak to an officer. Just as Cowling was replying, Linden arrived and a parley began. The general stood with his hands on his hips, gazing intently at Wicker, whose hands were clasped behind his back, almost in a position of military parade rest. The young lieutenant's stiff demeanor, neat uniform, and impassive, almost arrogant, expression personified the popular notion of an SS officer. As more individuals arrived, the group clumped together into a ragged semicircle around Linden and Wicker. Maurer acted as an interpreter, as did Sergeant Furst. With rifles and submachine guns in hand, Linden's soldiers stood respectfully at his side and behind him. Higgins hovered on the edges, close enough to hear the conversation but not so close as to be noticed. She wore heavy winter clothing and a fur hat to disguise the fact that she was a woman. Algoet and Cowling snapped photos. Through the interpreters, Wicker communicated his desire to surrender the camp to the Americans. Linden replied, "I am Assistant Division Commander of the 42nd Division and will accept the surrender of this camp in the name of the Rainbow Division [the unit's nickname] for the American Army."

Wicker said that two thirds of his men had already stacked arms and were waiting to surrender. The other one third—about 50 men—were still in the guard towers overlooking the Protective Custody Compound, maintaining order among the prisoners. "These are dangerous prisoners," he said contemptuously. "Watch out for your soldiers!" Maurer added that there were between 35,000 and 40,000 half-crazed inmates, many of them typhus-infected, in the enclosure. Wicker said he had given instructions to his guards in the towers not to fire at American soldiers. They were to forfeit their weapons and turn their respective posts over to the U.S. troops. General Linden pointedly asked the SS man to explain the death train. Wicker claimed no knowledge of it. Skeptical, Linden retorted that because he apparently knew nothing about the train, his first act as a prisoner would be to witness it.

Just then, they all heard rifle and machine gun shots coming from their left flank. Everyone took cover. Paul Levy, who had been listening to the parley, assumed that the fire represented some sort of SS treachery. "Some SS started to fire at our group," he wrote. General Linden was not pleased. He asked Wicker why, if he was really surrendering the camp, there was still shooting. "He said he knew nothing about it and could only state that he had given strict instructions that there would be no shooting," Linden wrote. Lieutenant Wicker was telling the truth. The fire almost certainly came from the battle that Sparks's force was fighting to seize the other side of the Dachau complex. It soon abated, and no one was hurt.

With the formal surrender now accomplished, General Linden's primary concern was to free the inmates and then hold them in place until relief arrived. (Sparks thought of his mission in exactly the same terms.) Linden ordered Lieutenant Cowling to take a small force and reconnoiter the prisoner compound. The general sensed that once the inmates understood what was happening, it might be difficult to keep them in the camp. He told Bauerlein and Donahue to take a jeep and return to the 222nd Infantry Regiment's command post with orders to send him two rifle companies to secure the compound and guard the surrendering SS men. In addition, the general ordered Major Herman Avery, the supply officer of the 222nd Infantry, to escort Lieutenant Wicker and his aide to the death train and show them the sights. Dr. Maurer would also tag along as a witness. While everyone went their separate ways, General Linden and the rest of his troops waited near Dachau's main entrance.

Cowling took Tech 5 Guido Oddi and PFC John Veitch on foot through the camp's main gate. Furst and Higgins trailed behind in their jeep. Cowling saw a guard tower ahead with German guards in it. "I hollered in German for them to come to me and they did," Cowling wrote. Twelve Germans filed out and surrendered. After disarming them, Cowling detached Veitch to take them back to General Linden's group. Then Cowling and Oddi hopped on the hood of Furst's jeep and continued in the direction of the Protective Custody Compound.[3]

Reprisal Killings

A few hundred yards to the west, Lieutenant William Walsh and I Company were clearing buildings, mostly capturing small groups of German soldiers but also engaging in sporadic firefights. In one case, they shot an enemy soldier just as he was rising from a toilet seat. The Americans overran a kennel area where SS guards had kept their dogs, mostly Doberman Pinschers and German Shepherds that they had turned into vicious killers, trained to do little else besides inflict pain. In many instances, the GIs shot and killed the dogs.

The train car summary executions had done little to calm Lieutenant Walsh's mood; he remained emotionally distraught. By now, his force had made contact with the smaller group led by Lieutenant Colonel Sparks. According to Sparks, he emerged from one building and saw Walsh chasing a

German and screaming, "You sons of bitches, you sons of bitches, you sons of bitches!" When Walsh caught up with the German, he began to beat the man over the head with his M1 carbine (a lightweight, small caliber rifle), shouting, "Bastards, bastards, bastards!" Sparks ran over and ordered Walsh to cease and desist, but the lieutenant ignored him. Sparks took his pistol out and struck Walsh over the head with it, knocking him to the ground. The young Massachusetts native sat crying hysterically. Sparks looked down and said, "I'm taking over command of your company." Walsh was so overwrought that, according to Private Sidney Horn, "it took seven men to take [him] into a room and get him quieted down."

Yet, despite Walsh's unbalanced state of mind and the fact that Sparks had apparently relieved him of his command, he nonetheless remained with his company and continued to issue orders. If the relief incident actually did happen—this was never corroborated by anyone else, and Sparks mentioned it in only a minority of the many Dachau-related accounts he gave during his life—then the colonel's subsequent inaction represents a major oversight on his part. He failed to follow through and make sure that Walsh was removed from the area. Sparks instead allowed him to remain in command, where he was certain to exact more vengeance for the atrocities he had witnessed. Surely an officer of Sparks's experience would have understood this and taken appropriate steps to prevent Walsh from further influencing an already tense, inflamed situation. For this reason, it is unlikely that the on-the-spot relief of Walsh ever took place.

When I Company soon thereafter came upon a hospital building, marked as such with a large red cross on the roof, Lieutenant Walsh was still firmly in charge. The Americans entered the building and found dozens of German military patients, doctors, nurses, orderlies, and even a few women and children. Lieutenant Walsh ordered his men to move everyone out of the hospital. "Several were in hospital beds with bandages on their arms and legs," PFC John Lee recalled. "Some of them were faking it. They put bed clothes on and were hoping we'd bypass the hospital and leave them there. Some were on crutches, feigning injury." There were regular German army soldiers in the hospital and also SS troopers, many of whom had tried to disguise themselves as ordinary soldiers. "There were also four or five inmates working in the hospital who became very helpful in picking out the real SS men, as well as those faking injury," Lee said. In one instance, when a former prisoner identified one German soldier as a member of the SS, the accused man loudly and fiercely denied it. The inmate roared back that he had been imprisoned in the camp for five years and fully recognized the soldier as SS. He punctuated his statement by punching his former tormentor.

The Americans herded everyone out of the building. SS Oberscharführer (Senior Squad Leader) Hans Linberger, who had been posted to Dachau after losing his left arm on the Eastern Front, claimed that one of the Americans hit him in the face and then shot a nearby wounded man. In Linberger's recollection, when one of the German doctors attempted to surrender, he "was beaten so hard that he received a skull fracture."

Once outside, the Americans thoroughly checked each person for weapons and then began separating all SS men from the rest of the group. "The reason the SS troops were segregated," Walsh later testified under oath to the Seventh Army's assistant inspector general, "was that I was told the SS were in command of the camp and they would need special watching, or be used for questioning." Walsh's convenient use of the passive voice obscured exactly who told him to separate the "SSers," as the Americans often called them. In all likelihood, the order originated from Walsh himself, and it was about much more than simply keeping these Nazis under special watch. Walsh and some of the other soldiers held the SS primarily responsible for the horrors of the death train. By separating the SS men from ordinary German military personnel, they were, whether consciously or unconsciously, singling them out for the possibility of special punishment.

When everyone had been moved out of the hospital, Walsh began angrily interrogating one of the officers. During the questioning, PFC Lee noticed a commotion behind the hospital. He and two other soldiers went to investigate and found a pair of inmates beating a white-coated German guard or medic on the head with a shovel. "By the time we got there, he was a bloody mess," Lee remembered. "We ordered them to halt. They said they were Poles." One of the inmates shouted in German and pointed at himself. A soldier with Lee was of German descent and understood the language well enough to translate for his buddies. The Polish man claimed that he had been castrated and that the German had somehow been involved in the operation. "The inmate dropped his pants to show us and, sure enough, he had been castrated," Lee said, with a visible shudder, to an interviewer. "I have to admit the three of us turned around and walked away. What ever happened to that man, I don't know." The incident was a harbinger of many other reprisal scenarios that would soon unfold during Dachau's liberation and confront the Americans with the moral dilemma of deciding whether or not to intercede.[4]

Once the SS were separated into their own group, Walsh's men herded them into a nearby coal yard. "The ground was covered with coal dust, and a narrow-gauge railroad track, laid on top of the ground, led into the area," Sparks wrote. The yard was located between Dachau's power plant and the hospital that I Company had just cleared. An L-shaped masonry wall about eight feet high partially enclosed the yard and divided it from the hospital. There were anywhere from 50 to 150 of the former-SS prisoners. The Americans lined them against the wall. "Keep your goddamn hands up and stay there!" they commanded the prisoners. The GIs could see the top floor and roof of the hospital, looming just over the wall.

Lieutenant Walsh supervised the placement of guards. He asked Lieutenant Daniel Drain of M Company for machine gun support. "I set my machine gun up in the direction of the prisoners," Drain said. Private William Curtin, the gunner, placed his Browning .30-caliber air-cooled gun on its tripod and lay down into a prone firing position. Private Martin Sedler assisted him as a loader. With his machine gun team in place, Drain turned and left. As Curtin hunched over his gun, Lieutenant Walsh addressed him. In Curtin's recollection, the lieutenant said that "he was going to shoot the machine gun and line up BAR [Browning Automatic Rifle] men."

There were only a few Americans, somewhere between six and ten, in the coal yard. They were covering a group several times their size. Lieutenant Colonel Sparks watched as the machine gun team and several riflemen set up and covered the prisoners. After a few moments, he formed the impression that the situation was calm and under control. One of his soldiers called him away to show him something. Sparks left the coal yard.

On the other side of the wall, PFC William Competielle, a medic, was attending to three civilians, a woman and two children, who had fainted. He had heard Lieutenant Walsh ask for the machine gun, and he assumed that nothing good was happening on the other side of that wall. In his later estimation, he "did not have the nerve to see what was going on. The word had got around that they were going to shoot all the SSers. I figured that is why they were taking them behind the wall."

Contrary to Sparks's impression, the coal yard was crackling with malevolent tension. In direct defiance of their captors' commands, many of the Germans refused to raise their hands. Some stood several paces in front of the wall, too close for American comfort. Many of them must have formed the same opinion about American intentions as had Competielle. The two groups stared at each other, hatred radiating in their eyes. There was no real communication between the antagonists, just the poisonous residue of the atrocities the Americans had beheld, their resultant anger, and the fearful contempt of the SS prisoners. The moment cried out for a strong leader on either side to calm the tension. None was present.

Private Curtin fed a belt of .30-caliber ammunition into his machine gun and pulled the charging handle to load the lead round into the chamber. The prisoners apparently took this as a sign that they were about to be shot. They moved toward the outnumbered Americans, many of whom now felt directly threatened (and few of whom had any positive feelings about their captives after what they had already witnessed in the camp). Walsh raised his pistol, pulled the trigger, and cried, "Let them have it!"

The soldiers opened up on the SS troopers. "Rifles were fired, the machine gun went off," said PFC Lee, the BAR man. He unloosed a magazine of about 20 rounds before his weapon jammed. Lieutenant Jack Busheyhead, the company executive officer, aimed his M1 carbine and squeezed off several shots. At least three other riflemen opened fire. Curtin also opened up with the most powerful weapon of all, the machine gun. In his estimation, he fired "about three long bursts."

In response to the barrage of bullets, most of the Germans moved forward several paces and dove to the ground. The man standing behind Oberscharführer Linberger was hit immediately. "The pigs are shooting at my stomach," he cried out as he fell forward. The man's blood splashed over Linberger's head and face. "I let myself fall immediately," Linberger later testified under oath to the German Red Cross. "To me it didn't matter if they would hit me standing or lying down." They did not hit him, though it looked otherwise because he was covered in blood. Some of the prisoners tried to yell out that they were not actually German or that they were not really SS men. None of this mattered. They were gunned down too. One of the more committed Nazis intoned, "Stay calm, we die for Germany." The prisoners lay in clumps along the wall. At a glance, it was hard to tell which were dead, which were wounded, and which were unhurt. "Most of them I don't believe were shot at all but fell to the ground and hid under each other or tried to hide," PFC Lee told the assistant inspector general. "They moved forward so they would have room to fall on their face [sic]. A few of them stooped . . . and jumped back when the firing ceased and held up their hands and were yelling."[5]

Lieutenant Colonel Sparks heard the shooting and immediately ran to the scene. He kicked Private Curtin off the gun, grabbed his collar, and asked sharply, "What the hell are you doing?" The young gunner was in tears. "Colonel, they were trying to get away." Sparks did not buy that. With his right hand, he drew his pistol, fired several shots into the air to get everyone's attention, and then raised his left hand, palm outward, in a clear signal to stop shooting. "There will be no more firing unless I give a specific order," he said firmly.

On hearing the shots, Lieutenant Drain had also returned to the scene. He was saddened and angered to see that his machine gunner had opened fire. "That is not the American way of fighting," he later commented to the assistant inspector general. According to Lieutenant Donald Strickland, Drain said that "it was one of the worst things he had ever seen since being in the army. He was sorry that it was his machine gun that had to be used for it." Noticing how upset Drain was, Sparks looked at him and said, "Lieutenant, let's not have any more firing here." Drain ordered his machine gun team to dismount their weapon and leave the coal yard.

In all, the shooting had probably lasted less than 30 seconds, but, in the estimation of one witness, it was "long enough to inflict damage." The question of exactly how much damage remains unsettled. In all probability, the majority of the prisoners lived. According to one of Sparks's bodyguards, PFC Frank Eggert, when someone gave the order for the prisoners to get up, most of them stood. "Only a small percentage were unable to walk." Some of the American medics refused to treat the wounded. Two wounded men supposedly finished themselves off by severing their own carotid arteries.

At some point, medics or other soldiers must have assisted the survivors, because they ended up at the Horhammer Inn in the town of Dachau. (Sparks also claimed that the wounded among them were treated by German doctors in the nearby hospital.) First Lieutenant Howard Buechner, the 3rd Battalion's surgeon, arrived on the scene soon after the shooting and testified under oath that he found 15 or 16 dead or wounded men. Forty years later, though, he wrote a fantastical account claiming that 520 SS troopers had been killed, including 346 supposedly dispatched by Lieutenant Busheyhead alone. Buechner ludicrously attributed Busheyhead's special bloodthirstiness to the fact that he was a Native American whose ancestors had been persecuted, thus

Mere moments after the coal yard reprisal shootings at Dachau, when Americans opened fire on unarmed SS men. Private William Curtin can be seen in the foreground on the machine gun. Private First Class John Lee is visible on the extreme right, walking with a Browning Automatic Rifle and a cigarette in his mouth. (National Archives)

eliciting a special kinship with Dachau's victims. Other 45th Division veterans quickly disavowed Buechner's claims, and he himself subsequently admitted that he grossly overestimated his numbers. Sparks estimated that his men killed between 30 and 50 SS soldiers, with the majority dying in firefights or reprisal killings in other places than the coal yard. Lieutenant Wicker, the acting German commandant, was probably among the dead who were murdered elsewhere. After the war, his family reported him missing, and he remains as such to this day. He might have been executed by angry Americans or by liberated inmates, many of whom beat or kicked their former guards and kapos to death in the course of that chaotic day. One American soldier even allowed vengeful inmates to borrow his rifle so that they could shoot a pair of guards to death.

Lieutenant Colonel Joseph Whitaker from the Seventh Army's inspector general section is probably the most reliable source for an estimate of the number of dead SS men, especially in the coal yard. He visited the scene four days after the killings and found 17 bodies in the yard, most of whom were clothed in SS uniforms. In the wall above the bodies, he found "12 marks or holes . . . such as might have been made by cal. 30 MG or rifle fire, with blood and small pieces of flesh in three of them; a number of .45 caliber slugs, some of which had blood on them." Most likely, the death toll at the coal yard was higher than the 17 bodies Whitaker found because some of the wounded undoubtedly died later on. At most, probably 20 to 25 men died, and that many or more were wounded.[6]

The killings, although understandable in view of what the soldiers had seen at the death train, reflected a clear failure of military leadership. The officers lost control of the situation and fostered a mood conducive to illegal, vigilante-style killings. From a humanitarian viewpoint, perhaps it was to Lieutenant Walsh's credit that he was so deeply affected by the sight of Nazi atrocities. However, as a company commander, Walsh did not have the luxury of giving in to his sorrow and anger, no matter how justified his emotions might have seemed. In such tragic and tense situations, soldiers often take their emotional cue from their commanders. When Lieutenant Walsh broke down and personally engaged in reprisal shootings, it legitimized that behavior for his soldiers, many of whom were naturally in the mood to lash out at whomever they felt was responsible for such unimaginable horrors. As an officer, Walsh's job was to rein in those feelings and focus his men on the mission at hand, not to stoke those emotions to a fever pitch. His behavior after witnessing the death train was unprofessional and self-indulgent.

As the ranking officer, Lieutenant Colonel Sparks bears the heaviest responsibility for what happened. Though he remained in control of himself and properly focused on his mission, he was unable, by his own later admission, to fully restrain his troops. "That was one situation that I was just unable to control for a short time," he said. Given the unprecedented horrors that he and his troops encountered, his inability to maintain control was understandable. However, he could have—and should have—realized how easily anger could lead to a thirst for revenge. He should have made it a priority to speak to his men and calm them down as best he could. Sparks was so highly respected and trusted among the troops that the force of his personality would likely have defused at least some of the murderous tension. Instead, he reacted after his men had already engaged in reprisal shootings.

Sparks's main mistake, though, was his failure to remove Lieutenant Walsh—not just from a position of responsibility but from the scene altogether. If, as Sparks later claimed, he did relieve Walsh of command, then it is absolutely inexplicable why he allowed the lieutenant to remain with I Company and continue issuing orders, especially in the coal yard. More likely, Sparks did not relieve Walsh. Instead, the colonel somehow failed to identify just how volatile and incendiary Walsh's emotional state had become under such trying circumstances. As a result of Sparks's oversight and lack of preemptive action, the situation spiraled out of control, at least for a short time.

Of course, it is easy to pass judgment from the safe emotional distance of many decades, but such is the inherent nature of history itself. As one 42nd Division soldier, who later retired from the army as a sergeant major, put it, "Clear thinking did not prevail on the part of our leaders and our troops. The liberators of the Dachau complex acted more like a mob force than an organized military unit." Indeed they did, and the main reason for this was a failure of leadership. No such widespread reprisal killings took place against guards at Buchenwald or, for that matter, any other camp liberated by the United States Army, though the shock and trauma experienced by the liberators was often just as profound.

For the men of Sparks's battalion, the coal yard killings forever tinged their liberation experience with the poison of instant retribution. Lieutenant Harold Moyer, who witnessed the aftermath of the shootings, told the assistant inspector general, "I believe every man in the outfit who saw those boxcars . . . was justified in meting out death as a punishment to the Germans who were responsible." The flaw in Moyer's logic was that the SS troopers in the coal yard were almost certainly not responsible for the death train. Even if they had been, this hardly would have justified such summary executions. Lieutenant Buechner, the surgeon, described the killings as "one of the most disturbing and stunning scenes . . . because it showed our own forces taking vengeance." Corporal Henry Mills, a combat-seasoned member of the intelligence and reconnaissance section and a witness to the shootings, remarked, "Geez, we've come over here to stop this bullshit and now here we've got somebody doing the same thing." Reflecting on it again many years later, he opined, "Once they were prisoners, they were prisoners. They were unarmed. You can't shoot 'em. You can't do that. That's an atrocity."

Sparks had mixed emotions:

I never like to see people killed unnecessarily no matter what their stripe is or what they have done. We did kill some people there I consider unnecessarily. Given the circumstances, well, I'm sorry about it. But it was just one of those things that no one could control. Actually the people that we killed died a much easier death than the people they tortured and killed. So in a way we were kinder to them than they were to the people that they murdered. But, at the same time, I never countenanced any unnecessary killing at any time during the war.

John Lee, whose rifle bullets most likely killed or wounded several Germans, felt anything but pleased with what he had done:

I didn't really feel good about what happened there. But also I have to admit I felt there was a certain amount of revenge. Even though these may not have been the men who perpetrated this sort of thing, at least you were paying back for these people and what happened to them. And I realize you can't resolve it by doing that. It was wrong what happened there. But you had to have been there to see what we saw. You've probably seen the pictures. They're just pictures to you. You've never walked up on something like that. It knocked you off your equilibrium. It's part of war, but nobody prepared us for it.

Walsh was unrepentant, never expressly admitting he did anything wrong. Years later, he still had strong feelings about the Nazis he encountered at Dachau. "Some goddamned day when I go to hell with the rest of the SS, I'm gonna ask them how the hell they could do it," he said with forthright passion. "I don't think there was any SS guy that was shot or killed in the defense of Dachau that wondered why he was killed. I think they all knew goddamned well right why some of them were killed down in the camp. Goddamn well right."

What few of the soldiers seemed to realize, though, was that the killings might have led to far broader consequences for the army and the moral authority of the liberators. The Allied governments had committed themselves to post-war trials for war criminals. The powerful message conveyed by such trials was that the Allies represented legality and human rights. Even the most murderous Nazi war criminal was to receive proper legal representation, due process, and a fair trial. This would not be victors' justice. It would be legal justice. However, if American soldiers could carry out arbitrary vigilante

The bodies of dead Germans lie along the coal yard wall at Dachau. Notice that the bodies have been heavily looted either by liberated prisoners or American soldiers. (U.S. Army Military History Institute)

executions by claiming extenuating circumstances, this could undercut the legal and moral authority of the Allied governments. If the liberating troops engaged in such behavior, what would differentiate them from the Nazis they so abhorred? As General Dwight D. Eisenhower wrote, "America's moral position will be undermined and her reputation for fair dealing debased if criminal conduct of a like character by her own armed forces is condoned and unpunished by those of us responsible for defending her honor." He was not referring directly to the Dachau incident, but he might as well have been. However, punishing perpetrators of revenge killings would also draw substantial public attention to American misdeeds, thus jeopardizing the perception of moral authority.

Lieutenant Colonel Whitaker, the investigating officer and assistant inspector general of the Seventh Army, seemed to concur with Eisenhower's viewpoint. He recommended court martial on murder charges for Walsh, Busheyhead, and Private Albert Pruitt. He further recommended that Drain and Buechner be charged with failure to do their duty—Drain for failing to keep his machine gunners from opening fire and Buechner for refusing to dispense medical care to wounded Germans lying along the coal yard wall. "Rumor had it that we were going to Leavenworth for the rest of our lives," Lee later said, "and I was scared to death." But Whitaker never recommended any charges against Lee, nor were those individuals he did recommend for court martial ever tried. General Wade Haislip, who had assumed command of the Seventh Army by the time Whitaker completed his investigation, chose not to act on his recommendations. "The investigation indicates an apparent lack of comprehension on the part of the investigating officer of the normal disorganization of small unit combat action and of the unbalancing effects of the horror and shock of Dachau on combat troops already fatigued with more than 30 days' continuous combat action," he wrote. Haislip further accused Whitaker of engaging in bias against the soldiers by trying to solicit damning testimony against them rather than investigating their actions impartially. Haislip recommended another, "true and unbiased," investigation. No such reinvestigation ever took place.[7]

The Liberation

Inside the protective custody compound, the prisoners had heard the sounds of shooting and knew that their liberators must be close. If the mood among the prisoners had been anticipatory at the start of the day, it was now, in late afternoon, akin to a hot kettle reaching the boiling point. Inside and outside of the barracks buildings, thousands of pairs of eyes and ears strained for any sight or sound, anything to confirm that the moment of deliverance had finally come. Nerin Gun was typical of the many prisoners. He looked to the west and glimpsed what he believed was the first American soldier. "He is still quite far away but I can already imagine that I see him chewing gum," Gun wrote. "He comes cautiously, yes, but upright, stalwart, unafraid. At that moment, for me as for all of us . . . he was like the cowboy of my youth, the one out of my favorite books and films."

Gun and the vast majority of the other inmates knew little of the United States beyond what they had seen in movies or magazines. To them, Americans were mysterious creatures from an impossibly distant land— swaggering, gum-chewing cowboys who were larger than life. "We had prayed, we had waited, we had lost all hope of ever seeing you," Gun wrote in tribute to the soldier he had glimpsed, "but you had finally come. Messiah from across the seas, angel and demon. You had come at the risk of your own life, into an unknown country, for the sake of unknown people, bringing us the most precious thing in the world, the gift of freedom." Word of the Americans' arrival spread with lightning speed. "Die Amerikaner sind hier!" prisoners excitedly told one another.[8]

One of the first soldiers on the scene was Lieutenant Cowling, whom General Linden had sent ahead to reconnoiter the compound after SS Lieutenant Wicker's formal surrender. Cowling and Tech 5 Guido Oddi rode on the hood of a jeep driven by Sergeant Peter Furst, the correspondent from *Stars and Stripes*. Marguerite Higgins sat in the passenger seat. A German prisoner served as a guide. They crossed a small concrete bridge over the canal that bordered the western side of the enclosure. In their path lay the dead body of a man who had been shot in the head. (Neither Cowling nor any of the others ever said whether the body was that of a guard or a prisoner.) The German POW dismounted and moved the body out of the way, and they proceeded straight ahead to the two-story jourhaus (entrance building) that served as the main guard post into and out of the compound. In the center of the jourhaus was the wrought iron gate emblazoned with the famous slogan, "Arbeit Macht Frei."

The German POW opened the gate, and the Americans entered the compound at the main assembly ground (appelplatz), an open area where prisoners had endured so many thousands of roll calls. "When we entered . . . not a soul was in sight," Lieutenant Cowling wrote to his family. "Then suddenly people (few could call them that) came from all directions. They were dirty, starved skeletons with torn tattered clothes and they screamed and hollered and cried. They ran up and grabbed us. Myself and the newspaper people and kissed our hands, our feet and all of them tried to touch us. They grabbed us and tossed us into the air screaming at the top of their lungs."

The Americans were tossed around so much that they were left with some bruises and scrapes. Furst was on the receiving end of such a strong bear hug that he was lifted off of the ground. Higgins's heavy clothing and fur hat obscured her gender for many of the joyful prisoners. She was picked up, hoisted from shoulder to shoulder, and hugged. At one point, though, one of the celebrants hugged her so hard that she could not breathe. When she called out in her high-pitched voice for him to stop, he was startled and immediately released her. "Mon Dieu, c'est une femme," he said in French. "Pardon, madame." The SS prisoner who served as a guide had made the great mistake of following the Americans into the enclosure. (Perhaps he had no choice.) In the confusion of the initial moments, the liberated inmates assumed he was an American. "It was weird to see the grimacing, unwilling SS man being toted around as a hero, cheered and applauded," Higgins wrote. "He was soon found out." She claimed that she later saw his body lying just outside the gate, beaten to death.

Cowling managed to extricate himself from the celebration and leave the enclosure. Inside the jourhaus, eight SS guards, who had been manning a guard tower atop the structure, surrendered to him. He collected their weapons and told them to stay put. Emerging from the jourhaus several moments later, Cowling noticed the presence of other American soldiers from the 42nd and 45th Divisions. Lieutenant Walsh and some of his I Company soldiers were there (and might actually have arrived just before Cowling). Reinforcements from A Company and F Company of the 222nd Infantry Regiment, 42nd Infantry Division, were nearby. General Linden had also arrived. Inside the compound, pandemonium reigned. "Now the square was completely filled with thousands of yelling, screaming prisoners," Cowling wrote. "They were all crowded up to the edge of a ditch just inside the barbed wire fence surrounding the encampment."[9]

The situation was now fraught with danger. The prisoners were in a delirium of excitement at the prospect of their liberation. Many were eager to exact revenge on their former tormentors, whether SS or kapos. The natural desire of every prisoner was to get out of the compound. Many had spent years nurturing such dreams of freedom. But there were still armed SS guards in some of the towers, and the orders Lieutenant Wicker had given them—to keep the prisoners in the compound and surrender to the Americans—were somewhat confusing. Under the best of circumstances, this would have been a delicate operation. Under these conditions, it was a near impossibility. Meanwhile, the American soldiers were in the process of orienting themselves to this chaotic and frenzied environment. They were absorbing the disturbing sight of the ragged, hungry prisoners, figuring out the geographic layout of the compound, and, probably most important to them, assessing the potential threat posed by the SS guards. Some had also gotten their first glimpse of the crematorium and gas chamber, located just west of the compound, where hundreds of emaciated bodies lay in heaps, awaiting incineration. These sights, together with all the others, ratcheted up the tension still further.

Thousands of prisoners converged on the jourhaus and the electrified barbed-wire fence enclosing the western side of the compound. An almost indescribable roar emanated from their throats, an otherworldly combination of cheering, crying, and shouting for joy. Gleb Rahr, who had survived the death train and was now lying semiconscious on a crude bunk in a quarantine barrack, heard the voices and later described them as "a sound, the like of which I had never heard in my life. It was a howling—not the howling of wolves—but of men!"

The excitement was nearing a fever pitch. The prisoners were so overjoyed that they came close to stampeding. "I saw prisoners running to the Main Gate [jourhaus]," Stephan Ross, a teenaged inmate, later wrote. "I was very weak and hardly able to walk, but I had to get to the gate. I walked for a while, but got dizzy and fell down." Several times, his brother had to pick him up. They were absorbed into the crowd of bodies. Just outside the enclosure, Tech 5 William Donahue, bodyguard for General Linden, stared in amazement at the sight of thousands of prisoners running and stumbling toward the wire. Many of them were looking right at him, and he was convinced they were reacting to the sight of him on the other side of the barbed wire. "I heard people cheering and hollering and screaming. It was the greatest feeling I ever had in the world. My heart was going a mile a minute." The sound of their jubilation made the hairs on the back of his neck stand up. The young soldier kept thinking to himself, "God, they're cheering me! Why?"

The crowd had become a tidal wave of single-minded humanity. The only thing that mattered was getting out of the compound and meeting the Americans. "All we could think about were Americans," Walenty Lenarczyk, one of the newly liberated inmates, later said. "For the past six years we had waited for the Americans, and at this moment the SS were nothing." He and the others ran or walked as fast as they could. In no time, they reached the fence. "This seething mass increased in intensity until the surge against the steel barbed wire fence was such that it broke in several places, and inmates poured out into the roadway between the fence and that moat," General Linden testified to the assistant inspector general. "In this process several were electrocuted on the charged fence." Lieutenant Cowling distinctly saw three people die of electrocution. Others thought the number was one or two. Higgins placed it at six.

Several more minutes passed before somebody figured out where and how to shut off the electricity. With the electricity off, the freed inmates tore holes in the fencing and barbed wire. Others pushed into the jourhaus. "We were able to keep control over those that poured through the holes in the fence along the moated roadway," Linden said, "but the surge through the gate house building and its bridge opening directly across the moat became a problem." Some of the inmates hugged soldiers, lifted them onto their bony shoulders, or kissed them. For the Americans, this was gratifying but rather overwhelming. The soldiers knew they had to get the crowd under control. Linden hopped onto the concrete bridge wall and barked orders at his men, supervising as the soldiers apprehended people or tried to push them back into the enclosure. At one point, he even drew his pistol and threatened to shoot anyone who moved over the bridge.

At the same time, many of the SS guards in the towers still had not surrendered. The chaos of these frenetic moments led to what may have been another illegal killing. Prisoners alerted the Americans to the presence of SS men in tower B, located a couple hundred yards north of the jourhaus along the barbed-wire fence. Some of the Americans later made the dubious claim that the SS troopers were shooting into the crowd of inmates. Though certainly not impossible, this would have been an act of self-destruction and stupidity. A group of soldiers led by Tech 3 Henry Wells, a German-speaking intelligence sergeant from the 222nd Infantry Regiment's headquarters, and covered by another group under Lieutenant Colonel Walter "Mickey" Fellenz, rousted 16 SS men from the tower. Wells and the others lined them up side by side, in two ranks, facing the tower with the canal to their backs. As one of the Americans searched them, one of the prisoners apparently made a sudden move, as if reaching for a gun. "The American soldier who had brought him from the tower stepped back and [another] soldier who had been guarding . . . with his gun went 'Brrrrrrt!!!' and it was finished," Marion Okrutnik, an inmate who witnessed the killings, later told Lieutenant Colonel Whitaker for his investigation. The bodies of some of the dead men were kicked or shoved into the canal. Others lay in a line underneath the tower. Whitaker recommended murder charges against Wells, but nothing ever came of his recommendation.

The American soldiers formed a cordon around the jourhaus and along the barbed-wire enclosure. Communication was a problem. They were, after all, dealing with a dizzying multiplicity of nationalities and languages. Ironically, the common denominator language was German. As best they could, the Americans tried to tell the prisoners that they must remain in place for now; that food, medical care, and water were on the way; and that they would be better off here than roaming the German countryside. To quell the bedlam, the soldiers sometimes fired their weapons into the air. "We were gesturing them back," one soldier recalled. "We didn't want to hurt their feelings after what they went through, but they smelled like hell." The soldiers also enlisted the assistance of any prisoner who seemed calm and could speak some English.

It took the Americans more than an hour to restore order, move the inmates back into the compound, and seal it off. This was at times a confusing and traumatic process for the soldiers, but more so for the liberated, many of whom had naively assumed that the Americans would allow them to go wherever they wished. As Nerin Gun wrote:

> The bars were still down and the GIs in uniform closed the doors and locked the gates . . . just as the Germans had done. Many who danced with joy in the twilight of April 29 were to face the supreme ordeal shortly afterward—at the very time when the hope of seeing their homes and loved ones had been given to them. I admit that letting the prisoners loose on the countryside would have entailed a certain amount of danger for the people, but if it had been a matter of sacrificing the lives of half the Bavarian population to save a fellow prisoner, I would not have batted an eye.

What Gun and so many others did not fully realize—understandably so— was that their restored health and dignity could be purchased only at the price of continued confinement at Dachau. Turning loose more than 30,000 malnourished, diseased, disoriented, traumatized, and displaced former prisoners of many nationalities into the turmoil of 1945 Europe would have been disastrous.[10]

The Great Sparks-Linden Controversy

At some point during this process of restoring order, Lieutenant Colonel Sparks made contact with General Linden. After querying Sparks (who Linden mistakenly thought was named "Squires") about the strength and disposition of his force, the general began to issue orders. He told Sparks that he and his men would be responsible for the administrative and training complex they had just secured. Lieutenant Colonel Fellenz and the soldiers of the 222nd would secure and guard the protective custody compound and its inmates. The canal and the barbed-wire fence would serve as the boundary line between the two units. "They would coordinate by having their CPs [command posts] close together somewhere in the officer section of the camp," General Linden wrote a few days later in a memo to his own commander. "This was agreeable to the Colonel [Sparks] and that order was put into effect."[11]

Decades later, Sparks told a radically different story of the meeting, one that demonstrates the bad blood that boiled between the two liberating divisions after the war. Sparks maintained that he and his troops got to the prisoner compound first and, after much effort, finally succeeded in calming the inmates down and restoring order. In his recollection, there were no 42nd Division soldiers at Dachau. According to Sparks, the SS guards at tower B were already dead when he and his troops arrived, and he simply assumed that his men had killed them in a firefight while taking over the compound. Then, as Sparks was standing at the jourhaus gate, Linden arrived with a small party of three jeeps, with Marguerite Higgins in tow, and demanded that Sparks allow her into the compound to interview notable prisoners such as Kurt von Schuschnigg, the former chancellor of Austria, and Martin Niemöller, a prominent anti-Nazi Lutheran pastor. Many in the media were eager to interview such famous prisoners who, they believed, were incarcerated at Dachau. They could not have known that the Nazis had already moved these so-called "VIPs" several days earlier.

The names of these prominent personalities meant nothing to Sparks, but he knew that, if Higgins entered the compound, chaos would ensue, and he had just now gotten the situation under control. He told General Linden as much. "At that time a sea of inmates pressed against the gate, awaiting an opportunity to get out," Sparks wrote 40 years later. "I advised the general that my specific orders were to prevent anyone from entering or leaving the compound." Linden replied, "Well, she's going in, and I'm taking charge." As the two officers argued, Higgins dismounted, opened the gate, and attempted to squeeze inside but was overwhelmed by the unrestrained mass of prisoners. Frightened, she turned around and ran back to the jeep while Sparks's men secured the gate.

Sparks then told Linden to vacate the area, and the general refused. Linden attempted to relieve Sparks of his command, but the colonel said that only his own superior officers could do that, not a general from another division who, according to Sparks, was outside of his proper area of operations. Sparks ordered one of his men to escort the general away. "This general was a dandy who carried a . . . leather riding crop. When the private stepped forward, the general, who was sitting in the front seat of his jeep, leaned forward and hit him over the helmet with his riding crop. It didn't hurt the boy. It might have rang his bell a little bit. Well, it had already been a long and trying day. I exploded at that point." Sparks said he pulled his pistol out of its holster and pointed it at the general. "You sonofabitch, if you touch another one of my men, I'll kill you." At gunpoint, he forced the general and his party away as Linden threatened a general court martial.

At the same time, Sparks also engaged in a verbal altercation with Fellenz, who said to him, "You can't talk to my general like that. I'll see you after the war."

"You sonofabitch, what's wrong with right now?" Sparks replied.

Linden's party and Fellenz drove away. Within two hours, an unidentified officer from the inspector general section of the Seventh Army visited Sparks and grilled him about what had happened with Linden. "I told him to leave, that I had no time for idle gossip. He got insulted, but he left." A few days later, Sparks's division commander, Major General Robert Frederick, visited his headquarters and told him that General Linden was making a stink, calling for an investigation of the incident at Dachau. "He said he thought he could handle the matter, but he considered it advisable that I leave for the United States at once." After a short leave in the states, he could then rejoin the division in time for the expected invasion of Japan later that year or the next.

Sparks said he left for Le Havre, France with three of his most trusted soldiers: Corporal Karl Mann, Tech 5 Albert Turk, and Private Carlton Johnson. At the docks of Le Havre, a military police lieutenant stopped him and said he was under arrest and was to be escorted back to Seventh Army headquarters. "I politely informed the lieutenant that I would not submit to an arrest but that I would voluntarily return to Seventh Army Headquarters." The three soldiers punctuated their colonel's proposal by pointing loaded rifles at the lieutenant, so he promptly agreed. Several days later, after going on a bender in Paris, Sparks ended up appearing in Augsberg, Germany, before General George Patton, who was now the military governor of Bavaria. "Colonel, I have some serious court martial charges against you and some of your men here on my desk," Patton said, apparently referring to the inquiry about the alleged illegal killing of SS guards and not to the troubles with Linden.

Sparks asked for an opportunity to explain, but Patton cut him off. "There is no point in an explanation. I have already had these charges investigated, and they are a load of crap. You have been a damn fine soldier. Now go home." With that, Patton supposedly tore up the inspector general's report on the killings and threw the papers into his wastebasket. Sparks maintained that he then rejoined his regiment.[12]

This colorful and rather self-serving story has predominated in most Dachau liberation accounts. Unfortunately for Sparks, virtually none of his story stands up to the scrutiny of documentary evidence. There is absolutely no doubt that Linden received the surrender of SS Lieutenant Wicker and then proceeded to the prisoner compound, where he took a leading role in quelling the pandemonium as the inmates attempted to leave the enclosure. This account was further corroborated by Brigadier General Charles Banfill, an Eighth Air Force officer whose mission was to assess bomb damage in Germany. In this capacity, Banfill accompanied Linden's party that day. He filed an official report of his observations, and his description of events mirrored those of Linden and the other members of his command group.

General Linden carried a small swagger stick, not a leather riding crop. Nor, in any fair manner, could he be described as a "dandy." This was a highly disparaging term used by combat soldiers like Sparks to describe rear echelon posturers who were loath to dirty their hands in real front-line action. Linden had seen a great deal of combat and was every bit as courageous as Sparks. The idea that Linden would exit a place he had helped secure only to return shortly thereafter in a small convoy of jeeps makes no sense. Multiple witness accounts demonstrate that Linden remained at the prisoner compound until well after the troops of both divisions had restored order. Higgins, as corroborated by Lieutenant Cowling and Tech 5 Oddi, was one of the first people to enter the enclosure. She then moved around on her own, interviewing people at will. She would not have had any cause or reason to leave the area and then place herself at Linden's disposal. If a reporter with her finely honed instincts for a good story had witnessed such a violent argument between two high-ranking American officers, she undoubtedly would have written about it, if not at the time then later. Yet, she never mentioned it in any of her writings. Nor did General Banfill, who presumably would have discussed such a court martial–worthy action in an official report. Peter Furst, the *Stars and Stripes* reporter who worked alongside Higgins that day, later said that he never saw any such incident between Linden and Sparks.

The dead SS guards at tower B, as Whitaker's report described, were killed by 42nd Division men—perhaps illegally—during the initial efforts to bring the compound under control and keep the prisoners from getting out. The fact that Sparks admitted to seeing their bodies is a near certain indicator that he did not arrive at the enclosure first. This is an important point only insofar as it collapses the fundamental reasoning behind Sparks's story of his violent altercation with Linden, namely that Sparks secured the compound first only to have that security threatened by an interloping, late-arriving, self-serving general. Sparks did not kick Linden out of Dachau; records show the general remained at the camp until about eight o'clock that evening. And there is almost no chance he threatened him with a pistol. Only two men from Sparks's battalion, Sergeant Donald Lesch and Corporal Hank Mills, ever claimed to see this happen, and neither of them was ever verified as a direct eyewitness. Corporal Karl Mann, an interpreter who was usually at Sparks's elbow, avowed that he never saw the confrontation occur. The same was true for General Banfill, Lieutenant Colonel Fellenz, and Linden's entire retinue. Tech 5 Donahue left Linden's side for only an hour or so over the course of the day; otherwise, he was with Linden the entire time. "If anybody threatened our general, he was a dead man," Donahue said. "I rebuke his [Sparks's] story."[13]

Within 24 hours of Dachau's liberation, Sparks was relieved of command, almost certainly because of the reprisal killings. The orders for his relief probably originated directly from General Eisenhower's headquarters in response to the troubling news of the killings. Sparks's relief probably had nothing to do with General Linden. He never preferred any court martial charges against Sparks. Instead, Sparks was ordered to report to the Assembly Area Command in Reims, France. He was gone from his battalion by 2:30 p.m. on May 1, 1945. Mann and Turk, two of the men Sparks supposedly took with him to Le Havre, later told two different historians (David Israel and Art Lee) that the story of Sparks's journey was not true. Turk had actually been wounded shortly before Dachau's liberation and never saw Sparks again. The third man, Johnson, could not possibly have been with Sparks because he appeared in Munich on May 5 to testify to the Seventh Army assistant inspector general for the murder investigation. Thus, the incident with the military police in Le Havre almost certainly did not happen, or at least not in the manner Sparks described.

The same is true of the meeting with Patton, whose headquarters were located in Regensberg until May 23 and then Bad Tölz, but never in Augsberg. Personnel records show that Lieutenant Colonel Sparks was present for duty at the Assembly Area Command in Reims and Suippes from May 8 through

July 14, 1945, when he returned to the United States. This means he could not possibly have met with Patton in Germany during that time, or he would have been listed in the Assembly Area Command records as absent without leave (AWOL). Moreover, Patton left Europe on June 7 for a 30-day leave in the United States. The 45th Division did not come under the administrative control of Patton's Third Army until June 9, after Patton had left, Lieutenant Colonel Whitaker had concluded his investigation, and General Haislip, the Seventh Army's new commander, had already decided to take no action. Thus, Patton had no real jurisdiction over the case. The idea that he would simply tear up the more than 200-page report and toss it into his wastebasket borders on the ridiculous. Besides, there were no formal court martial recommendations in that report against Sparks, so the meeting would have been pointless. Finally, there is no record of Sparks ever returning to his old regiment.

Beyond all of these unforgiving facts, there are other aspects of Sparks's story that are difficult to accept for anyone familiar with the World War II United States Army and its practices. For his claims to be accurate, several extraordinary, illegal instances had to have occurred with no adverse consequences for him. His commanding general, Robert Frederick, by attempting to send Sparks home, had to have disobeyed a direct order from Eisenhower's headquarters for the colonel to report to the Assembly Area Command. Sparks had to have gotten away with threatening the life of a general officer with a deadly weapon. Sparks had to have refused cooperation with an investigating inspector general officer and sent him away, saying he had no time for idle gossip. Finally, he and his men had to have threatened the life of an unnamed military police officer with multiple deadly weapons. Obviously, all of these stories strain credulity.

Given the major accuracy problems with Sparks's story of a confrontation with Linden, does this mean that he simply made the whole tale up? In all probability, some sort of argument or altercation did take place, though nothing remotely close to what Sparks described. Mann did confirm that "Sparks got pretty angry and red in the face." The trouble could have come from a disagreement over who had jurisdiction in the camp, especially because both divisions believed they had orders to secure the place and seal it off. General Linden, in his own statement, did mention that he eventually toured the compound with Higgins and two other reporters, so he might have argued with Sparks about whether the reporters should have had this kind of access.

The most likely of all explanations is that the altercation started as a result of a mishap between General Linden and one of Sparks's sergeants. While the Americans were attempting to quell the excitement of the inmates and put them back into the compound, one of Sparks's soldiers apparently picked up a set of chains and shackles and began to shake them in the direction of the inmates. Naturally, this only exacerbated their agitated state. "General Linden ordered the man, who was standing directly in front of him, to drop the chain at once," Lieutenant Cowling wrote three days later in his official statement on the liberation of Dachau.

> The man, however, disobeyed the General's order and turned his back on him, raising the chains above his head and shaking them again. In an attempt to get the man's attention, General Linden tapped the man on the helmet with a stick he was carrying. The man turned and the General again directed him to drop his chains. This time the man dropped the chains and walked off, although he was very sullen, showing no military discipline or respect.

Tech 5 Donahue contended that the soldier was drunk and had a bottle of wine tucked beneath his field jacket. "The supposed striking of the soldier was the general planting on the shoulder of one man with his swagger stick. He caught him on the shoulder and held him and said, 'Sergeant, I want you to take that bottle out of your jacket and throw it into the moat and go over there and sit down and cool off for a while.' That's all that was said." General Banfill did not even remember Linden striking the soldier. He watched as Linden "approached and directed the soldier to move over to a point some 20 feet away. I noticed Brig. Gen. Linden spoke emphatically to him for about a minute and then apparently directed him to rejoin his unit. The soldier walked away without delay."

If Linden did strike one of Sparks's soldiers with his swagger stick—and it seems very likely he did—then this certainly could have irked the colonel. Sparks was deeply protective of his men, and, at times, his temper could get the best of him. In all likelihood, he exaggerated this tense incident into a full-blown confrontation that might, in later years at least, explain his relief from command. Of course, the truth was far more complicated and less complimentary to Sparks. In a larger sense, Sparks serves as a metaphor for the American liberation of Dachau—well intentioned, but imperfect.[14]

6 Dachau
The Impact

WITH THE DACHAU COMPLEX SECURED, the Americans now had an opportunity to truly take in the awful sights and smells of the camp. Seeing the bodies at the death train had been bad enough, but there were plenty more in and around the compound, especially near the crematorium where prisoners had been forced to pile the dead in heaps during the days and weeks before liberation. A coal shortage and the turbulence of the military situation had led to delays in the burning of bodies, causing a significant buildup of decomposing corpses. As Sergeant Darrell Martin gazed at the crematorium, he imagined how the process of body disposal must have worked. "You could see how guys with wheelbarrows would haul the bodies to this . . . building and dump them through a window like they were delivering coal. And it was a big room. I know when I went in there that stack of bodies was damn near as high as my chest."

Lieutenant William Cowling remembered seeing "numerous piles of bodies, in piles of anywhere between twenty and fifty, stacked between numerous buildings; all showed signs of starvation and were mere skeletons; many showed signs of beating." All the corpses he saw were naked. Tech 5 Robert Stubenrauch, a photographer with the 163rd Signal Company, estimated that the bodies were stacked six feet high and spread over 150 feet along the expanse of the crematorium. "If you can imagine a human skeleton and his flesh becomes silver gray and is preshrunk on the skeleton so that every joint of the body is visible," he said, "you'd know everything you need to know about anatomy." Near the building and in adjacent warehouses, there were piles of clothing, shoes, coats, eyeglasses, and various other personal items.

Lieutenant Colonel Walter "Mickey" Fellenz spoke with members of the International Prisoner Committee (IPC) about the bodies. Based on this conversation, Fellenz reported to his division commander, Major General Harry Collins, that there were about 4,000 bodies in and around the crematorium and another 1,000 scattered throughout the compound. These numbers may have been overestimated, but there is little doubt that the human toll was immense—well into four figures. Fellenz, a 28-year-old West Point graduate and Texas native, personally witnessed a spot where guards had executed prisoners: "The mound of earth was still wet with blood." Elsewhere he saw a pile of naked corpses "thrown on top of one another like sacks of potatoes." General Henning Linden went into the crematorium and saw "several stacks of dead bodies, all of which showed signs of starvation, each body looking like a skeleton with skin stretched over it."

For many soldiers, the nakedness of these corpses made them even more disturbing than those in the death train. At least those bodies had been clothed, partially disguising their deteriorated physical condition. There was no such veneer to shield the depersonalized nature of these corpses, as if the Nazis had starved, mistreated, and tortured every last shred of humanity and individuality from them. Their taut skin, emaciated bodies, and distorted features lent them a macabre appearance. For PFC Robert Perelman, they were "so much like skeletons it was hard to tell the men from the women."

Sergeant Ernest Henry came upon a pile of nude, badly decomposed bodies, and it took several moments before he could process what he was seeing: "Suddenly it dawned on me what I was looking at. I had stumbled on the Charnal [sic] House of the Devil himself. The bodies were stacked like so much cord wood, and had been dumped there in anticipation of their being burned. All these people had either been shot through the head mercifully or bashed in the head sadistically or had tortuously starved to death." Private First Class Jim Dorris stared in disbelief at the bodies and thought to himself, "This has got to be what hell is like. God, help me get out of this place." To some, the bodies looked so bizarre that they almost seemed like wax dummies. "It's hard to associate these figures with anything that ever lived," one lieutenant said to a reporter. "They look like horrible caricatures of clothing store models. The way they're piled on top of one another—the indignity of it—why, it's an insult to the human race!"[1]

All day long, the troops had been cognizant of a gamey, rotten odor in the area. Once they were inside the compound, the stench intensified to nearly intolerable levels. Earlier that morning, during the advance to Dachau, Staff Sergeant C. Paul Rogers had even joked about the smell. "Somebody here needs a bath," he had wisecracked. Once Rogers and the others saw what was causing the odor, the jokes ended abruptly. "We were completely unprepared for what we saw and smelled," Rogers said. The odor was unforgettable and unique, like a suffocating blanket or the olfactory embodiment of evil. It was a combination of burned flesh, burned hair, decomposing bodies, disease, sweaty body odor, and raw sewage. "I never had experienced anything like it," said Lieutenant Thomas Spruell, a tank commander who had smelled many burning bodies in the course of combat. "It was just a deathly, sickening smell. Some of my men actually were so sick that they couldn't even carry on and some put their gas masks on." Private First Class Russell McFarland was so profoundly overwhelmed by it, he recalled, that "the stench from the Camp stayed in my lungs for about three days after leaving." The scent of the ovens stood out to PFC Howard Margol. It reminded him of when his mother would hold a freshly killed chicken over a gas stove to singe off the feathers. "Whether chicken or human flesh is burned, the odor is the same."

The closer to the bodies one stood, the worse the smell of putrefaction. Sergeant Henry walked past one pile and was taken aback at "the stench of decomposition and death." The crematorium odor "was enough to floor a person and all the rooms were full of bodies in every state of decomposition. I felt my marbles slowly starting to come up so I left there with as much speed as possible." Many others did get sick. "It was a day when young men cried and gagged and vomited," said Sergeant Hank DeJarnette. One of Sergeant Martin's buddies peered inside a room that was crowded with bodies and "just from the smell and how it looked, he got sick." No one was immune to the nausea, regardless of rank. Lieutenant Colonel Fellenz admitted as much in his report to General Collins. "The odor was terrific. I vomited three times in less than five minutes; it was the most revolting smell I have ever experienced." Sergeant Arthur Wallace was one of the many who retched right on the spot. "Did you ever see a man with his head slashed wide open with an

Liberated prisoners and American soldiers view the emaciated dead at Dachau.
(National Archives)

ax or beaten to death by clubbing?" he wrote to his family. "You'd run for the nearest latrine too."[2]

Mingling with the Survivors

Around the bustling enclosure and inside the filthy, cramped barracks, the GIs soon began to interact with the survivors. "Everywhere were sights which filled us with horror," PFC Clifford Barrett later wrote. "Human beings, in the shape of walking skeletons, were dropping dead at our feet. The dying were lying on the ground looking at us, and you wondered if they knew they were now free." Barrett and several other men, in their ignorance, gave them rations that they were in no condition to consume. Lieutenant Jack Westbrook made the same mistake, only to see the recipient devour the food and then vomit up the contents. "Another inmate picked up his vomit. But I do not remember if he ate it." As Westbrook stood on the other side of the fence, he stopped for a moment and looked around, taking in the sight of "masses of humanity, in their tattered and unkempt garb; filthy, hanging from their skeletal bodies—staring out of blank eyes, crying, screaming, reaching through the fencing, only wanting to touch us."

As First Sergeant Pat Stangl and another soldier explored one crowded barracks building, "we entered a twilight zone of hell. The prisoners in the barracks were sick and dying, and those who had expired during the night [lay] dead in their beds. The stench of unclean, dying and dead men living in close quarters was almost unbearable." Grateful to leave the building and breathe comparatively fresh air, he circulated through the compound. Inmates reached out to touch him. Their hands were calloused, and their nails were filthy. He recalled:

> As I touched the hands of those who reached out to me, I had the feeling that they were using touch to express themselves since there was a language barrier. Some of the prisoners . . . too weak to stand, feebly offered their hands as we walked past them. I always touched their hands and smiled. It was strange, but there was a magnetic bond as our hands touched; no further communication was needed.

The initial reaction of some soldiers was to shrink from physical contact, out of either revulsion or fear of disease. However, very few, if any, could bring themselves to reject contact with the survivors. In this regard, General Linden set the example. Sergeant Scott Corbett, a correspondent for the 42nd Division newspaper, and two or three others found themselves immersed in a veritable sea of inmates "who were hugging and kissing and slobbering all over us." Linden saw this, strode over, and immediately drew the crowd to him. "He let them give him the same treatment. He never flinched. Later, the Medics rounded up the lot of us and shot DDT Powder down the back of our necks and all over us. None of us were exactly unemotional that terrible day—and that includes General Linden in spades!"

Tech 5 Morton Barrish, a medic who was attached to one of the rifle companies, remembered the inmates he saw as "emaciated, walking scarecrows, no flesh on their body, just totally incomprehensible to describe, walking cadavers." One of them kept waving joyfully at the soldiers and yelling, "Brooklyn Dodgers! Brooklyn Dodgers!" This seemed to be the only English he knew, and the Dodgers seemed to be his main impression of American society. Tech

5 Stubenrauch, the photographer, raised his camera to snap a picture of about half a dozen severely undernourished inmates who were leaning against a barracks wall. After framing them for a moment, he lowered his camera, unable to bring himself to take the picture. "I just felt I was exploiting them."[3]

The faces of the liberated made a deep impression on Tech 5 William "Pat" Donahue. "To explain the look is almost impossible. Everything was in the eyes, the thank you, the love, the hatred, the sorrow, all rammed into one expression on the face. I just couldn't get over it. It was beautiful."

Staff Sergeant Ralph Fink, a machine gun platoon sergeant, was moving with several other soldiers in patrol formation along a line of barracks buildings at the far end of the compound from the jourhaus. No Americans had yet explored this area, and it looked deserted. Then a prisoner emerged from one of the buildings and started toward them. Fink and the other Americans stood watching warily, not knowing what to expect:

> He was in such a starved, weakened condition that he could just stagger a few steps and then fall on his face. He would then crawl a few feet, regain his feet and fall down again. After covering approximately 30 yards to reach us, his hands and face were covered with blood. He was hysterical; crying, laughing, sobbing, hugging, kissing. This scene prompted the other captives to come out and we were quickly engulfed by hundreds of prisoners, many barely able to crawl from their barracks. That was probably the most emotional . . . or most poignant experience of my life. I've often wondered if that man was ever nursed back to health . . . or whatever became of him.

The survivors were even more emotional than the soldiers. Gleb Rahr, who had survived the terrible ordeal of the death train, was transfixed by the sight of soldiers handing out cigarettes to anyone who crowded around them. "I will never forget them. They must have been my own age, twenty, or maybe twenty-two, or even younger. But we had become accustomed to looking at our own faces, prematurely aged, haggard, and ravaged—compared to us, they seemed to be twelve and fourteen—just boys!" Fourteen-year-old Stephan Ross had not seen his mother in five years. He and his brother had managed to survive ten different concentration camps, though both of them were in very poor physical condition. Amid the crowds of jubilant inmates, they spotted soldiers handing out food and cigarettes and carrying sick, emaciated victims in their arms. The Americans spoke to him, but he could not understand them. "I looked at them and they looked at me. I wanted to be a soldier just like them. I was so overwhelmed with joy and happiness when I saw such strong men who had saved my life. Had they arrived a few days later, I might not have survived."

Some of the most emotional liaisons took place between Jewish GIs and Jewish survivors. Corporal Morris Eisenstein noticed an elderly man whose lips were moving as if in prayer or mourning. He saw Eisenstein and, in Yiddish, asked him his name. Eisenstein, whose parents had immigrated to Chicago from Poland before the war, replied in Yiddish. The man seemed despondent rather than elated about liberation. He said that all was lost. Eisenstein wondered how he could comfort him. The night before, after a brief skirmish, Eisenstein had taken about 15,000 marks from SS prisoners. He took the money out and attempted to place it in the pocket of the man's prison uniform. The survivor shook his head and said, "I cannot accept this gift. It is not proper. I have nothing to give you in return."

Eisenstein noticed a yellow Star of David patch pinned to the man's uniform—a standard requirement for Jews in Hitler's empire. Eisenstein proposed to give the old man the money in exchange for the Star of David. He agreed. "It has been in my possession all the years since," Eisenstein wrote more than four decades later. "As a combat infantry soldier, I endured many experiences with dead and dying people. But I can tell you that when that emaciated, lost soul told me that he could not accept my gift because he had nothing to give me, I broke down completely. This moment of emotional expression and behavior will remain the highlight of my life." His fondest hope was that the money afforded the broken man an opportunity for a new and better life.

When Major Eli Bohnen, a Jewish chaplain in the 42nd Division, and his assistant, Corporal Eli Heimberg, arrived at Dachau, they first took in the terrible sights of the bodies, the weakened inmates, and the piles of clothes near the crematorium. Heimberg had a strong sense that these awful sights represented only the tip of the iceberg of Dachau's horror, "because there were people who wore those clothes once. And, believe me, they didn't have a second set of clothes to wear." In studying the survivors, he saw that "some didn't look too bad. But most looked terrible." He and Bohnen gravitated to the Jewish barracks. The building was packed with starving, bony people in various stages of deterioration. "Some were sitting lethargically on the ground with a far away, glazed look," Heimberg recalled. "Others were lying on their bunks, which were three tiers high with slats of wood as their mattresses." Some hardly seemed to notice the two Americans. Others stared at them with glassy eyes. In Yiddish, Major Bohnen told them that he was an American rabbi. "At that moment it was as if all pent-up emotions of all the years in misery and agony were unleashed in that room," Heimberg said. "There was a burst of wailing and crying. They ran over to us and hugged us and kissed our feet and I was very uncomfortable because it was I who should have hugged them and kissed them."

For nearly two hours, Bohnen and Heimberg recorded the names of these survivors so that they could place notices in American newspapers, in hopes of informing relatives that their loved ones were still alive. Then together they recited a memorial prayer for the dead. "I'm not ashamed to say that I wept very, very much," Heimberg commented. Deeply saddened by this experience, he could not help but ponder how different circumstances would have been for him had his parents not emigrated from Europe to America in the early twentieth century. Later, when he and Bohnen were alone, he asked, "Given all the trials, tribulations and vicissitudes of life, why live?" Rabbi Bohnen was just as sad, but he answered, "Life must go on."[4]

On April 29, 1945, and in the days that followed, as more soldiers visited Dachau, many struggled with a range of emotional reactions to the various sights, smells, and post-liberation experiences. Sergeant John Walker felt "disgusted, appalled, angered. [I] could not understand how one nation could treat other people so despicably." Many, like Sergeant DeJarnette, felt a sense of guilt for not conquering Germany sooner. "We were all heartsick that we got there too late for millions." One of the most common reactions was a stunned sense of incredulity; the intellect rebelled at the existence of such horrors even as the senses confirmed that they were real. "My mind refused to accept the testimony of my eyes," Tech 5 Donald MacDonald later commented. "I was numbed." Private First Class Fred Peterson, a 19-year-old infantry soldier, was overwhelmed by what he saw. He wandered around, taking in the sights, visiting several barracks buildings. He was so troubled that he wanted to leave as quickly as possible. "After we went into them, I really didn't want to go thru any more," he wrote in a letter years later. "Maybe that was a mistake, but at the time that was what I did."

Corporal Hank Mills was a hardened veteran with two years of combat under his belt. He had seen so much action already that he felt he was near the end of his endurance, both physically and emotionally. He prowled the camp, gazing at the gas chamber, the crematorium, and the bodies. Outside of the

Happy Dachau prisoners on liberation day. (National Archives)

crematorium, he saw decomposed pieces of a human being lying in a puddle of filthy water. He began to feel almost disoriented, as if he could not take even one more day of action. "That was a real turning point," he said to an interviewer. "I just wanted to get the hell out of there and go home. I couldn't go any farther. I'm telling you this because I never told anyone." He also had a powerful desire to visit his mother, whom he had not seen for three years. After he had survived so many months of ground combat and witnessed the ultimate in malicious human depravity, perhaps Mills's mother represented for him a sense of humanity, warmth, and decency of the sort he had not experienced since before the war.

Like Mills, quite a few of the soldiers had seen the tragedy and bloodshed of war firsthand. Although it would be an overstatement to say they had grown used to war's trauma, many had become inured to it. But what they saw in Dachau was something far more loathsome, sinister, and hard to process. "I saw death on the battlefield," Lieutenant Colonel Fellenz commented decades after the war, "and I killed many people . . . but that was a different kind of death. This was something against my heritage, the way my mother and father brought me up. How could people do this? How could they live with themselves? This was an organized scheme of destruction of a whole race of people!"

Private First Class John Lee, who had participated in the coal yard massacre at Dachau, had also seen a great deal of combat and had lost many good friends. He had come to understand the kill-or-be-killed nature of warfare, but his reaction to Dachau was that he could never truly comprehend it. "Maybe you don't like it, but out of fear you do it," he said of killing enemy soldiers. "But, God, when you go in and see people being treated like this, the human body being mutilated, starved and so mistreated . . . it's hard to believe that people in the [German] government could be in their right minds. Because how could you be in your right mind and actually do something like this to a human being, regardless of how you feel about 'em?"

Private First Class Barrett's main reaction was to think about the "Why We Fight" propaganda films he had viewed during basic training. This series of movies attempted to educate American soldiers about the causes of the war, its purpose, and Allied objectives. "I'm sure when we finished Basic and were headed overseas, we all forgot those films. But on April 29, 1945 in Dachau, we all indeed did know 'Why We Fight.'"[5]

Some men developed feelings of anger and contempt toward the Germans, whom they held collectively responsible for the camp's inhumanity. "This is not the nation we all believed to be lovers of art, beauty and culture," Captain A. Lewis Greene wrote home after seeing Dachau. "Quite the contrary. It is a nation of gangsters, no better than [John] Dillinger. We should never show them any mercy for these atrocities. All Germans can never be forgiven." Sergeant Scott Corbett, who wrote for the 42nd Division newspaper, listened as a German-speaking reporter interrogated some of the German military prisoners whom the Americans had captured at Dachau. One of the prisoners was tall, handsome, and blond, the embodiment of Hitler's notion of a racially superior German man. The reporter asked him, "How could you do this to these people?" "They're not people," the soldier sneered. "They're animals."

Such disturbing exchanges only hardened American attitudes against Germany. Captain Carlyle Woelfer, a company commander in the 222nd Infantry, felt strongly that no human being had any right to treat others the way some of these people were treated. Conversely, I felt any treatment that might seem harsh to the Germans . . . to a degree they had earned. Therefore, I made no effort to be easy on them. I did not mistreat them or allow my men to, but it was pretty clear to the German prisoners that if they made any effort to be obstreperous and escape or something of that nature, that it would go quite hard with them.

Staff Sergeant Fink, who had been mobbed by joyful, deathly looking survivors, had no love for the German people after that experience. "I myself am of German descent, but I had no good feelings about the German civilians at all. I still don't like 'em to this day." Although this was hardly a majority opinion among soldiers of German descent, it is fair to say that most were at least disturbed by what their ethnic cousins had done.

Along those lines, many of the Americans, regardless of their own heritage, struggled mightily to resolve the troubling question of how a nation known for impressive scientific, architectural, engineering, and literary achievements—and one whose cleanliness, work ethic, and order reminded them of America—could nonetheless perpetrate such monstrous crimes. "In Germany I have seen men and women who look and act just like mom and pop, grandma and granddad, back home," Sergeant Bill Harr wrote in the 45th Division newspaper. "It is difficult to believe that these ordinary-looking people are bloodthirsty murderers. And yet I have seen, also, the horrors of Dachau. It is altogether confusing." Lieutenant William Walsh had greatly respected the Germans as good soldiers and hard workers. The sight of Dachau was shocking and mystifying to him, creating an unsettling, unresolvable paradox in his mind that could well have been a factor leading to his reprisal killings. "How can you do this stuff?" he asked rhetorically many years later. "I mean, how can one human being treat another human being this way? Nobody could deny the fact that they were an intelligent, hard-working people, but I lost a lot of respect because of that incident."[6]

Most of the American soldiers who saw Dachau were quite skeptical when they heard Germans, whether soldiers or civilians, claim ignorance of what went on in the camp, sympathy for the victims, or powerlessness to do anything to help them. Private First Class Dee Eberhart's squad was billeted in a Dachau home. "The woman in the house . . . said she didn't know anything about the Camp. In the next door house, there was a tattooed human skin lamp shade." Lieutenant Lawrence Rogers, an artillery officer who served with the 20th Armored Division, was horrified and angered to see Dachau townspeople looting the death train:

The old villagers . . . began systematically to loot the dried corpses of anything of value that remained on them; shoes, jewelry, or what really awoke me [to] the irreconcilable horror of it—gold teeth fillings and dentures! All at once, there it was, like a feeding frenzy of a school of piranhas. It was respectable householders, mostly women, of a supposedly civilized society descended into the very bowels of human degradation.

Inexplicably, neither Rogers nor any of his men did anything to stop them—perhaps unwittingly demonstrating a disquieting point about the notion of passive complicity.

As at Buchenwald, the Americans forced the locals to view the camp and help bury the bodies. Often the bodies were loaded aboard wagons that took them to makeshift mass graves. German civilians briskly removed the skinny corpses and placed them onto the ground. "Watching the unloading was truly horrible," one American soldier wrote to his family. "The bodies squooshed [sic] and gurgled as they hit the pile and the odor could almost be seen." In the recollection of another American observer, "the bodies were in almost inestricable [sic] confusion, arms crooked in rigor mortis, legs intertwined, heads with staring eyes laid on abdomens so sunken you could almost see the backbones." Sergeant Ernest Henry, who was part of an engineering unit tasked with cleaning up the substantial mess at Dachau, including the removal and burial of bodies, made a point of watching the reactions of the Germans to these horrors. When they noticed Henry observing them, many shrugged their shoulders and shook their heads as if to convey the message that they were not responsible for these deaths. Henry wrote to his wife:

And they actually had the effrontery to think that we were ignorant enough to believe that they didn't know that such a thing existed in their city. The Germans have more to repay than they can ever atone for. And if the Combined Military Governments, do not do something about it, then may God have mercy on their souls for they will have failed dismally in the completion of the task for which thousands of our American boys gave up their lives.

Private Jerome Klein was exploring the town of Dachau during his off-duty hours when he stopped to admire sausages displayed in a butcher's window.

The owner noticed him outside and cordially invited Klein inside to have lunch with his wife and him. "While he was preparing what turned out to be an impressive feast in those lean days for Germany, he regaled me with the already familiar lament about how much suffering the war had caused and how innocent the average German was of any of the events. The Dachau camp was pivotal to his argument." The butcher and his wife said that they and their neighbors had known prisoners were utilized for labor projects, but otherwise they had no sense of what really happened in the camp. Because Klein knew the protective custody compound was nestled into an otherwise innocuous looking complex—Lieutenant Colonel Felix Sparks once commented that "from the outside it looked like an ordinary military post"—Klein initially agreed with the butcher.

He followed the man and his wife to their neatly maintained backyard, where they all prepared to eat lunch at a small table. Just then, Klein glanced at the back wall of their home and was surprised to see several old posters with Hebrew writing. When he asked the couple about them, they looked shocked and flustered. "It was instantly clear that [they] had completely forgotten that they were there. They claimed that long ago the property had been owned by a Jewish family but that they had moved and no one knew where they had gone." Klein knew immediately that their innocence was nothing more than a facade. They had probably appropriated the home and property of the absent Jewish family. Failing that, they had certainly known much more about what was going on than they had portrayed to Private Klein. Explaining pointedly that his appetite had vanished, he got up and left.

Captain Alvin Weinstein, a physician, once met a German doctor who told him he had worked in the Dachau camp. "Doing what?" Weinstein asked. "Research," the man replied vaguely. Curious, Weinstein probed him for more information and soon learned the truth: this doctor had participated in the cruel, exploitive hypothermia medical experiments on inmates. "His particular interest was the reproductive capacity," noted Weinstein. "He very proudly produced a sheaf of 'scientific studies' which demonstrated that, even when the human body was reduced to the extremely lowest limit of 30 degrees Celsius, his 'patients' could experience a full physical recovery—even to the ability to experience an erection." Disgusted with the man's casual, clinical cruelty, Weinstein asked, "How could you do this to human beings?" "Oh," the doctor replied dismissively, "they were all going to die anyhow."[7]

Dealing with a Humanitarian Catastrophe

United States Army medics, whose ethical values were markedly different from the German physician Weinstein had met, descended on Dachau to
care for the liberated inmates and to save as many lives as they could. Their
caregiving experiences were similar to the 120th Evacuation Hospital's experience at Buchenwald, only on a larger scale and in an urban setting. One of
the first medical specialists to arrive was Lieutenant Marcus Smith, a physician attached to a small unit (Displaced Persons [DP] Team No. 115) whose
mission was to feed, clothe, treat, care for, and repatriate displaced persons.
The commander was Lieutenant Charles Rosenbloom, who had once worked
with troubled youth in New York City. Smith was the only medical person
on the team; everyone else had an infantry background. Guided by inmates,
they toured the compound, taking in the sight of dead bodies, deplorable
overcrowding, and diseased inmates. They surveyed the camp hospital, which
was located in converted barracks buildings and was nearly as crowded as the
prisoner quarters. Naturally, Smith was appalled at the conditions and the
appearance of the survivors. "Everywhere is the stench of decomposition and
excrement. Some of the patients are too weak to reach the latrines, or, if they
do, too feeble to crawl back to their beds."

The leaders of the IPC told DP No. 115 that there were 4,205 patients in
the hospital barracks; 3,866 of them were bedridden. Another 6,000 inmates
required some kind of care. On average, 140 people—half of them anonymous—were dying each day without any medical attention. Smith and the
others were even shown an especially sordid part of Dachau: a brothel where
the SS had kept some 300 women as sex slaves. The women were wracked
with typhus, dysentery, and malnutrition, their physical condition completely
deteriorated.

By the time DP No. 115 finished its inspection, the team members felt
completely overwhelmed by the humanitarian crisis unfolding before them.
One of the men broke down and wept. Smith nearly did as well. He knew the
patients needed much more than the team could offer. They needed clean, ex-
pansive hospital wards, proper food, sterile bandages, around-the-clock care,
a dizzying assortment of medicines, clean clothing, clean water, soap, bathing
facilities, proper beds, medical equipment, and a host of other items. "It is
obvious that we need hospital beds, nurses, doctors, trained specialists such
as epidemiologists and sanitarians," Smith wrote after the tour. "A dietician

would be helpful . . . trained people who can seek out those afflicted with communicable diseases are urgently needed. Ideally, everyone here, with or without symptoms, should be evaluated medically."

Fortunately, higher command understood these needs quite well. Within a day of Dachau's liberation, Colonel Kenneth Worthing, the civil affairs officer for XV Corps, conducted his own inspection of the camp, as did the corps surgeon. Their own firsthand experiences, combined with reports from Rosenbloom and Smith, all made the urgency of the situation quite clear. (Information about the miserable conditions at Buchenwald had also prepared Worthing for what he might deal with at Dachau.) Worthing organized a new administration for Dachau, with various commanders in charge of food, sanitation, public health, security, shelter, medical care, and other tasks. He also incorporated members of the IPC into the camp's new organization and power structure. For communication purposes, he arranged for a loudspeaker truck from which leaders could make German-language announcements to the prisoners. Most importantly, he forwarded urgent requests for help to General Wade Haislip, his commander, and to the Seventh Army (even higher up the chain of command). The generals soon dispatched the 116th and 127th Evacuation Hospitals, both of which were major medical units. Together, the two outfits consisted of 40 medical officers, 40 nurses, and 220 enlisted medical specialists. They carried with them substantial quantities of medicine and equipment. Smith was thrilled to join forces with them.[8]

The process of setting up hospital wards was just as laborious as it had been for the 120th Evacuation Hospital at Buchenwald, although Dachau did offer much better infrastructure. "Both hospitals set up in existing SS barracks in the Outer Compound [administrative complex] of the camp," the 127th's unit history recorded. "Much rubble and debris had to be cleared and then all rooms plus beds and furniture were scrubbed down with a 2% solution of Cresol which necessitated a loss of many man hours." The wards were spread among 18 different barracks buildings, which were, according to Lieutenant Lucius Daugherty (a staff officer with the 116th), "convertible, by removing partitions, into large wards with latrines and washrooms. This work, which was considerable, was done by us with the aid of ex-prisoner help. Fortunately there was a large mess hall with excellent cooking facilities, cooler, and steam from central plant." As part of the cleanup, the Americans and the IPC leader re-established potable running water and electricity. "Later work consisted of painting, wiring, landscaping, and the improvement of the roads," Warrant

Officer (junior grade) David Schuman of the 116th reported in the unit history.

Together, the units set up a pharmacy, an X-ray building, a dispensary, and operating rooms. They coated all these buildings with a dusting of DDT. Initially, they were able to set up about 2,400 canvas cots (1,200 per hospital unit) among the wards. Later, the 116th added two more convalescent wards with 300 cots apiece. A German or United States army blanket covered each cot. The preparations took about a day and a half. Both hospitals were ready to receive patients by the evening of May 3, 1945. Aided by able-bodied inmates, orderlies retrieved patients and brought them, either by ambulance or by stretcher, to the new hospitals, where they were triaged, stripped down, dusted with DDT, bathed, outfitted in clean pajamas, and put to bed. "Many difficulties were encountered in the management of these patients," Lieutenant Daugherty wrote, "foremost of which was the language difficulties, as the patients were of many nationalities. Trained hospital personnel from among the liberated prisoners were used as ward men, interpreters, and utilities, and were of much assistance." Inmate physicians were also quite valuable because they could provide information on case histories and how to treat such deteriorated individuals. Some of these doctors were also effective interpreters.

Between May 3 and June 13, the 127th admitted 2,267 patients; 907 of these patients were suffering from multiple diseases, including some with both typhus and tuberculosis. Unit records report 246 deaths. The 116th admitted 2,057 patients, 85 percent of whom had typhus. Technicians who took chest X-rays found that nearly one third of those who were tested showed evidence of tuberculosis. A total of 190 patients died while under their care. "Malnutrition was contributory in most instances, and it was often difficult to determine the exact cause of death because of the presence of complicated pathology," Warrant Officer Schuman wrote. The doctors found time to do autopsies on 55 bodies. The most frequent killers were pneumonia and hemorrhaging as a result of disease, organ degeneration, and malnutrition. "The liver usually showed a great deal of fatty degeneration and the kidney evidence of nephritis. The heart was generally pale and very soft so that a finger could be easily thrust through it. An acute splenic tumor was usually present. About 50% had thickened colons . . . particularly in the rectum and sigmoid." At the time of death, some of the bodies were so underweight that it was possible for an orderly to place the corpse in a blanket and carry it away with the use of only two fingers on each hand. Doctors also autopsied, at random, ten bodies taken from the death train. Eight of the dead showed evidence of advanced tuberculosis; all had typhus and extreme malnutrition.[9]

To the American medics, accustomed to the blood and gore of battle casualties, the sight of the emaciated patients, many of whom seemed more dead than alive, was disturbing, disquieting, and almost bizarre. To maintain sanity and professionalism, some of the medics tried not to think of them as human. The Americans liberally doused themselves with DDT to guard against disease. "First you remove your hat and it's sprayed," one soldier wrote in a letter home, "then each arm, then down your trousers both in front and behind. We used louse powder here like you use face powder at home."

At all times in the wards, everyone wore surgical masks, hats, gowns, and rubber gloves. Private First Class Harold Porter, a bespectacled surgical technician who had once studied psychology at the University of Michigan, described the patients in a letter to his parents as

> living corpses. Ghandi [sic], after a thirty day fast would still look like Hercules compared with some of these men. They have no buttocks at all, and on some their vertebrae can be seen rubbing on their stomach. All have raw, ugly bed sores, pus dripping infections, scabs, scales, ulcers, bites plus typhus, beri-beri, scurvy, T.B., erysipelas, and 101 other symptoms. We don't even think of them as human. If we did, we'd never be able to do the work. They look like weird beings from Mars—with their shaven heads . . . knobby joints, huge hands, feet, and popping eyes. Many are toothless. They lie curled up in the oddest positions. Most have dysentery of the 'continuous bloody dribble' type—and of course are unable to drag themselves to the latrine. The alternative I'll leave you to imagine.

Far from being aliens from Mars, the patients were all very human. They were frightened and traumatized humans suffering from great pain and anguish. Porter and the other Americans did understand this, although they minimized such recognition to maintain an emotional distance. Porter was haunted by the macabre sounds emanating from the wards at night. "There are weird wails, sobs, groans, rattles, gnashing of teeth, and above it all the chant of men praying. I'll never forget it as long as I live."[10]

Some of the patients were terrified of anyone in a uniform, American or otherwise. They resisted medication out of fear that these strangers were poisoning them. Or, in many cases, they were simply too dazed and emotionally shattered to understand that they were now free and under the care of people who wanted to help them. However, most of the patients grasped quite well their newfound freedom and the benevolent intentions of the medics, even with the obstacle of a language barrier. There was an implicit tenderness and humanity inherent in the very fact that the GIs were working so hard to care for them. Their actions alone communicated a sense of deep concern for the patients' welfare. "Every member of the unit went away with a great personal pride in what he had been able to do for these unfortunate people, and with a far greater understanding of what we were fighting for and what the Nazi stood for," Lieutenant Daugherty wrote.

This fundamental decency stood in stark contrast to the terrible brutality, humiliation, and degradation so many of the survivors had experienced, often for years. "In the darkest hours of our life, when we completely lost faith in humanity, you appeared to us like angels from heaven, restoring in us new hope and will to live," wrote Michelle Korn, one of about 900 female prisoners liberated at Dachau, to the soldiers who freed her. "In many cases carrying us in your arms, disregarding the fact that every one of us was a dirty and smelly bundle of human bones. Your love and tender care had a much greater meaning to us [than] just the physical act."

Nearly all of the ex-prisoners were obsessed with food. Their hunger was such that they thought of little else besides eating as much as they could. "They eat and eat and eat, not only what we give them, but whatever they can," Dr. Smith wrote to his wife. "Every time I see them they are nibbling and chewing and crunching and gnawing and drinking and swallowing." Private First Class Porter reported to his family that "they fight among themselves, plunge head first into garbage cans and eat like pigs." He also claimed that several of them even resorted to stealing a bucket of entrails left over from an autopsy and attempting to eat them.

Their fragile digestive systems were not ready for high-calorie diets; overeating could be just as deadly as undereating. They needed to be nursed gradually back to health. The hospital staff fended off the patients' constant begging for more food. "We're having regular food riots on the wards," Porter wrote to his parents. "They don't understand why we give them so little, but if we don't it all comes up within minutes after it went down because they haven't eaten for so long." Nerin Gun, a Turkish survivor, actually ate his way into the hospital. As an interpreter and a member of the IPC, he had access to an American mess hall. For several days, he gorged on the buffet offerings, amazed at the quality and quantity of the food. "There were slices of buttered bread, rolls, toast, roast beef, bacon . . . pancakes and eggs, and all kinds of jams, juices—orange, tomato, grapefruit—and mysterious and extraordinary things like the gooey stuff they called peanut butter." His deteriorated digestive system could not begin to deal with all this rich food. His overeating led to vomiting, terrible cramps, acute diarrhea, and a long, fever-stricken stint in one of the hospital wards.[11]

Doctors supervised the implementation of a diet designed to fend off such gastrointestinal distress and steadily combat the malnutrition. "For the first two weeks patients received GI food plus two supplementary feedings of eggnog, chocolate, or fresh milk," the 116th's history chronicled. "Then a change was made to food from German ration dumps." This diet was still too rich, leading to cramps, diarrhea, and fever for many of the patients. "They couldn't digest meals," said Lieutenant Charlotte Chaney, a nurse in the 127th Evacuation Hospital. She remembered feeding them what she called "gruel," which was probably some concoction of oatmeal or concentrated soup. Often, the patients would hide crusts of bread under their pillows, just as they had done during their incarceration. "You'll get more," Chaney and the other nurses told them. "You don't have to do that any more." The habit died hard, though. Many patients made a common practice of licking their plates clean. They were also given vitamins, oranges, eggs, and other protein-rich foods. Those who had difficulty holding down any food were given intravenous feedings of vitamin-laden fluids and even blood plasma. "Trying to get into these patients' veins is really a job," Lieutenant Chaney wrote to her husband. "They are so thin that my hand fits around their upper arms."

May Craig, a 56-year-old war correspondent and columnist for the Gannett newspaper group, observed the medics with the keen eye of a veteran journalist. "On the wide parade ground, American GIs were playing ball," she wrote in one story. "Several were riding bicycles, showing off for the nurses sitting on the front porch of the building where the 116th live. Over at the 127th, somebody is playing the harmonica—Don't Fence Me In." She observed the wards firsthand, watching closely as the young doctors, nurses, and technicians engaged in the daily struggle to restore the patients back to health.

> It's hard and dangerous work they do . . . but they don't begrudge a minute
> of it. I . . . walked through the long, empty barracks, lined with cots, and
> some small metal beds. Rows of skeletons, shaved heads, great eyes looking
> at you, a few able to stagger around. Some are huddled completely under

drab blankets; they look like little children, they are so emaciated. Some lie in stupor; they are too far gone, or the high temperatures of typhus, as much as 105, hold them. Some are frightened and will not take treatment.

Craig saw a team of medics circulate around, attempting to give penicillin to patients who were battling infections. "I can't find enough muscle to get a hypodermic in," one of the nurses complained. In another corner of the ward, she saw a doctor vainly attempt to explain, by using pidgin words of several languages, to the patients why they could not have more food. "They get vitamins, frequent feedings, dressings for their sores when the skin has broken over bones, salves for their skin diseases," Craig wrote.

Over time, the treatment worked wonders. Patients gradually grew healthier, filled out, and could properly eat and digest larger quantities of food. Their collective energy level rose. Many, like death train survivor Joseph Knoll, were now able to get out of bed and exercise. "I can never forget the fantastic joy I experienced as I began to walk more and more, and better and better each day."

A greater variety of foods became available. At the end of May, an Army dietician brought in one million frozen eggs plus large amounts of carrots, frozen peas, asparagus, cauliflower, and beans. By this time, deaths had become much less common. In total at Dachau, of the 9,435 admissions to American hospitals, 1,598 died—a 17 percent mortality rate. Most of the deaths occurred within the first two weeks of liberation. When Dr. Smith and DP No. 115 got orders to leave Dachau on June 10, after a month and a half in the camp, Smith paid one last visit to the hospital wards, where he had spent so many hours tending to patients and saving as many lives as possible. "It has been sad to watch the critically ill patients die," he wrote in a letter, "but it has been an exciting experience to observe the steady physical and mental improvement of most of the patients. As I talk with some of them, I realize that their conversations are different from what they were six weeks ago. Then they could only talk about food. Now they mention their families, their homes, their plans for the future." Indeed, by this time, only about 12,000 former inmates remained at Dachau; most of the other liberated survivors had already been repatriated to their home countries. (The vast majority of those who remained were Eastern Europeans.)[12]

In a now familiar ritual, these post-liberation weeks included untold numbers of reporters, generals, soldiers, and politicians visiting the camp to bear witness and to document for posterity what they had seen. A special team from the Seventh Army, under the supervision of Colonel William Quinn, the chief of staff, prepared an informative booklet entitled *Dachau Liberated: The Official Report*. Quinn had thousands of copies printed up and circulated to soldiers and media members; the booklet remained in print many decades later as a repository of firsthand experience. As Quinn later explained, "I thought to myself, 'Nobody will believe this. I've got to document this now.'"

The same congressional delegation that had visited Buchenwald also toured Dachau, taking in all of the terrible sights, from the death train to the crematorium and beyond. "The committee feels that out of it all justice will emerge," they wrote optimistically, "and that through the sickening spectacle which we have witnessed . . . will come ultimately a firmer realization that men of all nations and all tongues must resist encroachments of every theory and ideology that debases mankind." Reflecting on the experience many decades later, Edouard Izac, one of the congressmen who helped write the report, said, "The truth is that we can never describe sufficiently the degradation that people were subjected to by the Nazis."

Most of the soldiers who liberated or visited Dachau also struggled to describe and define it in any coherent manner, but nearly everyone agreed that they could never forget it. Dachau brought them face to face with humanity's terrible potential for inflicting malevolence and destruction on a staggering scale. "Dachau was death reduced to such a state of ordinariness that it left you numb and feeling nothing," stated the history of one liberating company in a thoughtful summary:

> Your mind was in neutral, unconscious of pain. It was acres of bodies on bare ground where woods and fields used to be, green and growing under the warm spring sun. It was miles of barbed wire charged with electricity and guarded by machine guns in high stone towers. It was long low barracks crowded with 32,000 living, breathing, dying, and dead human beings who stink like nothing else on earth. It was a great parade ground where men were tied down and beaten until their flesh boiled and their mouths blubbered blood. Dachau was a fact for 12 years, a fact which will stink through generations of mankind's memory. Dachau was brain and skill and lives and destinies reduced to milestones of death.[13]

Epilogue

SEVERAL MONTHS AFTER the end of hostilities in Europe, Major Eli Bohnen, the 42nd Infantry Division chaplain who had prayed with Jewish survivors of Dachau on liberation day, was riding a train to Switzerland, where he planned to take some well-earned leave. During the journey, he struck up a conversation with a friendly lieutenant who had arrived in Europe well after the fighting ended. The young officer's job was to supervise German prisoners of war who were now cleaning and maintaining the grounds at Dachau. Rabbi Bohnen idly wondered if the crematorium, the gas chamber, and the ovens were still standing. The fresh lieutenant looked condescendingly at Bohnen and said, "Come, come, Chaplain, surely you don't believe that there were crematoria and gas chambers. You know that the Germans had their propaganda and we had ours. There were never any such things."[1]

Although this was an isolated incident, it illustrates a larger truth: in the wake of World War II, as the world inevitably moved on from history's most destructive, bloody, and cataclysmic war, the battle for memory of the Holocaust began. General Dwight D. Eisenhower had foreseen this battle and had made sure that as many soldiers, German civilians, media members, and dignitaries as possible witnessed and documented the realities of the Allied-liberated camps. Joseph Pulitzer, the publisher of the *St. Louis Post-Dispatch* who had led the media delegation that visited the newly liberated camps, shared this same commitment to verify the atrocities for current and future generations. On his return to the United States, he spoke to the Missouri legislature of what he saw. When the War Department showed him a graphic film, made by Army Signal Corps photographers, of the concentration camps, he strongly urged the government to show the movie far and wide. For Pulitzer, the images reinforced precisely what he had seen at Buchenwald and Dachau. "There is nothing in these films that the average adult cannot well stand seeing. Of course, they are shocking, but the cumulative effect . . . provides irrefutable evidence of the deliberate Nazi policy of ruthless disregard for the value of human life and the deliberate plan of torture, starvation and extermination." Aloys Kaufmann, mayor of St. Louis, agreed with Pulitzer, as did another Missourian, President Harry Truman, who had succeeded Franklin Roosevelt after his death on April 12, 1945. The film was shown to aghast audiences in American movie theaters, to American soldiers on occupation duty in Germany, and, most significantly, to German POWs and civilians.

Pulitzer's newspaper, in tandem with the federal government, put on a free exhibit that spring called "Lest We Forget" which showed enlarged Signal Corps still images of the camps and their victims, in minute and disturbing detail. Some of the photographs were life-sized or larger. They were displayed in the mechanical annex of the *Post-Dispatch* building in downtown St. Louis from 10 a.m. to 10 p.m. every day, including Sunday. At times, the exhibit was so crowded that people had to line up on the street outside the building and wait their turn to go inside. Over the course of 25 days, 80,413 St. Louisans, many of whom were of German descent, observed the display. The general mood was one of solemnity, respect for the victims, and disgust for the perpetrators. "The power of education is tremendous," declared Philip Hickey, superintendent of instruction for the St. Louis public schools. "These photographs show what madmen can impress on youthful minds." John Eckholdt, an elderly German-born man with three sons in the American military, told a reporter, "Atrocities are horrible, but it's all true. We must let the people know the truth about what happened—the German people too." Another man shook his head sadly and exclaimed, "It's not just the piles of dead prisoners. Look at the expressions on the faces of those living people!" One man who was observing the photos with his wife and three daughters said, "I'd like to make it a law to force all those who say they don't believe the atrocity stories to go through this gallery." R. W. Walker, an African American teacher, opined, "These pictures should teach people to love democracy more."

The most famous Missouri native to tour the exhibit was General Omar Bradley, the commander of the Twelfth Army Group, who had witnessed Ohrdruf firsthand. After looking at the photos, the general told the local radio station, KSD, "It is almost impossible to believe the atrocities committed by the Germans, particularly on political prisoners, without actually seeing them yourself. The next best thing is to show you such pictures of these atrocities and horrors as our photographers were able to take on the ground. These pictures are not exaggerated in any way. I saw some of [the atrocities] myself."[2]

The newspaper and the government also sponsored a free public showing of the unsettling Signal Corps film at the city's Kiel Auditorium Opera House. They originally planned for 14 showings, but demand was so high they eventually expanded to 44. Realizing that motion pictures tend to be much more affecting than photographs—especially for a pre-television generation unaccustomed to graphic, uncensored images—officials even arranged to have first aid staff on hand in case anyone fainted at the terrible sights. Fortunately, they were never needed. More than 81,000 people saw the film. "For the most part the audience, in which women outnumbered men about two to one, sat in shocked silence at the sight of living and dead victims of brutalities," the *Post-Dispatch* reported of one showing. "Some spectators turned their eyes from a few scenes, and one woman burst into tears when the camera showed survivors of the Buchenwald 'extermination factory.'" The crowd applauded at the sight of an American military policeman forcing a reluctant German medical officer to view a stack of dead bodies at Ohrdruf.

Throughout the showings, a diverse variety of people watched the movie, including housewives, businessmen, students, ministers, war industry employees, and servicemen. According to the *Post-Dispatch*, "audiences leaving the Auditorium were grim, and it was obvious the films had stimulated serious thought about world peace problems." No one expressed the opinion that the images were too gruesome for public consumption. Ushers overheard a number of people who spoke with German accents comment that, terrible though the atrocity footage was, it should be shown to as many spectators as possible.

One reporter covering the showings interviewed, at random, several viewers. "Some scenes will remain with me for the rest of my life," one of them said. Velma Jones, an African American woman from the city's north side, attested to the compelling nature of the images. "The pictures I've seen in the paper were awful, but the moving pictures are even worse." One man, thinking of the larger purpose served by the showings, commented, "I'm sure they'll teach the public what this war has been all about."

Although some newspaper editorials opposed the showings as too graphic or too blatantly anti-German, the murals and films were eventually shown to audiences at the Library of Congress in Washington, DC. The publicity surrounding these events helped establish the Holocaust as a defining, unique event, one that belonged at the center of World War II history, at least for those Americans who came to see the conflict as a good war fought for morality and justice. Though this is an oversimplified view of World War II—namely because there was plenty of Allied immorality—the Holocaust did provide some basis for the notion of the war having a larger meaning beyond the defeat of enemy armies.[3]

The Camps after the War

The camps themselves were affected by post-war events as well as the struggle for perspective and truth on what had actually happened—and what had not—in these infamous places. Ohrdruf became part of the Soviet zone of occupation and eventually of the Communist German Democratic Republic (East Germany) during the Cold War. At some point, the labor camp ceased to exist. The buildings were razed, and the area became a military training ground.

Buchenwald also ended up in the Soviet orbit. Tragically, its days as a repressive hellhole were not finished. As of August 1945, Soviet troops and security police occupied the concentration camp. Under their control from 1945 to 1950, the main camp became Soviet Special Camp Number 2 for Nazi Party members and other anti-Communist enemies. Conditions were brutal and inhuman. During the winter of 1946–1947, nearly one quarter of the 28,000 inmates died of hunger or disease. Overall, a total of 7,113 people died in the camp while it was under Soviet control. Most of them were buried anonymously in mass graves outside the perimeter, with no notice ever given to their families. In 1950, the newly established East German Communist government, heavily influenced by men who had once been inmates in the camp, decreed that most of Buchenwald would be torn down. Much of the site soon fell into disrepair. "The essence of Buchenwald Concentration Camp is not embodied in the barracks or the stone blocks," said Robert Siewert, one of the East German Communist survivors, in justification of this disrepair. "The essence was the deep comradeship, the mutual help, bonded and steeled by the struggle against fascist terror, organized resistance and deep faith in the triumph of our just cause!"

In 1958, the East German government built a grandiose, heavily politicized memorial complex at Buchenwald. The memorial emphasized the magnitude of Nazi crimes while focusing almost exclusively on the plight and resistance of the Communist and Socialist prisoners. There was no mention of Jews or of the Little Camp. Not surprisingly, the new memorial reinforced the questionable notion that the Buchenwald prisoners had liberated themselves. To the Communist authorities in the midst of the Cold War, the American role in Buchenwald's liberation was inconvenient, so they excised any mention of the Americans. The government cared little for honest historical inquiry. The memorial was designed to strengthen the East German state and stress the justice and inevitability of Communism, with a veiled implication that the new Federal Republic of Germany (West Germany) represented a post-war legacy of Nazi Germany.

The eventual collapse of the East German regime, the end of the Cold War in Europe, and the reunification of Germany led to sweeping changes at Buchenwald in the 1990s. A newly constituted historical commission spearheaded a major effort to turn the old camp into a museum, with guided tours, restoration of the crematorium and the disinfection station, a dedicated museum to Soviet Special Camp Number 2, and a commitment to communicating a well-balanced, truthful portrayal of the camp's entire history, including its years as a Soviet forced labor facility and the construction of various memorials to Jews and to the numerous other ethnic groups that suffered and died at the hands of the Nazis.[4]

Dachau over the Decades

Located in the heart of the American zone of occupation, within what eventually became West Germany, Dachau was hardly unaffected by the complex sweep of post-war events. By July 1945, nearly all of the liberated prisoners were gone. Most went home. Some went to displaced persons camps elsewhere in Germany, where they awaited repatriation to their homelands or emigration to adopted countries such as the United States. (Many of the

Jewish displaced persons hoped to go to Palestine to join with Zionists work-ing to establish the independent nation of Israel.)

To the American military occupation authorities, Dachau was a powerful symbol of the Nazi regime and its depravity. Thus, they deliberately chose Dachau as the place to incarcerate and try thousands of former kapos, SS, Nazi, military, and government war criminals subject to American military jurisdiction. Between 1945 and 1948, about 25,000 suspected criminals were imprisoned in the former concentration camp under generally decent condi-tions, with shelter, a library, regular subsistence meals, and proper legal rep-resentation available to them. Ironically, the protective custody compound was now used to house former concentration camp guards and Waffen-SS suspects. The Americans put them to work cleaning up and refurbishing the filthy barracks buildings. American guards forced them to tour the gas chamber and crematorium and to observe large photographs of Nazi atroci-ties. "Awful pictures of starved concentration camp inmates, piles of corpses, tortured creatures," SS Colonel-General Gert Naumann, a former member of Hitler's general staff, wrote in a secret diary he kept. "We have to post ourselves very close in front of the pictures." One American soldier slugged each of the prisoners on the neck, forcing them to press their faces against the pictures.

Most of the prisoners were investigated and released within several months or a year. Over the course of three years, 1,672 individuals were tried before a military court in proceedings that became known as the Dachau Trials. (The more famous Nuremberg Trials, conducted from late 1945 through late 1946, involved 22 of the highest-ranking Nazis.) Ironically, the Dachau Trials took place in a building that was located only steps away from the coal yard where American soldiers had massacred SS men on liberation day. Almost all of the accused Nazis were convicted; 297 were given death sentences, and 279 received sentences of life in prison. The condemned included Dr. Klaus Schilling, who had conducted medical experiments on Dachau concentra-tion camp inmates, Hans Mehrbach, who had overseen the brutal journey of the death train, and Martin Weiss, the former camp commandant. Ilse Koch, wife of Buchenwald's camp commandant, was sentenced to life in prison. As related in the Buchenwald chapter of this book, she served only two years of this sentence before the Americans commuted her sentence and released her. However, the Federal Republic of Germany tried and convicted her and sentenced her to life on charges of instigation to murder. In 1967, she committed suicide in prison.

In 1948, on conclusion of the trials, the Americans handed the protective custody compound over to the Bavarian Refugee Agency, which used the barracks to house people who had been displaced by the war. The United States Army maintained control of the old SS administrative complex and even used one of the buildings to house its own military prisoners, including some who were under suspicion of evasion or desertion during the Vietnam era. (The Army did not cede control of the complex back to Bavaria until 1972.) In the compound, most of the refugees were Germans who came from territories lost by Germany as a result of the war. At times, there were as many as 2,300 refugees at Dachau, and many of them spent years languishing in a state of limbo. Thanks to a tepid reception from the Dachau townspeople and other West Germans, their transition back to ordinary life in Germany was slow. The last refugees were not gone until the early 1960s.

In the meantime, former concentration camp prisoners who visited the site of the compound grew concerned about its descent into disrepair and neglect. They formed the Dachau Concentration Camp International Committee, an organization dedicated to preserving what was left of the compound and making it a permanent historical site. One former inmate had maintained a small museum in the crematorium and gas chamber, but otherwise there were few artifacts to show what had happened at Dachau. In fact, by the 1960s, many of the barracks buildings were gone as a result of dilapidation or because the refugees had stripped them down to help build new homes elsewhere. Eventually, the Dachau Concentration Camp International Committee persuaded the Bavarian government to preserve the camp as a permanent memorial and museum.

Located in the old service building in the southern end of the protective custody compound, adjacent to the roll call area, the Dachau Museum opened in May 1965. This original museum was heavily influenced by the perspective of German Communists and Socialists, and it made no mention that the camp had also included common criminals, social outcasts, and homosexuals. However, the museum's scope and content became far more comprehensive over the years, reflecting a balanced history of Dachau. This proper historical perspective was abetted by the growth of a first-rate archive. The entire compound was preserved and two of the barracks rebuilt to portray what they would have looked like in the 1930s and 1940s. Rectangular beds of gravel marked the location of the other barracks. The compound itself was adorned with Protestant, Catholic, Jewish, Russian Orthodox, and other international memorials as well as plaques for the liberating units. A Catholic chapel was built at the northern end of the compound. The crematorium and gas chamber remained centerpieces of the entire solemn place. In essence, Dachau became a place for reflection and commemoration, a potent and permanent symbol of the Holocaust as seen primarily from the perspective of the victims and the liberators. The commemorations regularly drew former liberators and survivors to the camp. (From the 1990s onward, the same was true at Buchenwald.)[5]

The Soldiers' Legacy

Although relatively few of the liberators of Ohrdruf, Buchenwald, and Dachau ever revisited the places they had once freed, most were deeply and forever affected by their experiences. In the short term, their experiences gave meaning and purpose to the tragedy and destruction they had witnessed through so many hard years of war. Combat soldiers tend to fight not for a lofty cause or abstract ideas of patriotism but for the men alongside them. This was certainly true for American soldiers in World War II. Although they believed in the Allied cause, it could not sustain them as they dealt with the privation, misery, and dangers of the war. Nowhere was this truer than in Europe, where hatred for the Germans was not a major motivating factor. Liberating and witnessing the camps, though, gave definition and meaning to the war these Americans fought.

"Up until then, we might not have been clear what we were fighting for . . . but after that, we damn well knew what we were fighting against!" John Searle, an infantryman, said of seeing Ohrdruf. After touring Buchenwald and meeting many survivors, Ernest Comito wrote, "It is these people for whom we are fighting . . . they are truly freed, they are the liberated ones, for they feel the breath of freedom." Elmer Joachim, who was at Dachau, wrote succinctly, "There may be a time . . . when we will wonder if the sacrifice is worth the while. The word Dachau will help us to make the decision." Ralph Fink, a machine gun platoon sergeant who fought through the hellish mud and mountains of the Italian campaign, endured it all, according to his own admission, mainly so that he did not look bad in front of his buddies and not out of any regard for a higher cause. When he and the other soldiers liberated Dachau, they said to one another, "Man, if this had happened a year ago, we would have known why we were fighting."

Although liberating the camps may have given the soldiers purpose, they found little uplifting or redeeming about the experience. For them, it was mainly a traumatic exercise in witnessing humanity at its lowest, most depraved state. There was no upbeat ending as in popular movies—just a boundless sense of tragedy and loss.

In the longer term, the liberation and witnessing experience left an indelible mark on everyone who was part of it. Some, like Harry Blumenthal, a medic who worked to save people at Buchenwald, tried hard to suppress the agonizing memories. "Reflecting on the Buchenwald experience . . . it is difficult to realize it was not just a bad dream. For many years I put it in the deepest recesses of my mind and avoided connections about it. It was like an ugly scar that I wanted to cover but knew it was there and could not forget." As Blumenthal found out firsthand, there was no way to un-see what he had seen, un-smell what he had smelled, and simply forget those traumatic days in April 1945. Lieutenant Colonel Don Downard, who pulled the lone survivor from the death train, served many more years in the army and attempted to forget everything that happened to him at Dachau, including his mission of mercy. "The sights at the Camp were so terrible that I have tried to block the whole thing out, and I have succeeded to some extent."[6]

Most soldiers were not successful at blocking and forgetting. In fact, the camps were, for many, the single most unforgettable aspect of their wartime service. "It's burned into my brain," said Hank DeJarnette, a Dachau liberator. "It is with me to my dying day." William Deierhoi, a truck driver with the 120th Evacuation Hospital at Buchenwald, never forgot the sight of impossibly skinny bodies piled cordwood-style onto a wagon. "Those views have not faded one-tenth from my mind. There are many experiences of my life that fade into the dim recesses of the mind, but Buchenwald is not one of them. What I saw there is indelibly printed in my memory and as clear today as it was then." Jerry Hontas, from the same unit, found that "the scenes were so deeply etched in my memory that it is impossible to cast them aside—or to forget—or to permit time to dull the sharpness of those horrifying images of hell on earth. The only thing that vanished was our innocence." Ralph Fink spent, by his estimate, no more than five hours inside the Dachau protective custody compound, and yet he noted that "my most vivid memories of all my time overseas center around the atrocities seen in Dachau." General Paul Adams, who, in his capacity as assistant division commander of the 45th Infantry Division, spent considerable time at Dachau, later wrote: "The smell of death and human filth is still there [in his mind] and I suppose it always will be."

A substantial minority held a lifelong grudge against the German people for what had happened. This was especially true for Jewish veterans like Morton Barrish, a medic who worked hard to save lives at Dachau. "I will never knowingly buy a product . . . made in Germany," he told an interviewer decades after the war. "I just have this feeling about Germans . . . whether younger or older or whatever. I don't have much tolerance for Germans. It irritates the living hell out of me to go to temple . . . and see Mercedes Benz's [sic] in the parking lot." Harry Blumenthal admitted "a strong animosity to most Germans." During a trip to Europe with his wife, they drove into Germany, but Blumenthal's deep antipathy was such that he could not continue. "After about an hour I was compelled to turn around and leave."

More commonly for liberators, time mellowed the hatred. "I hated the Germans for what I saw, all of them," Fred Peterson, a Dachau liberator, wrote to a friend in 1994. "Now I believe they were not all to blame. You can forgive but not forget."

Liberators Coming Home

The success of the *Post-Dispatch* exhibit and the Signal Corps film did not necessarily translate to a friendly cultural environment for discussion of Holocaust memories in post-war America. As World War II grew more distant and the Cold War unfolded, and as West Germany became a key ally of the United States, some Americans had little wish to revisit the traumatic past. More than that, many understandably had little appetite to dwell, especially in the context of normal everyday life, on such a troubling and barbarous moment in modern history. The subject could be awkward and uncomfortable. Or perhaps it was just so serious that there was no way to discuss it without delving into an examination of humanity's darkest side—hardly the fare of workaday discourse. In one former soldier's recollection, everyone he encountered "didn't want to hear any more. The war was over. Let's forget about it. That's the attitude I got."[7]

Most of the liberators were not inclined to discuss their experiences, but those who did sometimes met with a cold, bewildered, or skeptical reaction.

Howard Margol discovered this firsthand. "I found that the average person, when you brought up the Holocaust, would rather not talk about it. My wife in particular—she really did not want to hear about it or look at the few pictures that I took at Dachau. She wasn't too happy if I would show them to the kids when they got old enough to understand such matters." William Walsh, who went to his grave wondering how the terrible crimes at Dachau could ever have happened, once showed his father, a veteran of World War I, the Seventh Army booklet that documented atrocities at the camp. "He listened to me very politely. But quite honestly, I think what I was saying to him was going over his head. I don't think he could fathom what the hell the whole thing was all about. I don't know whether he was trying to forget or didn't want to hear about it or what. He couldn't imagine this kind of stuff going on."

Some family members denied that the atrocity stories could be true or simply urged their loved ones to discard their memories, as if they were like a worn old coat that was no longer useful. One ex-soldier's wife even went so far as to tear up the pictures he had taken. Another man sent photos home to his mother only to find out that she had destroyed them. Dennis Wile, whose unit had helped clean up Buchenwald, learned quickly that his family could never really understand what happened because they had not seen it with their own eyes. "I was disappointed in some of the responses that I got from my folks," he said.

In the face of such reactions, the natural inclination for most men was to clam up. Like veterans of all of America's modern wars, the liberators were generally reluctant to talk in great depth about their experiences to civilians and family members, especially for the first few decades after the war, when the ex-soldiers tended to be quite busy raising families, earning a living, and getting on with their lives. Moreover, finding the camps was probably the most traumatic wartime experience for many of the soldiers, so relatively few of them were eager to revisit their memories in great detail. "It's interesting that people who were in the camps as liberators couldn't speak about them for many years," Irving Lisman, a medic at Dachau, wrote to a fellow veteran in 1981. "I myself never referred to them directly or talked about them for many years. Only recently can I speak about what I saw, heard and smelled." Morton Barrish could not discuss anything until well into the 1990s. "I never told my family. I never told even my wife of where I had been and what I had seen." Often this led to a sense of emotional distance between veterans and their children, creating intimacy issues in the next generation and wounds that never really healed. This was a time, after all, when there was stigma attached to seeking psychological treatment. Jimmy Gentry, who witnessed Dachau as a soldier in the 232nd Infantry Regiment, 42nd Infantry Division, could not bring himself to discuss anything about it. "I wouldn't even talk about it for years and years and years." In one instance, a Jewish community center in his hometown of Nashville asked him to speak, but he refused.[8]

Whether or not they were willing or able to talk, the liberators remained deeply affected by their concentration camp experiences. Many felt that these experiences shaped their lives for the better. "Being in Dachau on that 'liberation day' was my wake-up call," George Jackson once wrote. "The rest of my life as a university professor of psychology has been informed and directed by that experience." Although Robert Perelman, a Dachau liberator and Jew, had many nightmares about the camp, he believed what he saw there made him a stronger individual; one who was able to face life's many adversities. "The smell of death, the stink, the stench of it stays with you all your life. You can't forget it. That will never leave me. I found I could cope and come back to a normal life and take it, but I feel so . . . small compared to the people that were in there." Eugene Glick, a philosophical former infantryman, ruminated for many years about his experiences in combat and at Dachau; he decided he was much the better for them. "Whenever the thought crossed my mind that I am really in a tough situation and things are rough, I stop and reflect on my experience at the front in World War II and at the Dachau concentration camp and all things are immediately put in perspective, my mood changes immediately I realize I don't really have a problem at all."

For Clifford Barrett, the sight of piles of dead bodies and emaciated survivors in the protective custody compound triggered a tremendous empathy for the downtrodden and persecuted. "We saw the Hell, but the inmates were the ones who had to live in it. And die there." The stark memory of treating patients in the aftermath of Buchenwald's liberation sparked a deep respect for humanity in Dr. James Mahoney. "I had a better understanding of the great extremes humanity could endure. I seemed to have less tolerance for those extremes. Gifted and less gifted people all deserve consideration and respect beyond their abilities. Each one is a child of a Supreme Being! Since Buchenwald I have tried to live with increased respect for my fellow man, though I have not always succeeded." General Adams was deeply struck by "how shallow is the veneer of civilization on mankind." Others, like Ralph Fink, devoted their lives to serving others. He had grown up as an orphan in the

Milton Hershey School in Hershey, Pennsylvania. He and his wife spent 31 years living in the school as house parents. "Over our long career, we cared for and nurtured nearly three hundred boys in the eleven-to-fifteen age bracket, each for a period of up to four years." After participating in the liberation of Dachau as a young officer, Clarence "Buster" Hart forged a lifelong respect for tolerance, representative government, and the dignity of individual liberties. "I will forever believe that we must constantly and fiercely protect our system of democracy and civil rights which guarantee due process of law."[9]

In contrast to those who found some good in their experiences, some of the former soldiers were forever haunted or disillusioned by what they had seen in the camps. They grappled with post-traumatic stress disorder. Some lost faith in humanity or in God. They could never quite come to terms with how human beings could treat their own with such wanton cruelty and calculated brutality. "Words can't express the feelings," wrote Neil Frey, a former machine gunner whose company was one of the first into Dachau. "I have tried to make myself feel it was a very bad dream that didn't happen. Then there are the times at nite [sic], you wake up & see those striped flimsy suits, those sunken eyes in those live skeletons wandering around like crazed animals." Sam Platamone, who was a 19-year-old rifleman on the day his company helped liberate Dachau, felt that this experience, in addition to combat, forever altered the course of his life. "I am certain I would have matured into a person far removed from the one I ended up being. Instead, I settled for a lot less than my scholastic potential indicated." He tried night school but could not concentrate. He was restless and troubled. "I could no longer glean information from the printed page as easily as before." In spite of his trauma, though, he still helped raise his younger siblings. He married, fathered several children, got a job with the U.S. Post Office, and dedicated much of his life to helping others.

Harold Davis, a veteran of the 45th Division, could never shake the specter of what he had witnessed. "I can never describe what Dachau really took from me," he wrote to a fellow veteran 40 years after the war. "The days and nights I lay studying and dreaming about Dachau and combat. It was about seven years I had to keep my weapons out of my reach." The bad dreams never left him. In a vain attempt to cope with what he experienced at Dachau and the terrible sense of guilt he felt over failing the victims, Bill Keithan tried to repress his memories, almost as if he could store them in the mind's equivalent of an attic:

Occasionally some sound, a word, some picture, some smell can return to consciousness most vividly the scene, with the shock, revulsion and the inevitable nightmares. Then comes the sense of guilt. Had we reached the camps sooner there might have been more survivors. There is also the guilt that I should have been . . . more vocal, more involved in telling the story of my direct and personal experiences.

Like Keithan, some came to feel a solemn obligation to talk, to tell the world what they had seen as some of the ultimate witnesses to one of history's darkest chapters. "I now realize it is my responsibility to discuss my Buchenwald experience to whomever and wherever," Harry Blumenthal said. "We are obliged to try to prevent a repeat of this tragedy." Indeed, many thousands of former soldiers contributed their recollections for history. Some wrote them down. Others gave interviews or spoke to groups large and small, especially in schools so that succeeding generations could learn from those who had experienced these events firsthand. In addition to writing extensively about Dachau and giving numerous interviews, Felix Sparks spoke to more groups than he could ever count. He especially relished the opportunity to speak to kids. In addition to telling them exactly what he had seen, he urged them to stay aware of political leaders and to always hold them accountable: "I've urged them to pay attention to your political system and to vote. The other thing I've told them is that this is not an isolated incident. Don't think this is an incident that is behind us. This is something that can happen at any time."

Fred Mercer, a signalman who saw Buchenwald, took many photographs and made a point of showing them to as many people as he could. "I'm quite proud of these pictures. I've shown them for years to friends, relatives, whatever." Donald Johnson photographed Ohrdruf and often studied the pictures to keep the memory fresh in his mind. When he served in the National Guard, he "made a point of showing them to the personnel, hoping we could prevent any such disasters from happening again." Bill Harr felt that photographs and other documentation should be ever present and accessible to political leaders at national and international levels. "They should be in plain sight for the lawmakers of the future to see a vivid reminder of what *did* happen . . . and what *can* happen if insidious minds should once again gain control over a large group of stupid but energetic people."[10]

Many were shocked and deeply angered by the late twentieth- and twenty-first century phenomenon of Holocaust denial or indifference by world leaders such as Iranian ex-president Mahmoud Ahmadinejad, clergy such as Gerald L. K. Smith, historians such as Harry Barnes and David Irving, and rabidly anti-Semitic groups such as the Institute for Historical Review and Don Black's White Pride World Wide. Elie Wiesel, a survivor of Buchenwald, once commented, "It's enough for all of those deniers of the Holocaust to meet these soldiers and these medics to learn that these things really happened. They are witnesses. They are our witnesses." Stephan Ross, a Dachau survivor, wrote to the men who liberated him, "You and I, who saw it all, must forever be willing to [bear] witness to the authenticity of the Holocaust."

Most of the liberators came to understand this concept and the deep historical meaning of what they had done in 1945, and, over subsequent decades, they embraced their responsibility to educate succeeding generations. This understanding imbued them with sense of mission to bear witness for posterity, not just in hopes of documenting the past but also to prevent similar tragedies from ever happening again. Kenneth Ivey, a Dachau liberator, felt pity for those who deny the concentration camps. "They were not with us," he said pointedly. Most of the veterans felt passionate anger or indignation. Anthony Cardinale, the first soldier to spot the death train survivor outside of Dachau, later wrote in response to the concept of denial, "To the revisionists who have written books denying the horrors of the concentration camps, I say, 'HIDE YOUR HEADS IN SHAME, LEARN THE TRUTH, GO THROUGH TONS OF PHOTOS, DOCUMENTS & TESTIMONIALS OF SURVIVORS THAT PROVE YOU WRONG!' "

Walter Fellenz, whose battalion was one of the lead units at Dachau, was so disturbed that anyone could deny what he knew to be true from his own firsthand experiences that he penned an emotional letter to the editorial page of *The New York Times*. "To me the Holocaust was one of the most shameful crimes since men walked this earth. More shameful, however, is the fact that forces of evil are trying to deny that this Holocaust ever took place. History is the truthful recording of the facts as they are. Our children are the adults of tomorrow. They must be factually informed of the Holocaust so they can prevent a recurrence."

John Lee, who was a 19-year-old rifleman on liberation day at Dachau and struggled for years to come to terms with his experiences, once said in a direct and devastating rebuttal to deniers, "I know what I saw at Dachau and it was no mirage, but the work of barbaric and uncivilized minds that have no place in this world." Like Lee, Eugene Glick reflected for years on the concentration camps and what he had witnessed, eventually forming the trenchant opinion that education was the ultimate key to ending denial and repression. "As more people become educated and are freed from superstition, prejudice, fear and want, the likelihood of such recurrence is dramatically reduced." He also urged the world's religious leaders to embrace messages of universal love and to reject dogmatism. Truly, such education offered the hope of a better, more caring world, one that respected the value of human life and multicultural toleration.

Dachau survivor Stephan Ross stands as perhaps the best single example of that lofty post-Holocaust vision. After World War II, he went on to become an American citizen and a preeminent psychologist. The bond he shared with his liberators—men and women he otherwise never would have met—lasted a lifetime. "You the G.I. Joes spoke the first kind words to us in years," he told them in a heartfelt, poignant letter:

> You held in your arms our living skeletons, too weak to talk, to eat, or to live. You gave us our first bites of decent food. You provided medical help as best you could. You left your homes and families and at times you were also hungry, cold and disillusioned. We owe you all our gratitude, recognition and our acknowledgment. You looked rough and tough and yet you showed so much empathy. You fought bravely and defeated the most vicious and evil empire the world has ever known.[11]

The soldiers who destroyed Nazism and liberated Ohrdruf, Buchenwald, and Dachau were not like the heroes often seen in action films. Most of them would never even think of using the word "hero" to describe themselves. They were ordinary people who found themselves enmeshed in extraordinary circumstances of a sort they could never have imagined. Their goal was to survive the war and go home. Before the spring of 1945, they were stunningly ignorant of both Nazi atrocities and Allied war aims. At these three camps—all of them monuments to humanity's worst capabilities—the soldiers peered into a frightening abyss. They saw death of the worst sort—starvation, the deterioration caused by contagious disease, burned flesh and bones caked in industrial ovens, the remnants of gray bones in sediment, and the gaping wounds of violent murder. They smelled death's nauseating byproducts of rot and putrefaction, a stench so profound they could almost taste it, often for the rest of their lives. They inspected mechanisms of torture and repression. They cleaned up cesspools of inconceivable filth. They encountered, conversed with, cared for, and often befriended survivors who looked all but dead and who stank of body odor, malignant disease, excrement, lice, and hopelessness. They found out firsthand how much trauma the human body and spirit could take and yet still somehow survive. They cared for the survivors in ways both guided and misguided. They nursed them back to health, restoring their dignity and their very lives.

Those who had lost friends in combat took some small comfort that perhaps their sacrifice had led to the diminution of someone else's suffering. In these camps, they occasionally behaved with indiscipline but, far more frequently, with sympathetic, soldierly correctness. In these actions, they found a sense of meaning and purpose amid a time of trouble, destruction, grief, and apathy. The liberation experience forever affected them in ways too numerous to count. And, in the cycle of time that inevitably consumes all generations, as the liberators exit the stage of history, their experiences should mark us, too, and those who succeed us, forever more.

NOTES

Abbreviations

AAR	after action report
CI	combat interview
CSWS	Center for the Study of War of Society
EL	Dwight D. Eisenhower Library
EU	Emory University Library
LOC	Library of Congress
NA	National Archives
RDVA	Rainbow Division Veterans Association
SHS	State Historical Society of Missouri Research Center
SLHOL	St. Louis Holocaust Museum Library
USAMHI	U.S. Army Military History Institute
USHMM	United States Holocaust Memorial Museum
UTEP	University of Texas El Paso

Prologue

1. Charles E. Wilson, diary and unpublished memoir, pp. 372–379; Charles Wilson Papers, Box 1, Folder 7, USAMHI, Carlisle, PA.

2. Clifford Barrett, letter to San Dann, June 16, 1996, RDVA Records, Series 3, Box 16, Folder 4, Archives and Special Collections, University of Nebraska.

CHAPTER ONE: Encountering Ohrdruf

1. 355th Infantry Regiment, AAR, April 1945, Record Group 407, Entry 427, Box 11027, Folder 1, NA, College Park, MD; 4th Armored Division, Combat Command A, Combat History and AAR, April 1945, U.S. Army Unit Records, Box 78, EL, Abilene, KS; Leavitt Anderson, unpublished memoir, p. 97, copy in author's possession courtesy of Colonel Don Patton, U.S. Army, Retired; Charles B. MacDonald, *The U.S. Army in World War II: The Last Offensive*, Washington, DC: United States Army, 1993, pp. 376–378.

2. Twelfth Army Group, Publicity and Psychological Warfare Group, Report on Ohrdruf, April 12, 1945, Record Group 331, Entry 54, Box 151; Third Army, G5 Historical Report, April 1945, Record Group 331, Entry 54, Box 147, Folder 1, both at NA.

3. Joe Friedman, interview with the Shoah Foundation, April 27, 1998, USHMM; Ralph Craib, "The Forgotten Death Camp," *San Francisco Chronicle*, April 9, 1995; Andrew Rosner, statement, April 23, 1995, www.89infdivww2.org.

4. 355th Infantry Regiment, AAR, April 1945; History, Record Group 407, Entry 427, Box 11027, Folder 1; Civil Affairs Summaries, April 1945, Record Group 407, Entry 427, Box 11029, Folder 2; Combat Command A, 4th Armored Division, AAR, April 1945, Record Group 407, Entry 427, Box 12416, Folder 1, all at NA; 4th Armored Division, Combat History, AAR, April 1945, U.S. Army Unit Records, Box 78, EL; 602nd Tank Destroyer Battalion, History, General Collection, Box 3, Folder 4, SLHOL; 89th Infantry Division Historical Board, *The 89th Infantry Division, 1942–1945*, Washington, DC: Infantry Journal Press, 1947, p. 129; 602nd Tank Destroyer Battalion, AAR, April 1945, copy in author's possession. Corroboration for the Holocaust Museum affording liberator status to the two divisions can be found at www.ushmm.org. Some veterans say they engaged in a brief firefight with Nazi guards in the process of liberating Ohrdruf. I believe this is highly unlikely. The photographic evidence in the aftermath of liberation shows no indication of recent fighting. It would have made no sense for the Germans to leave troops behind to guard what they thought was an empty camp. Moreover, surviving inmates do not mention the presence of any remaining guards.

5. Twelfth Army Group, Publicity and Psychological Warfare Group, Report on Ohrdruf, NA; Robert Cleary, oral history interview, May 29, 2003, Robert Cleary Collection 14879, Veterans History Project, LOC, Washington, DC; Herbert Lowe, statement, Box 1, World War II Survey 7781; George Armstrong, World War II Survey 3307, both at USAMHI; Benjamin Fertig, interview with the Shoah Foundation, September 9, 1998, USHMM; Michael Burge, "Remembrances: Bob Cleary, Fateful Steps into History," *San Diego Union-Tribune*, May 27, 2002; Bruce Nickols, statement, c. 1998, www.89infdivww2.org. After World War II, the Ohrdruf camp was torn down. No trace of it exists any more. In describing what it looked like in 1945, I have relied on eyewitness testimony and photographic evidence from that time.

6. Stanley Hodson, Memorandum for the Officer in Charge, War Crimes Branch, U.S. Army Judge Advocate General, March 6, 1946; Stanley Hodson, Letter to the Editors, *Lewistown Daily Sun* and *Lewistown Evening Journal*, April 13, 1945; Wencie Higuera, sworn statement, Pima County, Arizona Notary Public, March 7, 1946, all located in Box 1, World War II Survey 7781, USAMHI; Albert Hirsch, "Ohrdruf Remembered," April 2002, www.89infdivww2.org. To my knowledge, no one has ever been able to pinpoint the identity of the dead aviator at Ohrdruf. Many liberators of the camp made reference, usually just in passing, to the aviator in their testimony. I have relied exclusively on sworn eyewitnesses. The full story of who he was and what happened to him will probably never be known.

7. William Charboneau, interview with the Shoah Foundation, n.d., USHMM; William Coolman, letter to Dorothy and sons, April 29, 1945, Box 6, Folder 563, Collection 68, World War II Letters, SHS, Columbia, MO; Dick Colosimo, statement, September 2003, www.89infdivww2.org.

8. Twelfth Army Group, Publicity and Psychological Warfare Group, Report on Ohrdruf, NA; Abe Plotkin, interview with the Shoah Foundation, September 12, 1997, USHMM; Michael Hirsh, *The Liberators: America's Witnesses to the Holocaust*, New York: Bantam Books, 2010, p. xv; Albin Irzyk, *A Warrior's Quilt of Personal Military History*, Raleigh, NC: Ivy House Publishing Group, 2010, pp. 191–192.

9. Twelfth Army Group, Publicity and Psychological Warfare Group, Report on Ohrdruf, NA; Hodson, Memorandum for Record and Letter to the Editors, USAMHI; Charboneau interview, USHMM; Craib, "The Forgotten Death Camp," *San Francisco Chronicle*; Ralph Rush, statement, February 2001, www.89infdivww2.org; Irzyk, *A Warrior's Quilt*, p. 192.

10. Captain Fred Diamond, diary, April 13, 1945, Fred Diamond Collection, Record Group 04, .055, ACC.1994.A.164; Ben Logan, interview with the Shoah Foundation, February 25, 1998, both at USHMM; Private Arthur Santa, letter to wife, April 13, 1945, Box 31, Folder 2605, Collection 68, World War II Letters, SHS; Morris Abrams, interview with Sister Prince, January 11, 1983, Oral History Project, SLHOL; Thomas Curtin, unpublished memoir, no pagination, MS1608, Box 1, Folder 18, World War II Veterans Project, CSWS, Special Collections Library, University of Tennessee-Knoxville; Sol Brandell, unpublished memoir, p. 26, World War II Survey 6408, USAMHI; Jack Holmes, recollections, n.d., www.JackHolmes.weebly.com; Hirsh, *The Liberators*, p. 28; Irzyk, *A Warrior's Quilt*, p. 193.

11. Ralph Dalton, World War II Survey 2991; Ladd Roberts, World War II Survey 3431, both at USAMHI; Charboneau interview, USHMM; Hirsch, "Ohrdruf Remembered," www.89infdivww2.org; Irzyk, *A Warrior's Quilt*, p. 193. Charboneau was so upset at the memory of what he saw at Ohrdruf that he broke down sobbing and almost could not continue with the interview.

12. Santa letter, SHS; Diamond diary, USHMM; Curtin, unpublished memoir, no pagination, CSWS.

13. Third Army, G5 Historical Report, National Archives; Twelfth Army Group, Psychological Warfare Report, April 15, 1945, C. D. Jackson Papers, Box 7, Intelligence, Paris-7, EL; Andy Coffey, Letter to the United States Holocaust Memorial Museum, December 3, 1993, Record Group 09-.040, ACC 1994.A.0169 (underlined passage in original); Friedman interview, both at USHMM.

14. Third Army, G5 Historical Report, National Archives; Twelfth Army Group, Psychological Warfare Report, EL; Friedman interview, USHMM; Staff Sergeant Walter Seifert, diary, April 10, 1945, World War II Survey, no number, USAMHI; Saul Levitt, "Ohrdruf Camp," *Yank: The Army Weekly*, May 18, 1945; Earl Ziemke, *The U.S. Army in the Occupation of Germany, 1944–1946*, Washington, DC: Center of Military History, United States Army, 1990, p. 231; Jon Bridgman, *The End of the Holocaust: The Liberation of the Camps*, Portland, OR: Areopagitica Press, 1990, pp. 79–80; Osmar White, *Conqueror's Road: An Eyewitness Report of Germany 1945*, Cambridge: Cambridge University Press, 2003, pp. 90–92. White was an Australian war correspondent. He claimed, without citing any source, that the mayor and his wife somehow both hanged themselves and cut their wrists (a near physical impossibility) but he

did not witness the bodies. Graphic army footage of the Ohrdruf civilians touring the camp can be accessed at www.youtube.com.

15. John J. DiBattista, interview transcript, copy of Art Goldman letter, April 13, 1945, in footnotes, John Di Battista papers, Box 20, Folder 8, USAMHI.

16. General Dwight D. Eisenhower, letter to General George Marshall, April 15, 1945, George C. Marshall Collection, Box 80; Dwight D. Eisenhower, interview with Sherman Witt, March 1, 1965, Eisenhower Post-Presidential Papers, 1965 Principal File, Box 54, both at EL; George Patton, diary, April 12, 1945, excerpt copy in author's possession courtesy of Kevin Hymel; Omar Bradley, *A Soldier's Story*, New York: Henry Holt and Company, 1951, p. 539; Charles Codman, *Drive*, New York: Little, Brown and Company, 1957, pp. 282–283; George Patton, *War as I Knew It*, Boston: Houghton Mifflin Company, 1947, pp. 292–294; Jonathan Jordan, *Brothers, Rivals, Victors: Eisenhower, Patton, Bradley and the Partnership that Drove the Allied Conquest in Europe*, New York: NAL/Caliber, 2011, pp. 506–508; Brewster Chamberlin and Marcia Feldman, eds., *The Liberation of the Nazi Concentration Camps 1945: Eyewitness Accounts of the Liberators*, Washington, DC: United States Holocaust Memorial Council, 1987, pp. 76–77. Footage of the generals' tour can be seen at www.youtube.com. When compared with the photographic images of camp survivors, the tour guide does indeed look rather stout, unaffected, and healthy.

17. David Cohen, interview with the Shoah Foundation, n.d.; Richard Garrick, interview with the Shoah Foundation, May 15, 1998, both at USHMM; Major General Hobart "Hap" Gay, diary, April 12–14, 1945, Hobart Gay Papers, Box 3, Folder 4; Major Chester Hanson, diary, April 12, 1945, Chester Hanson Collection, Official Papers, War Diaries, Box 5, Folder 7, both at USAMHI; General Dwight D. Eisenhower, "Eyes Only" cable to General George Marshall, April 19, 1945, Eisenhower Pre-Presidential Papers, Box 134; Eisenhower letter to Marshall, April 15, 1945; Eisenhower, interview with Witt, all at EL; Rosner, statement, www.89infdivww2.org; Dwight Eisenhower, *Crusade in Europe*, New York: Doubleday, 1948, pp. 408–409; Carlo D'Este, *Eisenhower: A Soldier's Life*, New York: Henry Holt and Company, 2002, pp. 686–687; Bradley, *Soldier's Story*, p. 539; Codman, *Drive*, pp. 282–283. The detail about the lye soap bath comes from the scrapbook/journal of Colonel Paul Harkins, a member of Patton's staff. I would like to thank my friend and fellow historian Kevin Hymel for making portions of the scrapbook available to me. To cap off what had been a bad day for the three generals, later that same evening they received news of President Franklin Roosevelt's death. All italicized and underlined passages in quotations throughout this chapter are in the original sources.

CHAPTER TWO: "The Smell of Death Was Thick in the Air": Witnessing Buchenwald

1. 9th Armored Infantry Battalion, AAR, April 1945; Unit Journal, April 11, 1945, both in Record Group 407, Entry 427, Box 12608, Folders 16 and 6, respectively, NA; Robert Bennett, letter to Pierre Verheye, November 5, 1972, George F. Hofmann Col-

lection, Box 8, Folder 3, USAMHI; Captain Robert Bennett, S3, and Captain Frederic Keffer, S2, interview with Lieutenant Hollis Alpert, April 21, 1945, located in World War II CI-284, entire collection in author's possession; George Hofmann, *The Super Sixth: History of the 6th Armored Division in World War II and its Post-war Association*, self-published, 1975, pp. 404–405.

2. Egon Fleck and First Lieutenant Edward Tenenbaum, *Buchenwald: A Preliminary Report*, April 24, 1945, Twelfth Army Group Publicity and Psychological Warfare Group, Record Group 331, Entry 54, Box 151, Folder 3; Third Army, G5 Historical Report, April 1945, Record Group 331, Entry 54, Box 147, Folder 1, both at NA; Brigadier General Eric Wood, Lieutenant Colonel Charles Ott, and Chief Warrant Officer S. M. Dye, *Inspection of Buchenwald*, April 16, 1945, Walter Bedell Smith Papers, World War II Collection, Box 36; Marcel Blanc, unpublished memoir, no pagination, World War II Participants and Contemporaries Collection, both at EL; David Hackett, ed. and trans., *The Buchenwald Report*, Boulder, CO: Westview Press, 1995, pp. 32–36, 87–92; Christopher Burney, *The Dungeon Democracy*, New York: Duel, Sloan and Pearce, 1946, pp. 23–27. See also the U.S. Memorial Holocaust Museum website at www.ushmm.org for an overview of the camp's history. Marcel Blanc was a former resistance fighter and inmate at Buchenwald who experienced the camp's rigid hierarchy firsthand.

3. Fleck and Tenenbaum, *Buchenwald: A Preliminary Report*, NA; Wood et al, *Inspection of Buchenwald*, EL; Donald Robinson, "Communist Atrocities at Buchenwald," *American Mercury*, December 1946, pp. 397–404; Hackett, *The Buchenwald Report*, pp. 98–99; Burney, *The Dungeon Democracy*, pp. 33–35.

4. Wood et al, *Inspection of Buchenwald*, EL; Hackett, *The Buchenwald Report*, pp. 158–159.

5. Wood et al, *Inspection of Buchenwald*, EL; Robert Abzug, *Inside the Vicious Heart: Americans and the Liberation of Nazi Concentration Camps*, New York: Oxford University Press, 1985, pp. 46–47, 128; Hackett, *The Buchenwald Report*, pp. 335–341; www.jewishvirtuallibrary.org; www.ushmm.org; Flint Whitlock, emails to author, January 6, 2014, regarding the alleged guilt of Ilse Koch. Whitlock has written three books about Buchenwald, including one that focuses exclusively on the Kochs.

6. Fleck and Tenenbaum, *Buchenwald: A Preliminary Report*, NA; Hackett, *The Buchenwald Report*, pp. 317–319; Abzug, *Inside the Vicious Heart*, p. 46; Center for Holocaust and Genocide Studies, www.chgs.umn.edu.

7. Fleck and Tenenbaum, *Buchenwald: A Preliminary Report*, NA; Theresa Ast, "Confronting the Holocaust: American Soldiers Who Liberated the Concentration Camps," PhD dissertation, Emory University, 2000, pp. 30–31; Hackett, *The Buchenwald Report*, pp. 4–5, 325–333; Abzug, *Inside the Vicious Heart*, pp. 47–48; Burney, *The Dungeon Democracy*, pp. 123–136; www.buchenwald.de; www.jewishvirtuallibrary.org; www.ushmm.org. For an example of the Communist claim of self-liberation, see Rudi Jahn, ed., *Das war Buchenwald!* (This Was Buchenwald!), published in 1945 by the Communist party of Leipzig; and Walter Bartel, *Buchenwald: Mahnung und Verpflichtung* (Buchenwald: Warning and Duty), published in 1960 also by a Com-

munist source. Prisoners later claimed that Pister, with murderous duplicity, ordered a nearby air base commander to dive bomb the camp just after the SS withdrawal. According to the prisoners, the air base commander refused.

8. 9th Armored Infantry Battalion, AAR, April 1945; Unit Journal, April 11, 1945, both at NA; 6th Armored Division, AAR, April 1945, George Hofmann Papers, Box 8, Folder 4; Bennett, letter to Verheye, both at USAMHI; Bennett, Keffer, interview with Lieutenant Hollis Alpert, April 21, 1945, CI-284; Hofmann, *The Super Sixth*, 1975, pp. 404–406; Wayne Drash, "Buchenwald Liberator, American Hero Dies at 83," August 14, 2008, www.cnn.com. See also Buchenwald entries at www.scrapbook pages.com.

9. Fleck and Tenenbaum, *Buchenwald: A Preliminary Report*, NA.

10. Fleck and Tenenbaum, *Buchenwald: A Preliminary Report*, NA; Hackett, *The Buchenwald Report*, p. 5.

11. A Company, 317th Infantry Regiment, Morning Report, April 13, 1945, National Personnel Records Center, St. Louis, MO; Martin "Dick" Renie, "Buchenwald: I Was First and I Was Ashamed," *The Service Magazine*, Spring 1968; Martin "Dick" Renie, "Buchenwald Errata—I Was Not the First," *The Service Magazine*, Autumn 1968.

12. Fleck and Tenenbaum, *Buchenwald: A Preliminary Report*, NA; Wood et al, *Inspection of Buchenwald*, EL; Herman Cole, letter to Niles, March 30, 1981, Buchenwald Folders, Record Group 09.005.08; Victor Geller, unpublished memoir, p. 4, Victor Geller Collection, Record Group 09.042, ACC.1994.A.0257, both at USHMM; Ast, "Confronting the Holocaust," pp. 128–129.

13. 6th Armored Division, AAR, April 1945, NA; Jim Moncrief, "As You Were: Recollections of a Thirty Year Veteran," self-published, 1996, pp. 71–74; Major General Hobart "Hap" Gay, diary, April 14, 1945, both at USAMHI; Martin Blumenson, ed., *The Patton Papers, Volume II, 1940–1945*, Boston, MA: Houghton Mifflin, 1974, p. 686; Patton, *War As I Knew It*, Boston, MA: Houghton Mifflin, 1947, pp. 299–301; Codman, *Drive*, New York: Little, Brown and Company, 1957, p. 290.

14. Howard Cwick, unpublished memoir, pp. 1–4, 250–260; Anonymous Buchenwald survivor, unpublished memoir, pp. 47–49, both in Howard Cwick Papers, Record Group 09.069, Folders 1 and 2; Howard Cwick, interview with the Shoah Foundation, September 16, 1997, all located at USHMM.

15. First Army, G5 Historical Report, April 1945, Record Group 331, Entry 54, Box 151, Folder 2, NA; Alex Kormas, veterans' questionnaire, World War II Survey 3742, USAMHI; John Glustrom, interview with Ed Sheehee, November 6, 1978; Dwight Pearce, interview with Beth Machinot, August 7, 1978, both at Fred Crawford Witness to the Holocaust Project, Box 3, Folder 71, EU; Kenneth Gerber, letter to Miles Lerman, December 26, 1981, International Liberators Collection, Buchenwald Folders, USHMM.

16. First Army, G5 Historical Report, NA; Cwick, unpublished memoir, pp. 4–6, 258–261; Cwick, interview with the Shoah Foundation, September 16, 1997, both at USHMM.

17. Geller, unpublished memoir, pp. 9–11, USHMM; Margalit Fox, "Rabbi Herschel Schacter is Dead at 95; Cried to the Jews of Buchenwald: 'You are Free,'" *New York Times*, March 26, 2013; Brewster Chamberlin and Marcia Feldman, eds., *The Liberation of the Nazi Concentration Camps 1945: Eyewitness Accounts of the Liberators*, Washington, DC: United States Holocaust Memorial Council, 1987, pp. 35–36. Rabbi Schacter stayed at Buchenwald for several months, conducting religious services and spearheading humanitarian and resettlement efforts for the survivors. Marguerite Higgins, on pp. 77–81 of her memoir, *News is a Singular Thing*, Garden City, NJ: Doubleday & Company, 1955, claimed to have witnessed and put a stop to reprisal beatings by American soldiers against German prisoners at Buchenwald several days after the liberation.

CHAPTER THREE: Treating Buchenwald: Medicine and Murrow

1. 120th Evacuation Hospital, Unit History, Record Group 112, Entry UD1012, Box 86, Folder 10; 120th Evacuation Hospital, Unit Diary, April 14–16, 1945, Record Group 112, Entry UD1012, Box 86, Folder 9; Third Army, G5 Historical Report, April 1945, all at NA; Ralph Wolpaw, unpublished memoir, p. 2; May MacDonald Horton, unpublished memoir, p. 2; Jerry Hontas, unpublished memoir, p. 2, all at www.buchenwaldandbeyond.com; Jon Marcus, "War and Remembrance," *Boston Magazine*, May 2002.

2. 120th Evacuation Hospital, Unit History; 120th Evacuation Hospital, Unit Diary, April 15–18, 1945, both at NA; Lieutenant John Lafferty, letter to family, April 27, 1945; Hence Hill, letter to wife, May 25, 1945, both at www.buchenwaldandbeyond.com; David Hackett, ed. and trans., *The Buchenwald Report*, Boulder, CO: Westview Press, 1995, pp. 278–279.

3. 120th Evacuation Hospital, Unit History; 120th Evacuation Hospital, Unit Diary, April 15–18, 1945, both at NA; Warren Priest, unpublished memoir, at www.buchenwaldandbeyond.com; Marcus, "War and Remembrance," *Boston Magazine*; Hackett, *The Buchenwald Report*, pp. 278–279; Michael Hirsh, *The Liberators: America's Witnesses to the Holocaust*, New York: Bantam Books, 2010, pp. 119–121.

4. 120th Evacuation Hospital, Unit History; 120th Evacuation Hospital, Unit Diary, April 18–23, 1945, both at NA; Bill Whipple, letter to family, n.d., Box 37, Folder 3209, SHS; Walter Mason, unpublished memoir, no pagination; Lieutenant John Lafferty, letter to family, April 27, 1945, both at www.buchenwaldandbeyond.com.

5. James Mahoney, memoir, no pagination, at www.buchenwaldandbeyond.com; Yaffa Eliach and Brana Gurewitsch, eds., *The Liberators: Eyewitness Accounts of the Liberation of Concentration Camps*, Brooklyn, NY: Center for Holocaust Studies Documentation and Research, 1981, p. 17.

6. 120th Evacuation Hospital, Unit History, NA; Samuel Riezman, interview with David Eidelman, December 15, 1981, Oral History Project, SLHOL; Ralph Wolpaw, unpublished memoir, p. 7, at www.buchenwaldandbeyond.com; Eliach and Gurewitsch, *The Liberators*, pp. 17–18.

7. 120th Evacuation Hospital, Unit History, NA; Pierre Verheye, letter to Martin "Dick" Renie, August 29, 1972, 80th Infantry Division Survey Material, USAMHI; Elie Wiesel, *Remarks on Receiving the Congressional Gold Medal and Signing the Jewish Heritage Week Proclamation*, April 19, 1985, text of speech located at www.pbs.org /eliewiesel/resources/reagan.html; Hence Hill, letter to wife, May 25, 1945, at www .buchenwaldandbeyond.com; Brewster Chamberlin and Marcia Feldman, eds., *The Liberation of the Nazi Concentration Camps 1945: Eyewitness Accounts of the Liberators*, Washington, DC: United States Holocaust Memorial Council, 1987, p. 13; Eliach and Gurewitsch, *The Liberators*, pp. 17–18; Christopher Burney, *The Dungeon Democracy*, New York: Duel, Sloan and Pearce, 1946, pp. 138–139.

8. Corporal Howard Katzander, "Buchenwald Camp," *Yank: The Army Weekly*, May 18, 1945; Antoinette May, *Witness to War: A Biography of Marguerite Higgins*, New York: Beaufort Books, 1983, pp. 82–83; Marguerite Higgins, *News Is a Singular Thing*, Garden City, NJ: Doubleday, 1955, pp. 74–76.

9. Joseph Pulitzer, *A Report to the American People*, pp. 5, 81, 94, 109, General Collection, Box 5, Folder 27, SLHOL; Julius Adler, "Buchenwald Worse Than Battlefield," *New York Times*, April 28, 1945; Ben Hibbs, "Journey to a Shattered World," *Saturday Evening Post*, June 9, 1945; William Chenery, "I Testify," *Collier's Magazine*, June 16, 1945; Robert Abzug, *America Views the Holocaust, 1933–1945: A Brief Documentary History*, Boston, MA: Bedford/St. Martin's, 1999, pp. 198–202; Chamberlin and Feldman, *The Liberation of the Nazi Concentration Camps*, pp. 42–45.

10. *Buchenwald Camp: The Report of a Parliamentary Delegation*, 1945, pp. 2–7, located at USAMHI.

11. *United Nations War Crimes Commission Visit of Delegation to Buchenwald Concentration Camp in Germany*, pp. 1–3, Record Group 331, Entry 6, Box 1, Folder 4, NA; *Buchenwald Camp*, pp. 2–7, USAMHI; Hon. R. E. Thomason, *German Atrocities: Official Report of the Congressional Investigating Committee*, May 15, 1945, R. E. Thomason Papers, MS140, Series II, Box 6, Folder 10, Special Collections Library, UTEP; Edouard Izac, interview with Fred Crawford, May 7, 1981, EU; "Edouard Victor Michael Izac," located at Michael Robert Patterson, www.arlingtoncemetery.net; Percy Knauth, "Buchenwald," *Time*, April 30, 1945; Robert Abzug, *Inside the Vicious Heart: Americans and the Liberation of Nazi Concentration Camps*, New York: Oxford University Press, 1985, pp. 129, 138–139. Footage of the Weimar civilians visiting Buchenwald can be accessed at www.youtube.com. I would like to thank Claudia Rivers of the UTEP Library Special Collections for making the congressional report available to me.

CHAPTER FOUR: Dachau: The Approach

1. Hans-Günter Richardi, Eleonore Philipp, Monika Lücking, Greg Bond, eds., *Dachau: A Guide to Its Contemporary History*, Dachau, Germany: City of Dachau Office of Cultural Affairs, 2001, pp. 21–24, 74–79, 85–94; Andrew Rawson, *In Pursuit of Hitler: A Battlefield Guide to Bavaria*, South Yorkshire, UK: Pen & Sword, 2008, pp. 159–164; Thomas Harding, *Hanns and Rudolf: The True Story of the German Jew*

Who Tracked Down and Caught the Kommandant of Auschwitz, New York: Simon & Schuster, 2013, pp. 64–68; Barbara Distel, *Dachau Concentration Camp*, pamphlet, 1972, pp. 1–3, copy in author's possession; Dachau entries at www.holocaustresearch project.org and www.ushmm.org.

2. Andrew Mollo, "Dachau," *After the Battle*, No. 27, 1980, pp. 3–8; Richardi et al, *Dachau*, pp. 85–104, 132–143, 255–256; Rawson, *In Pursuit of Hitler*, pp. 160–174; Seventh Army, *Dachau*, self-published pamphlet, May 1945, pp. 15–20, 36–41; Distel, *Dachau Concentration Camp*, pp. 4–7. The question of the complicity or opposition of Dachau residents to the misdeeds of the SS is naturally quite controversial and prone to a great deal of latter-year political posturing and obfuscation. In my discussion, I used only what I considered to be the most unimpeachable, corroborated eyewitness accounts.

3. Father Stanislaw Wolak, statement, Curtis Whiteway Papers, Box 1, USAMHI; Rawson, *In Pursuit of Hitler*, pp. 174–177; Seventh Army, *Dachau*, pp. 20–23; Distel, *Dachau Concentration Camp*, pp. 10–12; see Dachau entries at www.scrapbookpages .com, www.holocaustresearchproject.org, and www.ushmm.org. After the war, Schilling was tried and executed as a war criminal. Rascher apparently falsified his results and lied to Himmler about them. In April 1945, the Gestapo (German state police) reportedly executed Rascher and his wife, either for his false data or for disobeying Nazi adoption laws.

4. Stephan Ross, unpublished memoir, pp. 1–2, Box 16, Folder 4, RDVA; Sam Dann, ed., *Dachau, 29 April 1945: The Rainbow Liberation Memoirs*, Lubbock, TX: Texas Tech University Press, 1998, p. 203; Marcus Smith, *Dachau: The Harrowing of Hell*, Albuquerque, NM: University of New Mexico Press, 1972, pp. 146–149; Robert Abzug, *Inside the Vicious Heart: Americans and the Liberation of Nazi Concentration Camps*, New York: Oxford University Press, 1985, pp. 88–89; Jon Bridgman, *The End of the Holocaust: The Liberation of the Camps*, Portland, OR: Areopagitica Press, 1990, pp. 63–65; Rawson, *In Pursuit of Hitler*, pp. 175–177; Seventh Army, *Dachau*, pp. 25–27; Distel, *Dachau Concentration Camp*, 17–19; Dachau entries, www.scrapbookpages .com, www.holocaustresearchproject.org, and www.ushmm.org.

5. Excellent background information on Wicker can be accessed at www.scrap bookpages.com and www.findagrave.com.

6. Dr. Victor Maurer's report is reproduced in *The Surrender of Dachau KZ Prisoner Compound, 29 April 1945: A Compilation of Documents and Photographs*, by Colonel John Linden, 1996, located in 42nd Infantry Division Papers, Box 32, Folder 7, and in Linden's self-published monograph, *Surrender of the Dachau Concentration Camp, 29 April 1945: The True Account*, 1997, both at USAMHI; Gleb Rahr, letter to Sam Dann, October 25, 1994, Box 16, Folder 8, RDVA; Mollo, "Dachau," *After the Battle*, pp. 11–12; Nerin Gun, *The Day of the Americans*, New York: Fleet Publishing Corporation, 1966, pp. 53–54; Rawson, *In Pursuit of Hitler*, pp. 177–178; David Israel, *The Day the Thunderbird Cried: Untold Stories of World War II*, self-published memoir, 2005, p. 149; www .scrapbookpages.com; www.findagrave.com. Some sources, such as Gun and Mollo, incorrectly claim that SS Lieutenant Heinrich Skodzensky was the commandant of

Dachau when it was liberated. It is possible that Skodzensky commanded the troops in the administrative complex and that he and Wicker did not coordinate their efforts. Indeed, the events of liberation lend some merit to this possibility. Wicker and company surrendered without a fight near the prisoner compound, whereas other Germans resisted among the administrative, residential, and factory buildings. This indicates two forces under separate commanders. However, two separate American units liberated these distinctly different parts of the Dachau complex, which also could account for the differing circumstances.

7. XV Corps, G5 (Civil Affairs) Report, April–May 1945; G5 Journal, April 29, 1945, both at Record Group 407, Entry 427, Box 4258, Folder 1, NA; 42nd Infantry Division, History, April 1945, U.S. Army Unit Records, Box 986; 45th Infantry Division, History, April 1945, U.S. Army Unit Records, Box 1020, both at EL; Major General Harry Collins, letter to Ed Weitzel, president of the 42nd Infantry Division Association, May 3, 1945, 42nd Infantry Division Papers, Box 11, Folder 10; Linden, *Surrender of the Dachau Concentration Camp*, pp. 1–11, all at USAMHI; James McCahey, letter to Art Lee, January 24, 1995, Box 13, Folder 10, RDVA. For this and the two subsequent chapters, I gathered hundreds of firsthand accounts from veterans of the 42nd, the 45th, and the 20th Armored Divisions. Very few had any prior knowledge of Dachau. Virtually no one understood the true horror of the place until he saw it firsthand.

8. Sid Shafner, letter to Sam Dann, June 5, 1995, Box 16, Folder 9, RDVA. The two teenagers who reported Dachau's presence to Shafner were Greek Jews from Salonika. According to Shafner, the unit adopted them as their own. He developed a lifelong friendship with the two survivors.

9. 222nd Infantry Regiment, AAR, April 1945; Unit Journal, April 29, 1945, Record Group 407, Entry 427, Box 9138, Folder 1; 157th Infantry Regiment, AAR, April 1945, Record Group 407, Entry 427, Box 9414, Folder 9; S3 Journal, April 29, 1945, Record Group 407, Entry 427, Box 9426, Folder 2, all at NA; 3rd Battalion, 157th Infantry Regiment, S2/S3 Journal, April 29, 1945, Box 22, Folders 4 and 5; Shafner letter to Dann, June 5, 1995, both at RDVA; Felix Sparks, unpublished memoir, pp. 1–2, World War II Survey 8182; Felix Sparks, "Dachau and Its Liberation," Monograph 14, January 1990, pp. 1–2, 8–10; Emmajean Jordan Buechner, ed., "Sparks: the Combat Diary of a Battalion Commander (Rifle), WWII, 157th Infantry, 45th Division, 1941–1945," self-published, 1991, pp. 138–141, all at USAMHI; Felix Sparks, personal account, p. 1, Felix Sparks Collection 41933, LOC; Felix Sparks, interview with the Shoah Foundation, September 12, 1996, USHMM; Flint Whitlock, *The Rock of Anzio From Sicily to Dachau: A History of the U.S. 45th Infantry Division*, Boulder, CO: Westview Press, 1998, pp. 354–356; Alex Kershaw, *The Liberator: One World War II Soldier's 500 Day Odyssey from the Beaches of Sicily to the Gates of Dachau*, New York: Crown Publishers, 2012, pp. 267–268.

10. Don Downard, letter to Dee Eberhart, May 17, 1988, Box 8, Folder 6; Kenneth Ivey, letter to Charles Paine, November 15, 1994, Box 16, Folder 6; Oather Wester, letter to Art Lee, June 26, 1995, Box 13, Folder 10, all at RDVA; Lieutenant William Cowling, letter to family, April 30, 1945, reproduced in Linden, *Surrender of the*

Dachau Concentration Camp, p. 51, USAMHI; Andrew Mollo, "The Webling Incident," *After the Battle*, No. 27, 1980, pp. 30–33; Smith, *Dachau*, pp. 79–80; Dann, *Dachau, 29 April 1945*, pp. 78–79. For a thought-provoking discussion of the Webling incident, see forum.axishistory.com.

11. Verheye is quoted in Michael Hirsh, *The Liberators: America's Witnesses to the Holocaust*, New York: Bantam Books, 2010, pp. 194–195; Richardi, Philipp, and Lucking, *Dachau*, pp. 224–225; Dann, *Dachau, 29 April 1945*, pp. 193–196, 210–211; www .scrapbookpages.com; Jurgen Zarusky, " 'That Is Not the American Way of Fighting': The Shooting of Captured SS-Men During the Liberation of Dachau," *Dachau Review*, 2002, pp. 138–140; Pierre Verheye, *The Train Ride into Hell*, unpublished paper, copy in author's possession courtesy of Carol Leadman and David Sun, Hoover Institution Archives, Stanford University. Mehrbach was tried for war crimes, convicted, and hanged in 1947.

12. Gleb Rahr, letter to Sam Dann, Box 16, Folder 8, RDVA.

13. Anthony Cardinale, letters to Art Lee, c. 1993, Box 10, Folder 5; Anthony Cardinale, letter to Sam Dann, November 8, 1996, Box 16, Folder 5; Joe Balaban, letter to Sam Dann, May 16, 1995, Box 16, Folder 4; Carl Bankovich, letter to Sam Dann, January 14, 1995, Box 9, Folder 3; William Hazard, letter to Art Lee, October 10, 1994, Box 12, Folder 1; Cliff Lohs, letter to Charles Paine, September 27, 1994, Box 16, Folder 7; Alvin Weinstein, letter to Sam Dann, September 9, 1994, Box 16, Folder 9; Downard letter to Eberhart, May 17, 1988; Wester letter to Lee, June 26, 1995, all at RDVA; *42nd "Rainbow" Division: A Combat History of World War II*, self-published (no byline), n.d., pp. 99–104, USAMHI; Joe Hazel, interview with Emmy Huffman, February 25, 2002, Joe Hazel Collection, 299, LOC; Anthony Cardinale, interview with the Shoah Foundation, July 29, 1999, USHMM.

14. *42nd "Rainbow" Division: A Combat History of World War II*, pp. 99–104; Clarence O. Williams, letter to Monroe Freedman, March 1, 1981, International Liberators Collection, Dachau Folders, RG-09.005.09; "Rescued from Pile of Dead Bodies, now Ordained as Rabbi," *Wisconsin Jewish Chronicle*, no author listed, June 15, 1956; Harvey Radish, "North Main Rescuers Offer Rabbi's Shawl to Lad They Saved," *International News Service*, August 27, 1956; Rabbi Abraham Feffer, "My Shtetl Drobin: A Saga of a Survivor," self-published, 1990, p. 65; Mrs. Beth Feffer, widow of Abraham, conversations with the author, July 10, 28, 2014; Miriam Feffer, daughter of Abraham, conversation with the author, July 15, 2014; Rabbi Abraham Feffer, interview with the Shoah Foundation, July 21, 1995, copy in author's possession courtesy of Beth Feffer. Hazel refused to talk about Dachau in his interview, but he was identified by several of his fellow soldiers as the man who put Feffer into the jeep. Moreover, the resemblance between a 1945 rescuer photo and the photo in his LOC collection is unmistakable. Williams, a 42nd Division medic, wrote to Freedman in 1981 of the death train: "Only one person was found alive and he later became a Chaplain in the U.S. Army. His name was Rabbi Abraham Feffer." In 1956, Sparks and some of his former soldiers presented the newly minted rabbi and chaplain Feffer with the gift of a prayer shawl. It seems that the 42nd Division veterans had no idea of this. Oddly

enough, Rabbi Feffer never spoke of the death train in his Shoah interview—he only vaguely related that he was liberated by the Americans "five or ten miles south of Dachau." Nor did he ever discuss the death train with his family members. Because of this inconsistency, I cannot say with certainty that he was the death train survivor, though I believe it is probable.

15. Arthur Haulot, letter to Colonel John H. Linden, October 9, 1995, reproduced in Linden, *Surrender of the Dachau Concentration Camp*, pp. 127–128; Sol Feingold, letters to Curtis Whiteway, September 27 and November 3, 1991, Curtis Whiteway Papers, Box 1, Folder 3, both at USAMHI; Felix Sparks, letter to Colonel Robert Sholly, U.S. Army Center of Military History, March 12, 1992, Box 15, Folder 3, RDVA; Ed Drea, "Recognizing the Liberators: U.S. Army Divisions Enter the Concentration Camps," *Army History*, Fall/Winter 1992–1993, pp. 1–5. The list of officially recognized liberator units is documented at www.ushmm.org.

16. 157th Infantry Regiment, History, April 1945; Unit Journal, April 29, 1945; S3 Journal, April 29, 1945, all at NA; Jack Hallowell, interview with Susan Singer, 1981 International Liberators Conference, Box 5, Folder 118; Thomas Spruell, "Witness to the Holocaust," panel participant, c. 1981, Dr. Fred Crawford, moderator, Box 5, Folder 125, both at EU; Sparks, unpublished memoir, p. 3; Sparks, diary, pp. 140–141; Sparks, "Dachau and Its Liberation," pp. 8–9, all at USAMHI; Sparks, interview with the Shoah Foundation, USHMM; James Kent Strong, *The Liberation of KZ Dachau* (documentary), Coronado, CA: Strong Communications, 1990. Strong was the son-in-law of a 45th Division veteran. His fascinating documentary includes extensive interviews with Sparks, Walsh, and several other former soldiers.

17. 157th Infantry Regiment, History, April 1945; Unit Journal, April 29, 1945; S3 Journal, April 29, 1945, all at NA; Sparks, unpublished memoir, p. 3; Sparks, diary, pp. 140–141; Sparks, "Dachau and Its Liberation," pp. 8–9, all at USAMHI; Sparks, interview with the Shoah Foundation, USHMM; Strong, *The Liberation of KZ Dachau*; Thomas Farragher, "The Secret History of World War II: Part V, Vengeance at Dachau," *Boston Globe*, July 2, 2001; Whitlock, *The Rock of Anzio From Sicily to Dachau*, pp. 359–360.

18. Strong, *The Liberation of KZ Dachau*.

19. Lieutenant Colonel Joseph Whitaker, Inspector General Division, Seventh Army, *Investigation of Alleged Mistreatment of German Guards at Dachau*, May–June 1945, Record Group 338, Entry 50170, Box 7, Seventh Army Report of Investigations (at the beginning of this document, there is a table of contents itemized by the names of the witnesses); 157th Infantry Regiment, History, April 1945, both at NA; another copy of Whitaker's inspector general report is in Box 22, Folder 2, RDVA; Howard Buechner, *Dachau: Hour of the Avenger, an Eyewitness Account*, self-published memoir, 1986, p. 29; Sparks, "Dachau and Its Liberation," pp. 8–10, both at USAMHI; Sparks, interview with the Shoah Foundation, USHMM; Strong, *Liberation of KZ Dachau*; Zarusky, "That Is Not the American Way of Fighting," p. 143; Farragher, "The Secret History of World War II: Part V, Vengeance at Dachau," *Boston Globe*; www.scrap bookpages.com. Rawson (*In Pursuit of Hitler*, p. 180) states that the man with the

Red Cross flag was Heinrich Skodzensky and that he was attempting to surrender his command. However, Rawson provides no citation or evidence to back up the point. Sparks was a very composed, effective speaker. During the interview for the Strong documentary, as he discussed the raw emotions of his soldiers, even he choked up for the briefest of moments.

CHAPTER FIVE: "My Heart Was Going a Mile a Minute": Liberating Dachau

1. Guido Oddi, letter to Charles Paine, n.d., Box 16, Folder 7; Harry Shaffer, letters to Howard Buechner and Sol Feingold, c. 1988 and 1990, letter to Art Lee, November 19, 1992, all in Box 14, Folder 7, RDVA; William Donahue, interview with the Shoah Foundation, June 10, 1997, USHMM. Background information on General Henning Linden is accessible at www.ww2gravestone.com and www.findagrave.com.

2. 42nd Infantry Division, AAR, April 1945, NA; Brigadier General Henning Linden, *Memo to Commanding General Regarding Dachau*, May 2, 1945, Box 22, Folder 5; Shaffer, letters to Buechner, Feingold, and Lee; Harry Shaffer, letter to wife, April 29, 1945, letter to Sam Dann, October 10, 1996, Box 16, Folder 9; Oddi, letter to Paine; Paul Levy, report, April 29, 1945, one-year retrospective on Dachau liberation, Folders 4 and 7, Box 8; Paul Levy, letter to Sol Feingold, February 29, 1992, Box 9, Folder 6; Paul Levy, answers to questions from Sol Feingold, August 16, 1994, Box 12, Folder 2, all at RDVA; Linden, self-published monograph, *Surrender of the Dachau Concentration Camp, 29 April 1945: The True Account*, 1997, pp. 11–12, 16–17, 109–114; Colin Hickey, "General Henning Linden: He Appreciates Life, Witnessed World War II Horrors," article for Chantilly (VA) high school newspaper, January 21, 1980, 42nd Infantry Division Papers, Box 32, Folder 2, both at USAMHI; Donahue, interview with the Shoah Foundation, USHMM; Sam Dann, ed., *Dachau, 29 April 1945: The Rainbow Liberation Memoirs*, Lubbock, TX: Texas Tech University Press, 1998, p. 13; Marguerite Higgins, *News Is a Singular Thing*, Garden City, NJ: Doubleday, 1955, pp. 89–90; www.findagrave.com. Within minutes of the camp's liberation, Levy did indeed reunite with Haulot, who had become one of the main leaders among the prisoners.

3. Brigadier General Henning Linden, PFC John Veitch, Tech 5 John Bauerlein, First Lieutenant William Cowling, testimony in Joseph Whitaker, *Investigation of Alleged Mistreatment of German Guards at Dachau*, May–June 1945, Record Group 338, Entry 50170, Box 7, Seventh Army Report of Investigations, NA; Linden, *Surrender of the Dachau Concentration Camp, 29 April 1945*, pp. 21–28, 61, 109–116, USAMHI; Lieutenant William Cowling, report, May 2, 1945, Box 8, Folder 4; Linden, *Memo to Commanding General Regarding Dachau*; Shaffer, letters to Buechner, Feingold, and Lee; Oddi, letter to Paine; Levy, report, one-year retrospective on Dachau liberation, letter to Sol Feingold, answers to questions, all at RDVA; Donahue, interview with the Shoah Foundation, USHMM; www.scrapbookpages.com; Dann, *Dachau, 29 April 1945*, pp. 22–23, 54–55; Flint Whitlock, *The Rock of Anzio From Sicily to Dachau: A History of the U.S. 45th Infantry Division*, Boulder, CO: Westview Press, 1998, pp. 370–372.

4. 157th Infantry Regiment, AAR, April 1945, NA; PFC John Lee, Lieutenant Wil-

liam Walsh, testimony in Whitaker, *Investigation of Alleged Mistreatment of German Guards at Dachau*; Felix Sparks, interview with the Shoah Foundation, September 12, 1996, USHMM; James Kent Strong, *The Liberation of KZ Dachau* (documentary), Coronado, CA: Strong Communications, 1990; Jurgen Zarusky, "'That Is Not the American Way of Fighting': The Shooting of Captured SS-Men During the Liberation of Dachau," *Dachau Review*, 2002, p. 143; Thomas Farragher, "The Secret History of World War II: Part V, Vengeance at Dachau," *Boston Globe*, July 2, 2001; Whitlock, *The Rock of Anzio From Sicily to Dachau*, pp. 361–364; Alex Kershaw, *The Liberator: One World War II Soldier's 500 Day Odyssey from the Beaches of Sicily to the Gates of Dachau*, New York: Crown Publishers, 2012, pp. 277–281. Linberger's sworn testimony is at www.scrapbookpages.com. Sparks was well aware of Walsh's volatility. Fifty years after Dachau's liberation, he referred to Walsh as "a loose bullet" in a conversation with a 42nd Division veteran. The documentation for this is in Box 18, Folder 8 at RDVA.

5. Lieutenant Joseph Whitaker, *Observation of Dachau, May 3, 1945, Diagram of Coal Yard Shooting, Report and Conclusions*; Lieutenant Donald Strickland, PFC William Competielle, PFC George Larson, Lieutenant Jack Busheyhead, Lieutenant William Walsh, PFC John Lee, Lieutenant Daniel Drain, Corporal Martin Sedler, Private William Curtin, Lieutenant Howard Buechner, PFC Frank Eggert, testimony all in Whitaker, *Investigation of Alleged Mistreatment of German Guards at Dachau*, NA; Felix Sparks, unpublished memoir, pp. 4–5, World War II Survey 8182; Felix Sparks, "Dachau and Its Liberation," Monograph 14, January 1990, pp. 11–13; Howard Buechner, *Dachau: Hour of the Avenger, an Eyewitness Account*, self-published memoir, 1986, all at USAMHI; Felix Sparks, personal account, Felix Sparks Collection 41933, LOC; Sparks, interview with the Shoah Foundation, USHMM; Howard Buechner, letter to Art Lee, March 14, 1993, Box 10, Folder 5, RDVA; Strong, *The Liberation of KZ Dachau*; www.scrapbookpages.com.

6. Whitaker, *Observation of Dachau, May 3, 1945, Diagram of Coal Yard Shooting, Report and Conclusions*; Whitaker, *Investigation of Alleged Mistreatment of German Guards at Dachau*, NA; Sparks, unpublished memoir, pp. 4–5; Sparks, "Dachau and Its Liberation," pp. 11–13; Buechner, *Dachau: Hour of the Avenger*, all at USAMHI; Sparks, personal account, LOC; Sparks, interview with the Shoah Foundation, USHMM; Buechner, letter to Lee, RDVA; Strong, *The Liberation of KZ Dachau*; Zarusky, "'That Is Not the American Way of Fighting,'" pp. 144–145; Farragher, "The Secret History of World War II: Part V, Vengeance at Dachau"; Whitlock, *The Rock of Anzio From Sicily to Dachau*, pp. 364–365; www.scrapbookpages.com. The woman and two children treated by Competielle may have been the wife and kids of a local doctor named Muller. According to Linberger, Muller's wife and two children poisoned themselves when the Americans liberated the camp. Competielle mentioned that he took his three patients to the hospital, where an unnamed German doctor gave them some kind of shot, "but that did not help them because all three of them passed away."

7. Lieutenant Colonel Joseph Whitaker, recommendations, report and conclusions, Lieutenant General Wade Haislip, summary of action and conclusions, Lieutenant Harold Moyer, testimony, *Investigation of Alleged Mistreatment of German Guards at*

Dachau, NA; Art Lee, letter to Sol Feingold, October 31, 1992, Box 10, Folder 3, RDVA; Strong, *The Liberation of KZ Dachau*; Farragher, "The Secret History of World War II: Part V, Vengeance at Dachau"; Whitlock, *The Rock of Anzio From Sicily to Dachau*, pp. 365–366, 388–391. The main flaw in Whitaker's investigation was his failure to get sworn testimony from Sparks. As we shall see, though, Sparks was quickly relieved of his command and transferred to the Assembly Area Command in Reims, France before Whitaker began his investigation in earnest.

8. Nerin Gun, *The Day of the Americans*, New York: Fleet Publishing Corporation, 1966, pp. 17–22.

9. Cowling report, May 2, 1945, letter to family; Oddi, letter to Paine; Linden, *Memo to Commanding General Regarding Dachau*, all at RDVA. For more information on the bitter controversy between veterans of the two divisions, see the Sparks letter to Colonel Sholly in Box 15, Folder 3, Lieutenant Colonel Hugh Foster's correspondence in Box 17, Folder 3, Sol Feingold's correspondence in Box 8, Folders 6 and 9, Box 12, Folders 3 and 4, and Box 14, Folder 7, all at RDVA; Linden, *Surrender of the Dachau Concentration Camp, 29 April 1945*, pp. 28–29, USAMHI; Strong, *The Liberation of KZ Dachau*; Gun, *The Day of the Americans*, pp. 17–22; Higgins, *News Is a Singular Thing*, pp. 91–92; Whitlock, *The Rock of Anzio From Sicily to Dachau*, pp. 372–373. According to Gun, the Frenchman who mistook Higgins for a man was actually a Catholic priest and was thus quite embarrassed to have made such close physical contact with her. Contrary to Higgins, Gun claimed that the SS prisoner guide was arrested by the International Prisoners Committee, sentenced to death, and executed that night by firing squad.

10. Lieutenant Colonel Walter Fellenz, Walteny Lanarczyk, Tech 3 Henry Wells, Sergeant Robert Killiam, Tech 5 John Bauerlein, Lieutenant William Cowling, Brigadier General Henning Linden, PFC John Veitch, Tech 4 Anthony Cardinale, testimony in Whitaker, *Investigation of Alleged Mistreatment of German Guards at Dachau*, NA; Jacques Songy, letter to Sol Feingold, Box 21, Folder 1; Gleb Rahr, letter to Sam Dann, October 25, 1994, Box 16, Folder 8; Stephan Ross, unpublished memoir, pp. 2–3, Box 16, Folder 4; Cowling report, May 2, 1945, letter to family; Linden, *Memo to Commanding General Regarding Dachau*, all at RDVA; Linden, *Surrender of the Dachau Concentration Camp, 29 April 1945*, pp. 29–30; Donahue, interview with Shoah Foundation, USHMM; Strong, *The Liberation of KZ Dachau*; Gun, *The Day of the Americans*, pp. 195, 200–202; Higgins, *News Is a Singular Thing*, p. 95; Yaffa Eliach and Brana Gurewitsch, eds., *The Liberators: Eyewitness Accounts of the Liberation of Concentration Camps*, Brooklyn, NY: Center for Holocaust Studies Documentation and Research, 1981, pp. 35–36; www.scrapbookpages.com.

11. Linden, *Memo to Commanding General Regarding Dachau*; Cowling report, May 2, 1945, letter to family, all at RDVA; Linden, *Surrender of the Dachau Concentration Camp, 29 April 1945*, pp. 29–30, USAMHI.

12. Sparks, unpublished memoir, pp. 4–6; Emmajean Jordan Buechner, ed., "Sparks: the Combat Diary of a Battalion Commander (Rifle), WWII, 157th Infantry, 45th Division, 1941–1945," self-published, 1991, pp. 142–154; Sparks, "Dachau and

Its Liberation," pp. 15–28; Buechner, *Dachau: Hour of the Avenger*, pp. 64–72, all at USAMHI; Sparks, interview with Shoah Foundation, USHMM; Strong, *The Liberation of KZ Dachau*. In the Shoah interview, Sparks implied that one of the reasons he never suffered any consequences for threatening Linden was because the married general was only at Dachau to impress Marguerite Higgins. "It didn't look good for . . . an assistant division commander to go out of his territory, into somebody else's territory with a nice looking young babe so she could conduct interviews. But that's the sole reason they were there." This allegation was as scurrilous as it was erroneous.

13. 222nd Infantry Regiment, Unit Journal, April 29, 1945; 157th Infantry Regiment, Unit Journal, April 29–May 1, 1945; S3 Journal, April 29–May 2, 1945; 3rd Battalion, 157th Infantry Regiment, S2/S3 Journal, April 29–May 1, 1945; Whitaker, *Investigation of Alleged Mistreatment of German Guards at Dachau*, all at NA; Brigadier General Charles Banfill, Deputy Chief of Operations, Eighth Air Force, memo, May 28, 1945, Box 23, Folder 1; Sol Feingold to Art Lee, *Report on Conversation with Peter Furst*, March 17, 1995, Box 12, Folder 3; Levy, letter to Feingold; Linden, *Memo to Commanding General Regarding Dachau*; Cowling report, May 2, 1945, letter to family; Oddi, letter to Paine, all at RDVA; Linden, "Dachau and Its Liberation," pp. 40–41, 69–92, 117, 143–149; Donahue Shoah interview, USHMM; Whitlock, *The Rock of Anzio From Sicily to Dachau*, pp. 377–381.

14. 157th Infantry Regiment, Unit Journal, April 29–May 1, 1945; S3 Journal, April 29–May 2, 1945; 3rd Battalion, 157th Infantry Regiment, S2/S3 Journal, April 29–May 1, 1945; Whitaker, *Investigation of Alleged Mistreatment of German Guards at Dachau*, all at NA; Brigadier Headquarters and Headquarters Company, 3rd Battalion, 157th Infantry Regiment, April 30–May 5, 1945; Headquarters, Assembly Area Command, April 30–July 14, 1945, all at National Personnel Records Center, St. Louis, MO; Art Lee, "Dachau and Its Liberators," 42nd Infantry Division Papers, Box 32, Folder 1, RDVA; Linden, *Surrender of the Dachau Concentration Camp, 29 April 1945*, pp. 40–41, 69–92, 117, 143–149; Sparks, "Dachau and Its Liberation," both at USAMHI; Charles R. Codman, *Drive*, New York: Little, Brown and Company, 1957, pp. 318–319; Andrew Rawson, *In Pursuit of Hitler: A Battlefield Guide to Bavaria*, South Yorkshire, UK: Pen & Sword, 2008, pp. 182–183; Higgins, *News Is a Singular Thing*, pp. 94–95; Whitlock, *The Rock of Anzio From Sicily to Dachau*, pp. 377–381. The accounts that most closely repeat the Sparks story verbatim are United States Memorial Holocaust Museum, *1945: The Year of Liberation*, Washington, DC: Holocaust Publications, 1995; Robert Abzug, *Inside the Vicious Heart: Americans and the Liberation of Nazi Concentration Camps*, New York: Oxford University Press, 1985, pp. 95–100; and Alex Kershaw, *The Liberator: One World War II Soldier's 500 Day Odyssey from the Beaches of Sicily to the Gates of Dachau*, New York: Crown Publishers, 2012, pp. 293–298, 309–320. Eisenhower's order was in paragraph 15, Special Orders 116. *Surrender of the Dachau Concentration Camp, 29 April 1945* might be a questionable source because it was written by the son of General Linden, largely in response to the Sparks story. However, this unpublished book is extremely well researched, with heavy reliance on primary sources, photographic evidence, and direct eyewitness testimony, both

contemporary and historical. Moreover, I have examined the primary sources myself and corroborated the original information. Although Higgins never mentioned any problem between General Linden and Lieutenant Colonel Sparks, she did claim to have had an argument with Linden when he told her to leave the compound because typhus was rife among the prisoners. Several other correspondents, including Paul Levy, Peter Furst, Sydney Olson of *Time*, and Howard Cowan of *The New York Times* were all present at Dachau that day. None ever wrote about a violent altercation between the two officers. General George Patton's visit to America is a well-known fact, especially because he made several public appearances, quite a few of which were documented in newspaper stories.

CHAPTER SIX: Dachau: The Impact

1. Darrell Martin, unpublished memoir, p. 30, Box 16, Folder 7; Bob Perelman, letter to Sam Dann, November 17, 1996, Box 16, Folder 8; Lieutenant Colonel Walter Fellenz, *Memo for the Commanding General*, May 6, 1945, Box 13, Folder 9; William Cowling, report, May 2, 1945, letter to family, April 30, 1945, Box 8, Folder 4; Brigadier General Henning Linden, *Memo to Commanding General Regarding Dachau*, May 2, 1945, Box 22, Folder 5, all at RDVA; Robert Stubenrauch, interview with the Shoah Foundation, December 12, 1996; Sergeant Ernest Henry, letter to wife, June 5, 1945, 1998.36; Jim Dorris, interview with the Shoah Foundation, June 11, 1997, all at USHMM; Bill Harr, *Combat Boots: Tales of Fighting Men, Including the Anzio Derby*, New York: Exposition Press, 1952, pp. 220–221.

2. C. Paul Rogers, letter to Sam Dann, November 4, 1993, Box 8, Folder 4; Russell McFarland, narrative statement, n.d., Box 16, Folder 7; Howard Margol, narrative statement, n.d., Box 16, Folder 7; Martin, unpublished memoir, p. 30; Fellenz, *Memo for the Commanding General*, all at RDVA; Thomas Spruell, "Witness to the Holocaust," panel participant, c. 1981, Dr. Fred Crawford, moderator, Box 5, Folder 125; Henry "Hank" DeJarnette, interview with Center for Holocaust Studies, October 29, 1981, Box 5, Folder 110, both at EU; Henry "Hank" DeJarnette, interview with the Shoah Foundation, July 9, 1997; Henry, letter to wife, both at USHMM; Andrew Carroll, ed., *Behind the Lines: Powerful and Revealing American and Foreign War Letters—and One Man's Search to Find Them*, New York: Simon & Schuster, 2005, pp. 336–338.

3. Clifford Barrett, letter to Sam Dann, June 16, 1996, Box 16, Folder 4; Jack Westbrook, unpublished memoir, p. 2, Box 9, Folder 2; Pat Stangl and Mary Stangl, *Unsung Heroes: Two Years in the Life of a Foot Soldier*, self-published memoir, 2000, pp. 282–284, all at USAMHI; Clifford Barrett, letter to Mr. Lerman, March 23, 1981, RG-09.005 09; Morton Barrish, interview with the Shoah Foundation, June 25, 1998; Stubenrauch, interview with the Shoah Foundation, all at USHMM; James Kent Strong, *The Liberation of KZ Dachau* (documentary), Coronado, CA: Strong Communications, 1990; Sam Dann, ed., *Dachau, 29 April 1945: The Rainbow Liberation Memoirs*, Lubbock, TX: Texas Tech University Press, 1998, pp. 13, 159–162.

4. Morris Eisenstein, narrative statement, n.d., Box 8, Folder 4; Eli Heimberg, un-

published memoir, pp. 1–3, Box 16, Folder 6; Gleb Rahr, letter to Sam Dann, October 25, 1994, Box 16, Folder 8; Stephan Ross, unpublished memoir, p. 3, Box 16, Folder 4, all at RDVA; Rabbi Eli Bohnen, letter to Mr. Lerman, March 1, 1981, RG-09.005 09; Ralph Fink, letter to United States Holocaust Memorial Council, March 26, 1981, International Liberator Collection, Dachau Folders; Ralph Fink, interview with the Shoah Foundation, August 19, 1997; Eli Heimberg, interview with the Shoah Foundation, October 24, 1997, all at USHMM; Eli Heimberg, interview with Michael Hirsh, September 21, 2008, Scholar Commons, University of South Florida; Strong, *The Liberation of KZ Dachau*; Dann, *Dachau, 29 April 1945*, pp. 13, 159–162.

5. John Walker, Veterans Survey 3038, 42nd Infantry Division Survey Material, Box 1; Donald MacDonald, Veterans Survey 5926, 45th Infantry Division Survey Material, both at USAMHI; Henry "Hank" DeJarnette, letter to Sam Dann, August 24, 1994, Box 16, Folder 5; Fred Peterson, letters to Sam Dann, c. 1994, Box 16, Folder 8; Walter "Mickey" Fellenz, interview with Yaffa Eliach, c. 1975, Box 21, Folder 4; Clifford Barrett, letter to Sam Dann, June 16, 1996, Box 16, Folder 4, all at RDVA; DeJarnette, interview with the Shoah Foundation; Clifford Barrett, letter to Miles Lerman, March 23, 1981, International Liberators Collection, Dachau Folders, RG-09.005 09, both at USHMM; DeJarnette, interview with Center for Holocaust Studies, EU; Strong, *The Liberation of KZ Dachau*; Flint Whitlock, *The Rock of Anzio From Sicily to Dachau: A History of the U.S. 45th Infantry Division*, Boulder, CO: Westview Press, 1998, p. 404.

6. Scott Corbett, letter to Art Lee, January 9, 1995, Box 16, Folder 5, RDVA; Captain Lewis A. Greene, letter to family, April 30, 1945, Box 2, Folder 43; Carlyle Woelfer, interview with unidentified, n.d., Box 4, Folder 101, both at EU; Harr, *Combat Boots*, p. 221.

7. May Craig, "In the Wake of the War," *Portland (ME) Press Herald*, May 29, 1945, Record Group 112, Entry UD1012, Box 86, Folder 6, NA; Dee Eberhart, narrative statement, n.d., Box 16, Folder 6; Jerome Klein, letter to Sam Dann, September 22, 1996, Box 16, Folder 7; Alvin Weinstein, letter to Sam Dann, Box 16, Folder 9, all at RDVA; PFC Harold Porter, letter to parents, May 7, 1945, World War II Participants and Contemporaries Collection, EL; Henry, letter to wife, USHMM; Lawrence Rogers recollections in *Field Dispatch*, Vol. 6, No. 1, Adolph Walter Collection, SLHOL; Strong, *The Liberation of KZ Dachau*; Whitlock, *The Rock of Anzio From Sicily to Dachau*, p. 402. The bodies were buried or cremated only after legal investigation teams had inspected and thoroughly documented them as evidence for war crimes trials.

8. XV Corps, G5 Journal, April 28–May 3, 1945; G5 Report, April–May, 1945, both at NA; Carol Byerly, "*Good Tuberculosis Men*": *The Army Medical Department's Struggle with Tuberculosis*, Ft. Sam Houston, TX: Office of the Surgeon General, 2009, pp. 292–294; Graham Cosmas and Albert Cowdrey, *United States Army in World War II: The Technical Services, the Medical Department: Medical Service in the European Theater of Operations*, Washington, DC: Center of Military History, United States Army, 1992, pp. 574–576; Marcus Smith, *Dachau: The Harrowing of Hell*, Albuquerque, NM: University of New Mexico Press, 1972, pp. 88–93, 98–99.

9. 127th Evacuation Hospital, Unit History, July 1, 1945, Record Group 112, Entry UD1012, Box 87, Folder 11; 116th Evacuation Hospital, Record of Events, May–June 1945; Unit History, May 1945; Unit History, June 30, 1945, all in Record Group 112, Entry UD1012, Box 86, Folder 6; XV Corps, G5 Report, April–May 1945, all at NA; Porter, letter to parents, May 7, 1945; Albert Cowdrey, *Fighting for Life: American Military Medicine in World War II*, New York: Free Press, 1994, pp. 288–289; Byerly, "*Good Tuberculosis Men*," pp. 294–296; Cosmas and Cowdrey, *United States Army in World War II*, pp. 576–577; Smith, *Dachau*, pp. 110–113.

10. PFC Harold Porter, letters to parents, May 10, May 19, May 31, June 28, 1945, all at World War II Participants and Contemporaries Collection, EL.

11. 127th Evacuation Hospital, Unit History; 116th Evacuation Hospital, Unit Histories, both at NA; Michelle Korn, letter, n.d., *Field Dispatch*, Vol. 11, No. 1, Adolph Walter Collection, SLHOL; Byerly, "*Good Tuberculosis Men*," pp. 295–296; Smith, *Dachau*, pp. 104–106; Nerin Gun, *The Day of the Americans*, New York: Fleet Publishing Corporation, 1966, pp. 208–224. Gun's fever was so bad that he nearly died.

12. May Craig, "In the Wake of the War"; XV Corps, G5 Report, April–May, 1945; 127th Evacuation Hospital, Unit History; 116th Evacuation Hospital, Unit Histories, Record of Events, all at NA; Charlotte Chaney, interview with the Shoah Foundation, May 23, 1995, USHMM; Yaffa Eliach and Brana Gurewitsch, eds., *The Liberators: Eyewitness Accounts of the Liberation of Concentration Camps*, Brooklyn, NY: Center for Holocaust Studies Documentation and Research, 1981, pp. 45–48; Smith, *Dachau*, pp. 243–244; Dann, *Dachau, 29 April 1945*, p. 211; Michael Hirsh, *The Liberators: America's Witnesses to the Holocaust*, New York: Bantam Books, 2010, pp. 214–218; Cosmas and Cowdrey, *United States Army in World War II*, pp. 577–578. Craig was a former women's suffrage activist who enjoyed a long and distinguished journalistic career. By World War II, she was already well known for her reporting as a White House correspondent. She wrote a popular national column called "Inside Washington."

13. William Quinn, interview with the Shoah Foundation, July 17, 1997, USHMM; William Quinn, interview with Dr. Fred Crawford, May 7, 1981, Box 3, Folder 74; Edouard Izac, interview with Fred Crawford, May 7, 1981, both at EU; Hon. R. E. Thomason, *German Atrocities: Official Report of the Congressional Investigating Committee*, May 15, 1945, R. E. Thomason Papers, MS140, Series II, Box 6, Folder 10, Special Collections Library, UTEP; E Company, 232nd Infantry Regiment, History, 42nd Infantry Division Papers, Box 27, Folder 7, USAMHI; Seventh Army, *Dachau*, self-published pamphlet, May 1945, p. 5.

Epilogue

1. Rabbi Eli Bohnen, letter to Mr. Lerman, March 1, 1981, RG-09.005 09, USHMM.

2. Joseph Pulitzer, *A Report to the American People*, a publication of the *St. Louis Post-Dispatch*, n.d., pp. 85–125, SLHOL.

3. Pulitzer, *A Report to the American People*, pp. 9, 85–125, SLHOL; Robert Abzug,

Inside the Vicious Heart: Americans and the Liberation of Nazi Concentration Camps, New York: Oxford University Press, 1985, pp. 132–137.

4. www.ushmm.org; www.scrapbookpages.com; www.chgs.umn.edu; www.bu chenwald.de.

5. Andrew Mollo, "Dachau," *After the Battle*, No. 27, 1980, pp. 20–29; www.ushmm .org; www.scrapbookpages.com; www.chgs.umn.edu; www.buchenwald.de; Barbara Distel, *Dachau Concentration Camp*, pamphlet, 1972, p. 21, copy in author's possession; James Kent Strong, *The Liberation of KZ Dachau* (documentary), Coronado, CA: Strong Communications, 1990; Hans-Günter Richardi, Eleonore Philipp, Monika Lücking, Greg Bond, eds., *Dachau: A Guide to Its Contemporary History*, Dachau, Germany: City of Dachau Office of Cultural Affairs, 2001, pp. 244–292; Andrew Rawson, *In Pursuit of Hitler: A Battlefield Guide to Bavaria*, South Yorkshire, UK: Pen & Sword, 2008, pp. 183–192; Dachau, personal survey by the author, c. 2004. A few veterans who visited the former camps were displeased and saddened by the commemorative museums. In the Strong documentary, Howard Buechner said of his latter-year visit to Dachau: "I came away with almost a greater sense of sadness than when I left it the first time."

6. John Searle, Veterans Survey 3012, USAMHI; Ernest Comito, narrative statement, n.d., General Collection, Box 1, Folder 27; Elmer Joachim, personal account, General Collection, Box 1, Folder 28, both at SLHOL; Don Downard, letter to Dee Eberhart, May 17, 1988, Box 8, Folder 6, RDVA; Ralph Fink, letter to United States Holocaust Memorial Council, March 26, 1981, International Liberator Collection, Dachau Folders; Ralph Fink, interview with the Shoah Foundation, August 19, 1997, USHMM; Harry Blumenthal, narrative statement, September 8, 2006, www.bu chenwaldandbeyond.com. For more information on the motivation to fight among American combat soldiers in World War II, see my book *The Deadly Brotherhood: The American Combat Soldier in World War II*, New York: Ballantine Books, 2003.

7. Henry "Hank" DeJarnette, interview with the Shoah Foundation, July 9, 1997; Morton Barrish, interview with the Shoah Foundation, June 25, 1998; Fink, interview with the Shoah Foundation, all at USHMM; Fred Peterson, letters to Sam Dann, c. 1994, Box 16, Folder 8, RDVA; William Deierhoi, narrative statement, n.d.; Jerry Hontas, narrative statement, n.d.; Blumenthal, narrative statement, n.d., all at www .buchenwaldandbeyond.com; Theresa Ast, "Confronting the Holocaust: American Soldiers Who Liberated the Concentration Camps," PhD Dissertation, 2000, Emory University, pp. 259–270.

8. Irving Lisman, letter to Curtis Whiteway, January 13, 1984, Curtis Whiteway Papers, Box 2, Folder 4, USAMHI; Jimmy Gentry, interview with Dr. G. Kurt Piehler and Kelly Hammond, July 22, 2000, CSWS; Howard Margol, interview with Kaethe Solomon, June 14, 1979, Box 3, Folder 60; Dennis Wile, interview with Dr. Fred Crawford, August 8, 1978, Box 4, Folder 98, both at EU; www.buchenwaldandbeyond.com; Ast, "Confronting the Holocaust," pp. 259–270; Strong, *The Liberation of KZ Dachau*; Marcus Smith, *Dachau: The Harrowing of Hell*, Albuquerque, NM: University of New Mexico Press, 1972, pp. 278–279.

9. George Jackson, unpublished memoir, pp. 2–3, Box 16, Folder 6; Clarence "Buster" Hart, correspondence, 1994–1996, Box 16, Folder 6, both at RDVA; Robert Perelman, interview with Chicago Judaica Museum, December 10, 1980, Box 3, Folder 72, EU; Eugene Glick, letter to Mr. Lerman, October 12, 1981, International Liberators Collection, Dachau Folders; Clifford Barrett, letter to Miles Lerman, March 23, 1981, International Liberators Collection, Dachau Folders, RG-09.005 09, both at USHMM; James Mahoney, narrative statement, n.d., www.buchenwaldand beyond.com; Whitlock, *The Rock of Anzio From Sicily to Dachau: A History of the U.S. 45th Infantry Division*, Boulder, CO: Westview Press, 1998, p. 402.

10. Neil Frey, letter to William Paine, October 7, 1994, Box 16, Folder 6; Sam Platamone, letter to Sam Dann, November 29, 1996, Box 16, Folder 8; Bill Keithan, narrative statement, n.d., Box 16, Folder 7, all at RDVA; Harold Davis, letter to Curtis Whiteway, January 5, 1984, Curtis Whiteway Papers, Box 1, Folder 2, USAMHI; Fred Mercer, interview with Kaethe Solomon, June 8, 1980, Box 3, Folder 63, EU; Donald Johnson, letter to United States Holocaust Memorial Council, April 13, 1981, International Liberators Collection, Ohrdruf Folders, USHMM; Blumenthal statement, www.buchenwaldandbeyond.com; Strong, *The Liberation of KZ Dachau*; Bill Harr, *Combat Boots: Tales of Fighting Men, Including the Anzio Derby*, New York: Exposition Press, 1952, p. 219; Smith, *Dachau*, p. 279.

11. Stephan Ross, letter to Donald Segal, August 10, 1990, Curtis Whiteway Papers, Box 1, Folder 3, USAMHI; Walter Fellenz, letter to the editor, *New York Times*, December 22, 1977, copy located in Box 14, Folder 9; Kenneth Ivey, letter to Charles Paine, November 15, 1994, Box 16, Folder 6; Anthony Cardinale, letter to Sam Dann, November 8, 1996, Box 16, Folder 5, all at RDVA; Glick, letter to Mr. Lerman, USHMM; Jon Marcus, "War and Remembrance," *Boston Magazine*, May 2002; Whitlock, *The Rock of Anzio From Sicily to Dachau*, p. 404. For an introduction to the historiography of Holocaust denial/skepticism, see Gerald L. K. Smith, *The Cross and the Flag* magazine; Paul Rassinier, *The Drama of European Jewry*, Paris: Aux Sept Couleurs, 1964; articles by Harry Elmer Barnes in the *Rampart Journal*; Austin App, *The Six Million Swindle*, self-published pamphlet, 1973; Arthur Butz, *The Hoax of the Twentieth Century: The Case Against the Presumed Extermination of European Jewry*, Uckfield, UK: Historical Review Press, 1976; David Irving, *Hitler's War*, London: Hodder & Stoughton, 1977; Willis Carto's Liberty Lobby organization; Lewis Brandon's Institute for Historical Review; Bradley Smith's Committee for Open Debate on the Holocaust; and Don Black's White Pride World Wide at www.stormfront.org. Black is associated with the Ku Klux Klan.

SUGGESTED FURTHER READING

The Holocaust is one of the most heavily studied and best-documented events in human history. The topic is multidimensional, so much so that it is nearly impossible for any single individual to absorb all of the available literature. Several ambitious studies do attempt to relate the larger story as a whole. They serve as a nice starting point for those who wish to get acquainted with the basics of the Holocaust. Lucy Dawidowicz's *The War Against the Jews, 1933–1945* (New York: Holt, Rinehart and Winston, 1975) asserts that World War II in Europe was primarily about Germany's struggle to subdue and eliminate the continent's Jewish population. Martin Gilbert's *The Holocaust* (New York: Henry Holt and Company, 1985) is a vast, sprawling examination of the rise of anti-Semitism in Germany and Nazi atrocities against Jews, especially in eastern Europe. *The Destruction of the European Jews* by Raul Hilberg (New York: Holmes and Meier, 1985) takes more or less the same approach. Originally published in 1961, Hilberg revised it over the next several decades with much original research on the genocide of the Jews. In *The Holocaust: The Fate of European Jewry, 1932–1945* (New York: Oxford University Press, 1990), Leni Yahil argues that Hitler had a long-term, consistent plan to make war on the Jews and destroy them and that this informed nearly all of his wartime decisions. She also challenges the notion that Jews meekly acquiesced to their own destruction, demonstrating that they actively resisted with partisan warfare and multiple uprisings.

The limitation of all these studies is that they see the Holocaust as predominantly an anti-Jewish event, when in fact the Nazis targeted many ethnic and political groups for enslavement and destruction. (In fact, one could argue that the Holocaust was every bit as much about the exploitation of slave labor as the genocide of targeted groups.) More recently, Donald Bloxham in *The Final Solution: A Genocide* (New York: Oxford University Press, 2009) has broadened our understanding of the Holocaust through extensive coverage of Hitler's many non-Jewish victims. He also places their experiences in the larger context of traditional European ethnic cleansing. *The World Must Know: The History of the Holocaust as Told in the United States Holocaust Memorial Museum* by Michael Berenbaum (Baltimore: Johns Hopkins University Press, 2005) takes a similarly comprehensive approach while relating the many tragic human stories associated with such a traumatic event. Some of the best reference works on the topic include Israel Gutman's *Encyclopedia of the Holocaust*, Volumes I and II (New York: Macmillan Library Reference, 1995), Martin Gilbert's *Atlas of the Holocaust* (New York: William Morrow & Company, 1993), and *The Holocaust Encyclopedia* (New Haven, CT: Yale University Press, 2001) by Judith Tydor Baumel and Walter Laqueur.

A rising and controversial subfield centers on the actions and attitudes of the perpetrators. Daniel Goldhagen's groundbreaking book *Hitler's Willing Executioners* (New York: Knopf, 1996) argues that the German people enthusiastically persecuted and killed Jews, largely because of deep-seated anti-Semitic notions of Jews as evil, dangerous, and inherently anti-German. The scope of Christopher Browning's *Ordinary Men: Reserve Police Battalion 101 and the Final Solution in Poland* (New York: HarperCollins, 1992) is limited to one military unit, though he conclusively shows that those who committed some of the worst atrocities were often apolitical, average Germans, not fanatical SS men or diehard Nazis. Raul Hilberg's *Perpetrators, Victims and Bystanders: The Jewish Catastrophe, 1933–1945* is perhaps the most balanced study of the troubling question of how otherwise normal, law-abiding individuals could commit such terrible crimes. He explores not only the perpetrators but the "bystanders" of history, such as the Vatican, the United States government, and millions of Europeans who might collectively have done much more to prevent the Holocaust.

The experiences of American concentration camp liberators and witnesses, the particular focus of this book, comprise only a small aspect of Holocaust studies. Indeed, compared with other aspects of the Holocaust, the literature on American soldiers who liberated or witnessed camps is very limited. *The United States Army in World War II: The Last Offensive* (Washington, DC: United States Army, 1993), the official history by legendary military historian Charles B. MacDonald (a former rifle company commander who fought in Europe), offers basic descriptions of camp liberations. Earl Ziemke's *The U.S. Army in the Occupation of Germany, 1944–1946* (Washington, DC: Center of Military History, United States Army, 1990) sheds some light on the army's efforts to provide food, medical care, and shelter to camp survivors. Graham Cosmas and Albert Cowdrey's *United States Army in World War II: The Technical Services, The Medical Department: Medical Service in the European Theater of Operations* (Washington, DC: Center of Military History, United States Army, 1992), Cowdrey's *Fighting for Life: American Military Medicine in World War II* (New York: Free Press, 1994), and Carol Byerly's *"Good Tuberculosis Men": The Army Medical Department's Struggle with Tuberculosis* (Ft. Sam Houston, TX: Office of the Surgeon General, 2009) all furnish an in-depth look at the many challenges faced by army medics to control disease and nurse survivors back to health.

Robert Abzug is the leading scholar of the American liberation experience. His book *Inside the Vicious Heart* (New York: Oxford University Press, 1985) is the foundational work on the subject. He has also authored smaller studies, including *G.I.s Remember: Liberating the Concentration Camps* (Washington, DC: National Museum of Jewish History, 1994) and *America Views the Holocaust, 1933–1945: A Brief Documentary History* (Boston, MA: Bedford/St. Martin's, 1999). Jon Bridgman's *The End of the Holocaust: The Liberation of the Camps* (Portland, OR: Areopagitica Press, 1990) is a useful, well-written introduction to the topic. More recently, Michael Hirsh in *The Liberators: America's Witnesses to the Holocaust* (New York: Bantam Books, 2010) provides us with a rich portrait of former GIs who liberated or visited concentration camps. The book is based primarily on dozens of personal interviews Hirsh conducted with veterans. Leila Levinson's father cared for Holocaust survivors as a physician in the 104th Infantry Division. In the soul-searching book *Gated Grief: The Daughter of a GI Concentration Camp Liberator Discovers a Legacy of Trauma* (Brule, WI: Cable Publishing, 2011), she traces the long-term effect his experiences had on their family many decades later. In 2000, Theresa Ast wrote an excellent, superbly researched overview of the topic in an Emory University dissertation—unfortunately never published—titled "Confronting the Holocaust: American Soldiers Who Liberated the Concentration Camps." Brewster Chamberlin and Marcia Feldman's *The Liberation of the Nazi Concentration Camps 1945: Eyewitness Accounts of the Liberators* (Washington, DC: United States Memorial Holocaust Council, 1987) and Yaffa Eliach and Brana Gurewitsch's *The Liberators: Eyewitness Accounts of the Liberation of Concentration Camps* (Brooklyn, NY: Center for Holocaust Studies Documentation and Research, 1981) both contain a wealth of edited oral histories from American liberators. The latter book is primarily based on accounts recorded at the 1981 International Liberators Conference in New York City.

The remaining works center primarily on individual camps or soldier memoirs in which liberation is seldom the main focus. There is no single book about Ohrdruf. The best historical information on this camp—outside of primary archival sources—can be found at www.89infdivww2.org, the website of the liberating 89th Infantry Division. The division history, *The 89th Infantry Division, 1942–1945* (Washington, DC: Infantry Journal Press, 1947), contains fascinating information about the horrors the soldiers of the 89th encountered at Ohrdruf. Generals Dwight D. Eisenhower, Omar Bradley, and George S. Patton all wrote about what they personally witnessed during their visit to the camp. Eisenhower, who was a gifted writer, discussed his experiences in his memoir *Crusade in Europe* (New York: Doubleday, 1948). Bradley did the same in *A Soldier's Story* (New York: Henry Holt and Company, 1951). Patton, who died shortly after the war, wrote descriptive passages about Ohrdruf in his diary. The edited version of his writings is in Martin Blumenson's *The Patton Papers, Volume II, 1940–1945* (Boston, MA: Houghton Mifflin, 1974). Most of the numerous biographies of these famous generals only briefly mention their Ohrdruf visit. The best single description of the visit was written by Jonathan Jordan in *Brothers, Rivals, Victors: Eisenhower, Patton, Bradley and the Partnership That Drove the Allied Conquest in Europe* (New York: NAL/Caliber, 2011). The finest published soldier account of Ohrdruf is Albin Irzyk's *A Warrior's Quilt of Personal Military History* (Raleigh, NC: Ivy Publishing Group, 2010).

For an excellent introduction to Buchenwald, the best place to start is with David Hackett's edited and translated volume *The Buchenwald Report* (Boulder, CO: Westview, 1995). Eugen Kogon's *The Theory and Practice of Hell: The German Concentration Camps and the System Behind Them* (New York: Farrar, Straus and Giroux, 2006) is a useful, chilling study, surprisingly dispassionate considering the fact that Kogon was an inmate of Buchenwald. Flint Whitlock has written a Buchenwald trilogy: *The Beasts of Buchenwald* (Brule, WI: Cable, 2011) focuses on the infamous Koch couple; *Survivor of Buchenwald: My Personal Odyssey Through Hell*, coauthored with Louis Gros

(Brule, WI: Cable, 2012), is one of the best accounts in print by a former inmate; finally, *Buchenwald: Hell on a Hilltop* (Brule, WI: Cable, 2014) delves deeply into the twisted world of the camp's perpetrators. Christopher Burney's *The Dungeon Democracy* (New York: Duell, Sloan and Pearce, 1946) lends some fascinating insights into the repressive hierarchy that existed among the prisoner population in the camp. Marguerite Higgins, a war correspondent who witnessed the liberation of both Buchenwald and Dachau, wrote about her experiences in *News Is a Singular Thing* (Garden City, NJ: Doubleday, 1955). The only cautionary note is that Higgins at times grossly exaggerated her own role in the liberation of these camps, especially Dachau. Also, some of the "facts" she reported are contradicted by documentary evidence.

The best single source on Buchenwald's liberation and its inner workings is *The Buchenwald Report*, written in the spring of 1945 for General Bradley's Twelfth Army Group by Egon Fleck and Edward Tenenbaum. The original report is in the National Archives. Copies can be accessed easily through a basic Google search. As with Ohrdruf, published soldier accounts focusing primarily on Buchenwald are rare; in most instances, soldiers devoted only a chapter or two to their experiences at Buchenwald as part of a larger recollection of their overall wartime experiences. James Ray Clark of the liberating 80th Infantry Division misleadingly titled his memoir *The Fiery Furnaces of Buchenwald: Journey to Hell*, even though his book contains only a small, rather generic chapter on the liberation of the camp. The best description of the camp's liberation by the army is in Dr. George Hofmann's *The Super Sixth: History of the 6th Armored Division in World War II and Its Post War Association* (self-published, 1975).

As the largest and most complex camp liberated by western Allied soldiers, Dachau has generated the richest body of literature. *Dachau: A Guide to Its Contemporary History* (Dachau, Germany: City of Dachau Office of Cultural Affairs, 2001) by Hans-Günter Richardi, Eleonore Philipp, Monika Lücking, and Greg Bond is an outstanding, detailed study from a latter-day German viewpoint of both the concentration camp and the town that reluctantly lent its name to such a horrible place. *Concentration Camp Dachau, 1933–1945* (Munich, Germany: Dachau International Committee, 1978) by Barbara Distel and Ruth Jakusch is also first-rate. As the director of the Dachau Concentration Camp Museum from 1975 to 2008, Distel lends an especially authoritative voice to this book. The Seventh Army's original report *Dachau Liberated* is available in published form (Seattle, WA: Inkling, 2000) and is certainly worth a look. Andrew Rawson's *In Pursuit of Hitler: A Battlefield Guide to Bavaria* (South Yorkshire, UK: Pen & Sword, 2008) is, in spite of its title, much more than a battlefield guide. It is surprisingly detailed on Dachau's liberation and a worthwhile guidebook for anyone wishing to visit the site today. *The Last Survivor: Legacies of Dachau* (New York: Vintage, 2000) by Timothy Rayback explores the memories of Dachau residents decades after the war and reveals the long-term impact of the concentration camp on this otherwise quiet, unremarkable Munich suburb.

As with the other camps, published soldier accounts from those who liberated, visited, or witnessed Dachau are uncommon. Flint Whitlock's *The Rock of Anzio from*

Sicily to Dachau: A History of the U.S. 45th Infantry Division (Boulder, CO: Westview Press, 1998) includes several excellent chapters about the experiences of one of the liberating divisions. The strength of Whitlock's narrative comes from a large cache of personal interviews he conducted with the veterans. Along those lines, Sam Dann's edited volume *Dachau 29 April: The Rainbow Liberation Memoirs* (Lubbock, TX: Texas Tech, 1998) is loaded with captivating, vivid personal accounts from members of the 42nd Infantry Division, the other primary liberating unit at Dachau. David Israel's self-published *The Day the Thunderbird Cried* (2005) relates some well-researched insight about the coal yard reprisal shooting of SS guards and other events on liberation day. *Where the Birds Never Sing: The True Story of the 92nd Signal Battalion and the Liberation of Dachau* by Jack Sacco, son of a veteran, relates the experiences of several soldiers at the camp; in spite of the title, the focus of the book is on the war as a whole. *The Liberation of KZ Dachau*, a documentary film by James Kent Strong (Strong Communications, 1990), confines its scope entirely to a series of interviews with 45th Infantry Division liberators, some of whom participated in the reprisal shootings. Because many of these veterans have since died, Strong's film has become a foundational, highly valuable source on Dachau's liberation. *The Day of the Americans* (New York: Fleet Publishing, 1966) by Nerin Gun, a Dachau survivor, is often jumbled and inaccurate, yet it is the best single published account of the liberation from the prisoner's point of view. It also provides fascinating details on life (and death) in the camp during the tense, desperate weeks before its liberation. Michael Selzer's *Deliverance Day: The Last Hours at Dachau* (Philadelphia, PA: J.B. Lippincott, 1978) is based almost entirely on participant interviews and is geared for a popular audience, almost as a novelistic account. As such, it is often quite inaccurate. Even so, it is a worthwhile read for those who are interested in the raw emotions experienced by both the liberators and the liberated. Finally, the single best soldier memoir is *Dachau: The Harrowing of Hell* (Albuquerque, NM: University of New Mexico Press, 1972) by Dr. Marcus Smith, one of the first physicians to arrive at the camp and treat the emaciated survivors. Smith reveals a compelling tale of human catastrophe and redemption. It is a story that stands the test of time.

INDEX

Numbers in *italics* refer to illustrations.